PRESENTED BY

Toews Photo
Studio Ltd.

PHILOSOPHY OF RELIGION AND THEOLOGY:   1975 PROCEEDINGS


PREPRINTED PAPERS
FOR THE SECTION ON PHILOSOPHY OF RELIGION AND THEOLOGY


Compiled by

James Wm. McClendon, Jr.


AMERICAN ACADEMY OF RELIGION

ANNUAL MEETING

1975


WITHDRAWN

Distributed by

SCHOLARS PRESS
University of Montana
Missoula, Montana  59801

PHILOSOPHY OF RELIGION AND THEOLOGY:   1975 PROCEEDINGS

Compiled by
James Wm. McClendon, Jr.

Library of Congress Cataloging in Publication Data

American Academy of Religion
     Philosophy of religion and theology, 1975 proceedings.

     Includes bibliographical references.
     1.  Religion--Philosophy--Congresses.   2.   Theology--
Congresses.   I.   McClendon, James William.   II.   Title.
BL51.A54  1975          200'.1          75-26618
ISBN 0-89130-024-4

Printed in the United States of America

Printing Department
University of Montana
Missoula, Montana  59801

TABLE OF CONTENTS

iii

PHILOSOPHICAL HERMENEUTICS
AND
THEOLOGICAL HERMENEUTICS

Paul Ricoeur
The University of Chicago

Translated by R. Bradley DeFord


The title of this paper is more ambitious than its actual scope. My present purpose is limited in two ways. On the one hand, it does not reach an all-encompassing level where both terms of the comparison would be thoroughly comprehended. On the other hand, it does not cover the entire field of philosophical hermeneutics.

As concerns the first point, I must say at the start that I shall confine myself to the contribution of a philosophical hermeneutics to theology, as I conceive it from the philosophical side. To go directly to the point, what has interested me is the ambiguity in the relation between the two hermeneutics. In one sense, theological hermeneutics appears to be a particular case of philosophical hermeneutics, to the extent that it contains the major categories of the latter: discourse, writing, explanation, interpretation, distanciation, appropriation, etc. The relation, then, would be one between a general and a regional hermeneutics. But in another sense, theological hermeneutics displays specific traits which question the claim to universality of such a philosophical hermeneutics as that of H.G. Gadamer. The relation between the two hermeneutics tus seems to be inverted, philosophical hermeneutics becoming the organon of theological hermeneutics. Yet, it must be clearly understood that it is still from the philosophical point of view that I will attempt to disentangle this interplay of opposing relationships.

The second limitation of my paper concerns the philosophical enterprise itself. My purpose is to use the notion of the text as the guideline of my whole inquiry. It may appear, therefore, that my hermeneutics is limited to a reflection on exegetical disciplines at large, i.e., to text-interpretation. This apparent limitation will be obvious for those acquainted with Gadamer's work. For him, hermeneutics raises a claim to universality which is expressed in three ways.

First, hermeneutics claims for itself a universality equal to that of the sciences, at least to that of the social sciences: just as the social sciences develop a concept of truth based on the same model of objectivity as the formal-empirical sciences and supports this with a methodology comparable to that of those sciences, Gadamer's hermeneutics relates its concept of truth to the experience of belonging-to (Zughörigkeit) and dependence-on (Abhängigkeit) with respect to a reality which always precedes us. Compared to this experience, objectivity appears as an alienation (Verfremdung) which it is the task to overcome. This struggle against Verfremdung is what gives to hermeneutics the universality of a purpose and a goal.

Hermeneutics, furthermore, claims a universality of extension. It is known that Gadamer pursues his struggle against alienated objectivism in three realms: that of aesthetics, that of the philosophy of history, and that of the philosophy of language. Three vast provinces of the cultural experience of humankind are thus incorporated into hermeneutics.

Finally, the claim to universality raised by hermeneutics is determined by the specific character of the third sphere taken into account, that of the Sprachlichkeit — or the language-dimension — of all experience. This trait does not, indeed, define one realm among others; it defines the universal medium which gives an articulation to the fundamental experiences of dependence-on and belonging-to. In that way, the universality of the mediation of language must be added to the universality of purpose and of extension of hermeneutics. Hermeneutics is the discourse which tells how belonging-to language provides the universal medium of belonging-to being.

In that sense, my hermeneutical conception may seem much narrower than Gadamer's. It will appear, at first glance, as an attempt to re-regionalize hermeneutics, to return to a regional concept of hermeneutics. The problem of the text which I take as the center of reference will appear, with good reason, as a second-order mediation in relation to the primordial Sprachlichkeit. A fortiori, it will seem to overlook the historical and aesthetical dimensions, and still more, it will seem to be doomed to forget the experience of belonging-to and dependence-on being which confers on Gadamer's hermeneutics its ontological character.

Nevertheless, I think that this apparent limitation to the precise subject-matter of the text has some advantages which further analysis will reveal. In spite of its pretention to universality, the hermeneutical experience advocated by Gadamer constantly refers back to its origin in a specifically delineated problematic: "my own attempt," Gadamer says,"is related to the revival of the heritage of the German romanticism of Dilthey, to the extent that it takes as its central topic the theory of the Geisteswissenschaften, while laying for them a new and broader foundation. The experience of art, with the victorious claim to contemporaneity which characterizes it, provides the proper response to the challenge of historical distanciation in the Geisteswissenschaften." (Rhetoric, Hermeneutics and Ideology-Critique, in Kleine Schriften, I, p. 113.) It is, then, perfectly convenient for a philosophical hermeneutics "to choose its starting point in limited experiences and experience-fields." (Ibid.) Everyone speaks from some place, and all claims to universality are raised from a priviledged position.

The priviledged place from which Gadamer speaks is the one where Verfremdung and Zughorigkeit come to terms. This confrontation is inherent in the kind of initial experience about which Gadamer questions, i.e., the experience of belonging to a cultural tradition which precedes us, encompasses us and supports us, but which we can never grasp from without, place in front of us and judge. This experience is already pregnant with all the antinomies which lace through his work and which develop at each level the initial antinomy of the primordial hermeneuitcal experience, the antinomy which is signified by the very title of his work, Warheit und Methode. In the field of aesthetics, this antinomy is between the experience of being captured by the work of art and the pretention of the judgement of taste to impose its criteria on the aesthetical object. In the field of the social sciences, the antinomy is between the experience of belonging to a tradtion and the pretention, since the Enlightenment, to be free of all prejudices in the attempt to know the historical past. In the philosophy of language, the antinomy is between the previous mutual understanding which supports "the dialogue that we are" (Holderlin) and the pretention to treat linguistic signs as available tools. This opposition, which cuts through all the areas of the hermeneutical inquiry, affects its most ultimate purpose and goal.

Two modalities of "world-experience" (Welterfahrung) are competing: the first one submits to our arbitrariness and puts at our disposal an objectified world; the other subordinates scientific statements to the fundamental laws of our being, removed in that manner from our arbitrariness. It is no longer our concern to make them, but to honor them.

("The Universality of the Hermeneutical Problem," <u>Kleine Schriften</u>, I,
p. 101.)

The following inquiry is an attempt to overcome this antinomy between the
objectivity of the sciences and the fundamental experience of the world. By choosing a starting point in <u>another</u> experience, as limited and particular as that of
Gadamer, I hope to reveal other traits of universality than those of a hermeneutics
dependent on its origin in the "revival of the heritage of German idealism in
Dilthey."

The return to the problematics of the text is in fact a return to the
most precise and rigorous problematics of Schleiermacher and Dilthey. In the case
of Dilthey, that is obvious: the problem of hermeneutics starts with "the expressions of life fixed by writing." Oral discourse poses, of course, some problems of
interpretation, but it does not call for an art distinct from conversation itself.
As for Schleiermacher, it is true that he did not oppose writing to speaking.
Nevertheless, only a reflection on ancient philosophy and Biblical exegesis may support his theory of the twofold hermeneutics — "grammatical" and "technical" (or
"psychological").

Whatever may be the authoritative caution that Schleiermacher and Dilthey
provide us, I propose to take the theory of the text as <u>one</u> point of departure for
the hermeneutical question. I shall henceforth call "hermeneutical" an inquiry
about the art of understanding involved in the interpretation of texts. The object
of my investigation will be, therefore, the relation between the text-being of discourse and the art of interpretation. My task will not be to give a hermeneutics
<u>of</u> the text, but a hermeneutics <u>based on</u> the problematics of the text.

This problematics will be organized around four poles: the text as a relation between writing and speaking; the text as a structured work; the text as the
<u>projection</u> of a world; and the text as the mediation of self-understanding. To
each of these characteristics of "textuality" (text-being) correspond some specific
modalities of interpretation.

If such are the tasks of a philosophical hermeneutics based on the problematics of the text, then, accordingly, my initial problem of the contribution of
a philosophical hermeneutics to a theological hermeneutics must be reformulated as
the contribution to a theological hermeneutics of a hermeneutics based on the problematics of the text.

At first glance, theological hermeneutics will appear as a mere <u>applica-
tion</u> of this general problematics of the text. But a more complex relationship will
emerge as we go along, a relationship which can be expressed in terms of a mutual
inclusion. Certainly religious texts are primarily texts, texts among other texts.
Therefore, theological hermeneutics must remain at first glance, a <u>province</u> within
the broader field of textual hermeneutics. But my thesis is that only the treatment of theological hermeneutics as regional, as applied to a certain category of
texts — in our case Biblical texts — can prepare a reversal in the relation between
both hermeneutics. Only the specificity of the task of interpreting these specific
texts will require that theological hermeneutics ultimately encompass philosophical
hermeneutics and transform it into its own organon. Such is the kind of inverted
relationship which I propose to investigate now, by following the order of the
<u>categories</u> provided by a hermeneutics centered on the notion of the text.

Nothing is more able to reveal the "ex-centric" character of theology than
the attempt to "apply" to it the general categories of hermeneutics.

## I. From the Word to the Scriptures

A.        Writing is obviously the first problem to discuss in connection with the theory of the text. But, if the problem does not need to be underscored, neither must it be overemphasized. Writing and text are not one and the same problem. This is true, first, because there are other problems than writing involved in text theory. Secondly, the problem raised by writing is not writing alone but the relation between writing and speaking. Indeed, writing only makes more explicit traits which already belong to oral discourse, to speaking. And all the traits of the text besides writing — work, world of the text, self-understanding before the text — presuppose the achievement of discourse as discourse. Discourse, then, is the overriding category, under which the transition from speaking to writing has to be put.

         The distinctive traits of discourse are those which are not to be found in language as a set of codes (philosophical, lexical, syntactical codes) and which make of discourse a message. First, discourse is an act — the speech-act — and in this sense, an event, whereas language as a set of codes is a system of signs which has only a virtual and not an actual existence. As the event of speaking, discourse is the act of a subject who expresses himself through it; furthermore, this expression is addressed to another subject, to whom he intends to convey information or whom he intends to influence. As for the act of discourse itself, it displays a structure of its own, irreducible to that of the code of language, which only consists of a system of oppositions between discreet entities. This specific structure is that of the sentence. It relies on a unique operation, the predicative act, whose objective correlate is what logicians call a proposition. This objective correlate of the predicative act makes discourse capable of communication. The entire enigma of discourse is captured in this act/object structure. On the one hand, we have a transient, fleeting act. On the other hand, we have the propositional content, which can be identified and re-identified according to its meaning. This dialectic between the utterer's utterance and the utterance's meaning is the basis of the problem of writing. Let us add a last distinctive trait which will become prominent when we introduce the concept of the "world of the text:" only discourse has simultaneously both a sense and a reference. In other words, it has an inner-composition (the relation of the predicate to the subject) and a relation to outer reality, which implies a claim to truth.

         Such are the main features of discourse which, in the transition from speaking to writing, give rise to significant changes, which in turn provide a principle access to the hermeneutical problem.

         What happens to discourse when it moves from speaking to writing? At first glance, writing seems to introduce a mere exterior and material factor, i.e., the fixation which rescues the event of speech from destruction. In fact, fixation is only the exterior appearance of a process which affects all the features of discourse.

         First of all, writing provides the text with a certain antinomy as concerns the intention of the author. What the text means may no longer coincide with what the author meant. Verbal meaning (i.e., textual meaning) and mental meaning (i.e., psychological intention) are henceforth disconnected.

         This first kind of antinomy invites us to give a more positive meaning to Verfremdung than it has in the context of Gadamer's work. The semantic autonomy of the text is the support of what Gadamer calls the "thing" of the text, because this autonomy creates the possibility that what is at issue in the text escapes the narrow intentional horizon of the author. In other words, thanks to writing, the "world" of the text can shatter the world of the author.

What is true of the psychological conditions of the production of the text must also be true of its sociological conditions. The text is essentially a work of art, a literary work, which transcends its own psycho-sociological conditioning and which becomes open, in that way, to an indefinite range of readers and readings, within different socio-cultural contexts. The text must be able to be de-contextualized, both from a sociological and a psychological point of view, in order to be able to be re-contextualized in fresh situations: this is what really occurs in the act of reading.

This liberation regarding the author has its counterpart regarding the reader. Whereas in the dialogical situation the interlocutor is determined by the very situation of discourse, the written text is free to seek its own audience or public, which virtually extends to anyone who can read. The most striking aspect of writing is this liberation of the written subject-matter from the dialogical condition of discourse. The consequence is that the relation between writing and reading is not one particular case of the relation between speaking and hearing, but is, in this way, a different matter altogether.

This semantic autonomy of the text has an immediate hermeneutical implication. Distanciation is not the product of methodology, something superimposed and parasitic. Rather, it belongs to the genuine constitution of the text as writing. Verfremdung is not only something that understanding must overcome, but a condition for and a mediation in understanding. We are inclined, therefore, to view the relationship between **objectivation** and **interpretation** not as dichotomous, as the romanticist tradition has, but as complementary.

The transition from speaking to writing affects discourse in many more ways. In particular, the referential function is deeply altered by the fact that, in written discourse, it is no longer possible to show the thing about which one "speaks;" this remains possible in the common situation of both speaker and hearer in dialogue. But we may postpone this problem, since it is not so much in writing as such, but some other features which have not yet been introduced which affect the destiny of reference, mainly the case of literary works. The problem of reference will therefore be treated under the title of "the world of the work."

We may now raise the question of the significance for theological hermeneutics of this relation between speaking and writing. The following analysis will be a typical "application" of a general hermeneutic to a regional hermeneutics.

B.      Above all, theological hermeneutics receives from philosophical hermeneutics an early warning, a warning not to be too quick to construct a theology of the Word which does not include initially and in principle the passage from speech to writing. This warning is not without a certain aptness insofar as theology seeks to lift the Word above the Scripture. It does not do this without good reasons: Does not speech precede all writing? Was this not true of the speech of the teller of the sagas, of the prophet, the rabbi, the preacher? And was not Jesus, like Socrates, a preacher and not a writer? Did not primitive Christianity see him as the Word made flesh? And his apostles, did they not announce the Gospel as the Word of God? Thus it is that Christian theology willingly calls itself a "theology of the Word," unifying within this phrase the origin of its faith, the object of its faith and the expression of its faith. And these aspects of speech become a unique word-event (Wort-Geschehen).

Yet we will miss what constitutes the first hermeneutical situation of Christian preaching if we do not pose the question of the speech-writing relation-

ship at the origin of the problem of interpretation. At every stage speech maintains a relationship to writing. First, it relates itself to an earlier writing
which it interprets. Jesus himself interpreted the Torah, and St. Paul and the
author of the letter to Hebrews interpreted the Christian event in the light of the
prophets and the institutions of the old covenent. In a general way, a hermeneutic
of the Old Testament, inasmuch as it is a given writing, is implied by the proclamation that Jesus is the Christ. All the titles that exegetes call Christological
titles proceed from a reinterpretation of figures received from the written Hebraic
and Hellenistic cultures: King, Messiah, High priest, Suffering Servant, Logos. It
seems therefore that writing must precede speaking, if that speaking is not to remain only a cry. The very newness of the event requires that it be transmitted by
means of an interpretation of the preliminary signs — already written down — and
available within the cultural community. In this sense, Christianity is, from its
very beginning, an exegesis. (Think of the role of "figures" and "types" in Paul.)
But this is not all: new preaching is not just tied to an earlier writing which it
interprets; it becomes in its turn a new writing. The letters written to the Corin-
thians become letters for all Christianity. Mark, followed by Matthew and Luke,
then John, wrote a gospel. Newer documents were added until, one day, the church
closed the canon, constituting the achieved and closed writings as the corpus of the
witnesses. Henceforth, any preaching which takes the Scriptures as its guide is
called Christian. It does not refer to one scripture — the Hebrew Bible — but to
two writings, the Old and the New Testaments.

Thus a hermeneutical situation was created which was not immediately
recognized as such. But if the formulation of the problem is modern, the problem
itself has underlain the very existence of Christianity. From its beginning, preaching rested upon witnesses interpreted by the primitive community. Testimony and
interpretation of the testimony already contained the element of distanciation
which make writing possible. If we add that a certain variation in the testimony
was part of the testimony of the church from its beginning, it seems as though a
certain hermeneutical liberty, as strikingly evidenced by the insurmountable differences among the four gospels, belonged to the entire primitive hermeneutical situation.

The result of this reflection on the hermeneutical situation of Christianity is that the speech-writing relationship is constitutive of what we call proclamation, Kerygma, preaching. Thus what occurs is the chain speech-writing-speech, or
writing-speech-writing, in which sometimes speech mediates two forms of writing, as
Jesus' speech does between the two Testaments, or in which sometimes writing mediates between two forms of speech, as the Gospels do between the preaching of the
primitive church and all contemporary preaching. This chain is the condition of the
possibility for a tradtion in the fundamental sense of the transmission of a message.
Before being added to writing as a supplementary source, tradition is the historical
dimension of the process which links speech and writing to each other. Writing
brings distanciation which detaches the message from its speaker, from its initial
situation, and from its primitive destination. Thanks to writing, speech reaches
all the way to us and touches us through its "meaning" and its "issue" which is at
stake in it, although no longer through the "voice" of its proclaimer.

Here someone might ask, "What accounts for the particularity of Biblical
speech and writing among other forms of writing and speech?" We would answer that
it is nothing that belongs to the relation between speech and writing as such. The
originality of the text is connected with its "issue," i.e., its way of refering to
a world which is the world of the text.

But we still have to postpone this suggestion until after we have developed the second category of textual hermeneutics.

## II. The Structure of the Work and the Forms of Biblical Discourse

A.        A text is not merely a written discourse. It is a discourse written in the form of a work. Three distinctive traits may characterize this notion of work. First, a work is a sequence longer than a sentence. It displays a composition of a second order which makes discourse into a finite and closed whole. Second, the work is submitted to a kind of codification which rules the composition and generates such forms as narratives, poems, essays, etc. According to this codification, a work belongs to a certain literary "genre." Finally, a work receives a unique configuration, due to its relation with a particular individual, which can be called the style of the work.

Composition, compliance to genres, and individuality of style characterize discourse as work. The term "work" indicates the nature of these new categories: thay are categories which have to do with production and labor. To impose a form on a matter, to submit production to genres, to generate individuals: all of these procedures imply that language appears as a raw material to be fashioned and shaped. In that sense, discourse falls under the scope of praxis and techne; from this point of view there is no clear cut difference between intellectual work and manual work.

Consequently, discourse displays a quite high level of objectification, similar to that of the products of work in relation to the process of production. Man objectifies himself through the works of his discourse, as he does through the products of his craftmanship, and his art. Other alterations of the initial features of discourse proceed from this general trait of objectification. First, the speaker appears as an author; this expression indicates that an author is more than merely an "utterer;" it designates the artisan at work in discourse. The writer, as an author, is less than even a psychological entity. He can be only a category of the interpretation, related to the interpretation by the work itself.

But the most decisive feature is implied by the notion of composition. The work of discourse presents characters of organization and of structure which legitimate the extension to discourse of structural methods first applied to linguistic entities shorter than the sentence, either in phonology or in lexical semantics. One knows how successfully these methods were applied first by Russian formalists to folktales, then by Levi-Strauss to myths borrowed from the cultural area of totemism, and then by French structuralists to narrative and poetic structures.

Both this objectification of discourse in work and this structural charcter of composition, when added to the kind of distanciation linked to writing, compell us to question radically the opposition, originating with Dilthey, between "understanding" and "explanation." Explanation was supposed to be borrowed from the field of the natural sciences, whereas understanding meant the transfer into a foreign psychic life on the basis of this life's expression in external signs. This opposition no longer holds as soon as the structural features of discourse are taken into account. It is no longer obvious that "explanation" is borrowed from the natural sciences, since it is provided by the very sciences on language itself, i.e., semiotics. The only difference here concerns the scale of application of semiological models. Whereas semiotics, before its extension to narrative and poetic structures, addressed itself to linguistic entities shorter than the sentence, structural analysis of texts extends the structures of language to the structures of discourse, i.e., to the formal characters of discourse qua work, as displaying inner composition, generic rules and individual style.

In that way, a new era of hermeneutics is necessarily opened by the success of structural analysis. "Explanation" has become the unavoidable road to "understanding." This does not imply that explanation, in turn, could make understanding expendable. Objectivation of discourse in a structured work does not abolish the first and fundamental trait of discourse, i.e., that it is a set of sentences, in which somebody says something to somebody else about something. Hermeneutics, I would say, remains the art of identifying the discourse within the work. However, it is true that this discourse is given nowhere else than in and by the structure of the work. Consequently, interpretation cannot rely on the opposition between "explanation" and "understanding," but on their combination. "Method" and "truth", as well, must be encompassed in a unique dialectical process.

B.        A hermeneutic centered on the text thus finds a second "application" in the use of structural categories in Biblical exegesis. But at the same time that this exegesis is given as a simple "application" to the Biblical domain of an analysis applicable in principle to all texts, it develops traits which will be affirmed when we pass from the "structures of the text" to the "world of the text."

Once again, we shall limit ourselves here to sketching the framework of problems which are considerable in themselves and, furthermore, to sketching it from the point of view of the philosophy of discourse.

The fundamental point on which I would like to concentrate is this: The "confession of faith" which is expressed in the Biblical documents is inseparable from the forms of discourse there, by which I mean the narrative structure of the prophecies, the parables, the hymns, etc. Not only does each form of discourse give rise to a style of confession of faith, but the confrontation of these forms also gives rise to, in the confession of faith itself, tensions and contrasts which are theologically significant. The opposition between narration and prophecy, so fundamental for the mentality of the Old Testament, is perhaps only one of the pairs of structures whose opposition contributes to engendering the global shape of its meaning. We shall speak later of other contrasting pairs at the level of literary genres. Perhaps we would even go so far as to consider the closing of the canon as a fundamental structural act which delimits the space for the interplay of forms of discourse and determines the finite configuration within which each form and each pair of forms unfolds its signifying function.

There are three problems to consider under the aegis of forms of Biblical discourse: (1) the affinity between a form of discourse and a certain modality of the confession of faith; (2) the relation between a certain pair of structures (e.g., narration and prophecy) and the corresponding tension in the theological message; and finally (3) the relation between the configuration of the whole of the literary corpus and what one might correlatively call the space of interpretation opened by all the forms of discourse taken together.

I should say here that I am particularly indebted to Gerhard von Rad for my understanding of this relation between the form of discourse and the theological content. I find a confirmation of his method of correlation in similar works applied to the New Testament, especially those of Amos Wilder (The Language of the Gospel, Early Christian Rhetoric) and Beardslee (Literary Criticism of the New Testament).

The example of narration is perhaps the most striking, since it is also in the domain of narrative forms and structures that structural  analysis has its most brilliant success. This example, systematically developed, no longer allows us to construct theologies of the Old and New Testaments which understand the narrative category to be a rhetorical procedure alien to the content it carries. It seems, on the contrary, that something specific, something unique, is said about Yahweh and about his relations with his people, Israel, because it is said in a narrative form, in the form of a story which recounts the events of deliverance in the past. The very concept of a "theology of tradition" which provides the title for the first volume of von Rad's Theology of the Old Testament expresses the indissoluble solidarity of the confession of faith and the story. Nothing is said about God, or about man, or about their relations, which does not first of all reassemble legends and isolated sagas and rearrange them in meaningful sequences, in order to constitute a unique Story, centered upon the kernal-event, which has both an historical import and a kerygmatic dimension. It is well known that Gerhard von Rad organizes the whole story on the basis of the primitive creed of Deuteronomy 26. This way of tying together the narrative dimension and the kerygmatic dimension is, for us, of the greatest importance.

On the one hand, taking the narrative structure into consideration permits us to extend structural methods into the domain of exegesis. A comparison between von Rad and the structuralists trained in the school of Russian formalism and post-Saussurian semiology would be very interesting in this respect.

On the other hand, the relation between these two hermeneutics begins to reverse itself once we begin to consider the other side of the narrative, namely the confession of faith. But this other dimension remains inseparable from the structure of the story. Not just any theology whatsoever can be tied to the narrative form, but only a theology which proclaims Yahweh to be the grand Actor in a history of deliverance. Without a doubt, it is this point that forms the greatest contrast between the God of Israel and the God of Greek philosophy. The theology of tradition knows nothing of the concepts of cause, foundation, or essence. It speaks of God in accordance with the historical drama instituted by the acts of deliverance reported in the story. This manner of speaking of God is no less meaningful than that of the Greeks. It is a theology homogeneous with the narrative structure itself, a theology in the form of Heilsgeschichte.

I have developed here to some extent a single example, that of the narrative structure and the theological signification which corresponds to it. The same could be done with the other literary forms in order to bring to light in theological discourse the tensions which correspond to the confrontation of the structures. The tension between narrative and prophecy is exemplary in this regard. The opposition of two literary forms — that of the chronicle and that of the oracle — is extended even to the perception of time, which the one consolidates and the other dislocates, and even to the meaning of the divine, which alternatively seems to have the stability of the founding events of the history of the people, only to unfold the menace of deadly events. With prophecy, the creative dimension can only be attained beyond the valley of the shadows: the God of the Exodus must become the God of the exile if he is to remain the God of the future and not merely the God of memory.

Unfortunately, I cannot say more about this within the limited framework of this article. To do so, it would be necessary to explore other forms of discourse and perhaps other significant contrasts, such as that of wisdom and the law, or that of the hymn and the proverb. Throughout these discourses, God appears differently each time: sometimes as the Hero of the saving act, sometimes as wrathful or compassionate, sometimes as He to whom one can speak in an I-Thou relation, or sometimes as He whom I meet only in a cosmic order which ignores me.

Perhaps an exhaustive inquiry, if one were possible, would disclose that together all these forms of discourse constitute a circular system and that the theological content of each of them receives its signification from the total constellation of forms of discourse. Religious language would then appear as a polyphonic language sustained by the circularity of the forms. Then again, perhaps this hypothesis is unverifiable and confers on the closing of the canon a kind of necessity which would not be appropriate to what should perhaps remain an historical accident of the text. At least this hypothesis is coherent with the central theme of this analysis, that the finished work which we call the Bible is a limited space for interpretation in which theological significations are correlatives of forms of discourse. It is no longer possible to interpret the significations without making the long detour through a structural explication of the forms.

## III. The World of the Text: Toward the "New Being"

A.          This new trait will bring us still further from the positions of any romanticist hermeneutics, but also from those of structuralism, which I hold to be the mere opposite of romanticism. The task of hermeneutics is not to recover a certain contemporaneity with the act of creation; but neither is it merely to reconstruct the structure of the work. I would say that the task of hermeneutics is to explicate the "world of the text."

This notion corresponds, at the level of the whole work, to that of reference at the level of an isolated sentence. Whereas the sense of a sentence is its ideal object and is immanent in the proposition, the reference is its truth-value, its claim to reach reality. This trait is specific of discourse, in opposition to the code of language, which has no relation to extra-linguistic reality. Only discourse is intended toward reality.

Even if the notion of the world of the text is analogous to that of the reference of the sentence, it displays its own specific traits. Writing and, above all, the inner-structure of the work make reference quite problematic. In oral discourse, the problem is solved by showing the thing referred to, or by locating it by means of uniquely refering descriptive definitions in the unique spatio-temporal network to which both the speaker and the hearer also belong. Writing already abolishes the common reference within which an ostensive reference could point. What we call "literature" is to a large extent a consequence of this abolition of the ostensive dimension of reference. But it is mainly with particular literary genres, generally (but not necessarily) linked to writing, that this suppression of the reference to the world is pushed to its most extreme consequences. It seems to be the function of a great deal of literature to "destroy" reality. That is true not only of fictional literature — such as folktales, myths, novels, plays, — but also of lyrical literature, in which language seems to celebrate itself at the expense of the referential function such as it is achieved in ordinary language.

In spite of this inwardly directed use of language, no discourse is so introverted that it no longer addresses itself at all to reality. Writing, such as fiction, rejoins reality, however, at another, more fundamental level than the one on which this descriptive, confirmative, didactic form of discourse which we call ordinary language functions. My thesis is that the suspension of a first-order reference, such as is achieved by fiction and poetry, is the condition of the possibility for yielding a second-order reference. This second-order reference no longer touches the world at the level of manipulatable objects, but at the deeper level which Husserl designated by the term "life-world" (Lebenswelt) and Heidegger by that of being-in-the-world (in der Welt-Sein).

Such is the referential dimension of the work of fiction and poetry which, to my mind, raises the most fundamental hermeneutical problem. If we are no longer able to define hermeneutcs as the inquiry into another's psychic life, into his psychological intentions concealed behind the text, yet if we do not want to reduce interpretation to an analysis of strucutres, what is left to interpretation? My answer is the following: To interpret is to explicate the kind of being-in-the- world displayed before the text. What is then submitted to interpretation is the pro-position of a world in which I could dwell, a world created by the projection of my utmost possibilities. For every unique text, there is such a "world of the text."

The world of the text, therefore, is not that of everyday language. In that sense, it implies a new kind of distanciation, that of fiction, to our ordinary grasp of reality. A narrative, a tale a poem are not without referents, but there is a gap between their referents and that of ordinary language. Through fiction, through poetry, new possible modes of being-in-the-world are opened up in the midst of reality. Fiction and poetry intend being, not as given being but as potentiality of being. Consequently, everyday reality undergoes a metamorphosis, thanks to what could be called the "imaginative variations" which literature displays. Metaphorical language is the kind of discourse which is most able to generate these imaginative variations and, in that way, to redescribe reality according to the new model created by the poet. Metaphorical — and, more generally, poetic — language aims at a mimesis of reality. However, this language "imitates" reality only because it recreates reality by means of a mythos, a "plot," a "fable," which touches upon the very essence of things.

Such is the third category of hermeneutical theory. I might say that this is the central category, as much for a philosophical as for a theological hermeneutics. All the other categories are based on it: distanciation by writing and objectfication by structures are only the preliminary conditions for the text's saying something which is its "issue." As for the fourth category — self-understanding — we will see to what extent it depends on the world of the text in order to come to language. Simply, the "issue" of the text, the "new being" of the text, is the object of hermeneutics.

B.     It is in applying these considerations to Biblical exegesis that we clarify the veritable finality of the latter. That is, it is in applying what has been said of this third category to the Bible as one category of text among others that we make possible the reversal which makes general hermeneutics the organon of Biblical hermeneutics.

Let us therefore follow the route of the simple "application" of the general theme to the text whose internal structure we have just pointed out.

This "application," far from submitting Biblical hermeneutics to an alien law, restores it to itself and delivers it from several illusions. First, it delivers us from the temptation of prematurely introducing existential categories of understanding to counter-balance the eventual excesses of structural analysis. Our general hermeneutics invites us to say that the necessary stage between structural explanation and self-understanding is the unfolding of the world of the text. It is this latter which finally forms and transforms the self (être-soi) of the reader according to its intention. The theological implications here are considerable: the first task of hermeneutics is not to proceed immediately to a decision on the part of the reader, but to allow the world of being which is the "issue" of the Biblical text to unfold. Thus, above and beyond emotions, dispositions, belief or non-belief, is the proposition of a world, a new covenant, the Kingdom of God, a new birth. These are the realities unfolded before the text, which are certainly for us, but which begin from the text. This is what one might call the "objectivity" of the new being projected by the text.

A second implication is this: To put the "issue" of the text before everything else is to stop asking the question of the inspiration of the writings, in the psychologizing terms of an insufflation of meaning by an author who projects himself into the text. If the Bible can be said to be revealed, this ought to be said of the "issue" of which it speaks: the new being which is displayed there. I would go so far as to say that the Bible is revealed to the extent that the new being unfolded there is itself revelatory with respect to the world, to all reality, including my existence and my history. In other words, revelation, it the expression is meaningful, is a trait of the Biblical world.

Now this world is not immediately carried by psychological intentions but mediately by the structures of the work. All that we said above about the relation between for example, the narrative form and the signification of Yahweh as the actor, or about the relation of the form of prophecy with the signification of the Lord as menace and promise beyond destruction, constitutes the only possible introduction to what we are now calling the Biblical world. The power of the most powerful revelation is born in the contrast and convergence of all the forms of discourse taken together.

A third theological implication of the category of the world of the text: Because it is here a question of a world, in the sense of a global horizon, of a totality of meanings, there is no privilege whatsoever for an instruction addressed to the individual person, and in general none for personalistic aspects, in the form of I-Thou or in the relation of person to God. The Biblical world has aspects which are cosmic — it is a creation; which are communitarian — it speaks of a people; which are historical and cultural — it speaks of Israel and the kingdom of God; and which are personal. People are reached through a multiplicity of dimensions which are as much cosmological, historical and worldly as they are anthropological, ethical and personalistic.

The fourth theological application of the category of the world of the text: We have said above that the world of the "literary" text is a projected world which is poetically distanced from everyday reality. Is not the new-being projected and proposed by the Bible a case par excellence of this trait? Does not the new-being make its journey through the world of ordinary experience and in spite of the closedness of this experience? Is not the force of this projected world a force of rupture and of opening? If this is not so, must we not accord to this projected world the poetic dimension, in the strong sense of the word, the poetic dimension which we have acknowledged in the issue of the text?

Pursuing this line of reasoning to its logical conclusions, must we not say that what it is thus opened up in everyday reality is another reality, the reality of the possible? Let us recall at this point one of Heidegger's most priceless remarks on Verstehen: for his Verstehen was diametrically opposed to Befindlichkeit in the measure to which Verstehen is addressed to our utmost possibilities and deciphers them in a situation which cannot be projected because we are already thrown into it. In theological language this means: "the kingdom of God is coming;" that is, it appeals to our utmost possibilities, beginning with the very meaning of this kingdom, which does not come from us.

The route which we have followed thus far is that of the application of a general hermeneutical theory to the Biblical hermeneutic seen as a regional hermeneutic. My thesis is that this route is the only one at whose end we can recognize the specificity of the Biblical "issue." In this Ebeling is correct: it is only in listening to this book to the very end, as one book among many, that we encounter it as the Word of God. But once again, this recognition does not appeal to a psychological concept of inspiration, as though its authors repeated a word which was whispered in their ears. This recognition is addressed to the quality of the new being as it announces itself.

One of the traits which makes for the specificity of the Biblical discourse, as we all know, is the central place of God-reference. The result of our earlier analysis is that the signification of this reference of Biblical discourse is implicated, in a special way which we have yet to describe, in the multiple, uni- fied significations of the literary forms of narration, prophecy, hymn, wisdom, etc. "God-talk," to use MacQuarrie's phrase, proceeds from the concurrance and conver- gence of these partial discourses. The God-referent is at once the co-ordinator of these varied discourses and the index of their incompleteness, the point at which something escapes them.

In this sense, the word "God" does not function as a philosophical con- cept, such as Being in either the medieval cr the Heideggerian sense. Even if one is tempted to say — in the theological meta-language of all these pre-theological languages — that "God" says more: it presupposes the total context constituted by the entire gravitational field of stories, prophecies, laws hymns, etc. To under- stand the word "God" is to follow the "direction of the meaning" of the word. By "direction of the meaning" I mean its double power: that of gathering together all the significations which issue from the partial discourses, and that of opening up a horizon which escapes from the closure of discourse.

I would say the same thing about the word "Christ." To the double func- tion which I have described of the word "God," this word "Christ" adds the power of incarnating all the religious significations in a fundamental symbol, the symbol of a sacrificial love, of a love stronger than death. It is the function of the preaching of the Cross and Resurrection to give to the word "God" a density which the word "being" does not possess. In its meaning is contained the notion of its relation to us as gracious, and of our relation to it as "ultimately concerned" and as fully "re-cognizant" of it.

It will be the task of Biblical hermeneutics to unfold all the implica- tions of this constitution and of this articulation of God-talk.

We can now see in what sense this Biblical hermeneutics is at once a particular case of general hermeneutics and at the same time a unique case. It is a particular case of a more general enterprise because the new being of which the Bible speaks is not to be sought anywhere but in the word of this text among others. It is a unique case because all the partial discourses refer to a Name which is the point of intersection and the index of incompleteness of all our discourse on God, and because this Name has become bound up with the meaning-event preached as Resur- rection. But Biblical hermeneutics can only claim to say something unique if this unique thing speaks as the world of the text which is addressed to us, as the issue of the text.

IV. To Understand Oneself Before the Text

A. The fourth and last category of text-interpretation has been anticipated in the introduction to the theory of text interpretation: the mediation of the read- ers self-understanding through the text. It was necessary to postpone this discus- sion until last, lest the subjectivity of the reader be substituted for that of the writer and thereby a new fallacy take the place of the "intentional fallacy" exposed by Wimsatt in the Verbal Icon.

The position of the reader in the whole hermeneutical process is analogous to that of the hearer in the dialogical situation and retains some of these charac- teristics, to the extent that a text remains a discourse said by someone and addres- sed to someone. In that sense, reading is a kind of response to what the text says and, also in that sense, it is that act by which a certain recognition takes place. But whereas in the case of oral discourse, the addressee is given within the dialog- al situation itself, the one to whom a text is addressed is, so to speak, created

as a reader by the work itself, which paves its own way toward its potential addressee.

The hermeneutical problem related to this specific position of the reader
as distinct from the "Thou" of the "I-Thou" relationship was known in the most traditional hermeneutic as the problem of the "applicatio" (in German, Anwendung) of
the teaching of the text to the present situation of the audience. It has been expressed in more modern terms as that of the "appropriation" (Aneignung), in order to
underscore the movement from the alien to the proper. My purpose is to relate the
problematic of the appropriation to the preceding analysis and to the categories
which rule it. The problem of appropriation receives its genuine meaning from being
introduced as the last one, mediated by all that precedes.

First, the concept of appropriation has to be connected dialectically to
that of distanciation, its specific counterpart. This connection results mainly
from the status of the text as written discourse. Thanks to the semantic autonomy
of the text, appropriation presents none of the traits of emotional identification
with the intention of the text. Appropriation does not mean contemporaneity or con-
geniality. Rather, it is understanding through distance, at a distance. The recognition of the author is therefore itself an indirect acknowledgement of the writer as
"implied author," in the words of Wayne Boothe in Rhetoric of Fiction.

But the correlation between distanciation and appropriation proceeds even
more from the objectivation of discourse as work. The appropriation is mediated by
the structure of the text, which articulates its "sense" as its inner-connectedness.
This mediation by the sense and the structure of the sense is philosophically of the
highest significance. In opposition to the tradition of the Cogito and to the claim
of the subject to know itself by immediate and direct intuition, we must say that we
understand ourselves via the detour of the signs of humanity sedimented in the works
of culture. The structure of the work is the tool of this sedimentation and therefore also of this highly mediated mode of transmission. What would we know of love
and hatred — and in general of the feelings and the values which support the Self —
if they had not been brought to language and articulated by works of art and discourse? The texture of the text is the bearer of this mediation.

Finally, the real vis à vis of appropriation is neither writing as such,
not the structure of the work as such, but the world of the text that both the categories of writing and of work introduce. What I may make my own — in other words,
appropriate — is the pro-position of a world, i.e., the mode of being-in-the-world
displayed by the text, before the text, and not behind the text, as the intention of
the author would be.

To understand, therefore, is to understand oneself before the the text,
i.e., before the "what" and the "about what" of the text (or, as Gadamer would say,
before die Sache des Texts, the "thing," the "issue at stake" in the text, the in re
of the text). This implies that the reader does not submit the meaning of the text
to his own finite capacity for understanding, but that he lets himself be exposed to
the text, in order to receive from it a Self. By Self I mean a non-egoistic, non-
narcissistic, non-imperialistic mode of subjecitvity which responds and corresponds
to the power of the work to display a world. The Self is the correlate of the
"thing" of the text.

This dialectical relation between distanciation and appropriation can be
given several concrete illustrations. It may be compared to a translation of one
idiom into another idiom, where the same meaning has to be transfered into another
medium. It may also be compared to the performance of a musical score containing
specific instructions; an interpretation must be both faithful and original. The

dialectic may be more radically compared to what happens to a formal system when it
is applied to a specific domain of experience, and interpreted according to specific
rules of correspondence.

All of these comparisons tend to show that the need for interpretation is
proportional to the degree of formalization of the medium in which meaning is to be
found. That is yet another way of saying that distanciation and appropriation are
dialectically related.

In spite of all these qualifications of the concept of appropriation,
misunderstandings keep recurring, as if the whole field of hermeneutics was always
in danger of succumbing to the spell of subjectivism. Two strategies may be acti-
vated in order to discard these misunderstandings.

First of all, stress may be placed upon the ludic aspect of reading. In
that way, the theory of understanding is connected to an entire mediation of the
concept of "play," as Gadamer does in the section of Warheit und Methode devoted to
aesthetics. This connection is not far-fetched — to the extent that we have start-
ed to elucidate the referential function of narratives and poetic works on the basis
of the concept of heuristic fiction. The concept of "play" provides a new dimension
to these previous remarks. "Play" has a philosophical bearing, to the extent that
play is not ruled by the consciousness which plays. "Play" is an experience which
transforms those who enjoy it. What happens in play determines the attitude of the
players. In "play" consciousness forgets itself, until in "earnest" it recaptures
its awareness.

If we apply this general description of "play" to the hermeneutical situation, one may say that "play" not only rules the metamorphosis of reality through
fiction, but that of the writer and of the reader as well. Both become ludic figures by assuming the imaginative variations suggested by the work. The imaginative
variations of the author, expressed in writing, become the paradigm for corresponding imaginative variations on the part of the reader. Fiction, in that way, is no
less a fundamental dimension of the reader's subjectivity than it is of the referential being of the text. Thanks to "play," the metamorphosis of the world extends
to that of the ego.

The second strategy concerns the application on the self-consciousness of
the ego of a technique of distanciation which owes more to critique tha   to play.
It addresses itself to the illusions of subjectivity and submits them to a radical
suspicion. Psychoanalysis and ideology-critique are, at present, the methodological
paradigms of this attack on the systematic distortions which affect both communication and self-understanding. They both have in common the bracketing of the testimony of consciousness about itself and the reconstruction of conscious meanings on
the basis of an objective inquiry into the unconscious, underlying forces. This
reconstruction, in turn, may provide a higher degree of self-awareness and lucidity
to the subject, to the extent that explanation is reconverted in self-understanding.

These two strategies converge in one point: they tend to connect appropriation and dispossession and to introduce within self-understanding itself the same
kind of dialectic between comprehension and objectivation as was introduced between
discourse and text, sense and structure, reference and fiction. At all levels,
distanciation is the condition of interpretation.

I shall end my essay by investigating the theological implications of the
fourth category of our text-centered hermeneutics.

B.      First, it must be said that what in theological language is called faith
is constituted, in the strongest sense of the term, by the new being which is the

"issue" of the text. In thus recognizing the hermeneutcal constitution of the
Biblical faith, we are resisting all psychologizing reductions of faith. This is
to say that faith is authentically an act which cannot be reduced to linguistic
treatment. In this sense, faith is the limit of all hermeneutics and the non-her-
meneutical origin of all interpretation. The ceaseless movement of interpretation
begins and ends in the risk of a response which is neither engendered nor exhausted
by commentary. It is in taking account of this pre-linguistic or hyper-linguistic
characteristic that faith could be called "ultimate concern," which speaks of the
laying hold of the necessary and unique from which basis I orient myself in all my
choices. It has also been called a "feeling of absolute dependence," underscoring
the fact that it responds to an initiative which precedes me. Or it could be called
"unconditional trust," pointing out that it is inseparable from a movement of hope
which makes its way in spite of the contradictions of experience and which turns
reasons for despair into reasons for hope according to the paradoxical laws of a
logic of superabundance. In all of these traits the thematic of faith escapes from
hermeneutics and testifies to the fact that the latter is neither the first nor the
last word.

But hermeneutics reminds us that Biblical faith cannot be separated from
the movement of interpretation which elevates it into language. "Ultimate concern"
would remian mute if it did not receive the power of a word ceaselessly renewed by
its interpretation in signs and symbols which have, we might say, educated and formed this concern over the centuries. The feeling of absolute dependence would remain
a weak and inarticulate sentiment if it were not the response to the proposition of
a new being which opens new possibilities of existence for me. Hope, unconditional
trust, would be empty if it did not rely on a constantly renewed interpretation of
sign-events reported by the Scriptures, such as the Exodus in the Old Testament and
the Resurrection in the New Testament. These are the events of deliverance which
open and disclose the utmost possibilities of my own freedom and thus become for me
the Word of God. This is also the first theological consequence of the indissoluble
correlation which we have discovered between the world of the text and appropriation.

A second consequence follows from the sort of distanciation which hermeneutical reflection has caused to appear in the very midst of self-understanding as
soon as this is a "self-understanding in the face of the text." As soon as one submits the understanding of oneself to the Selbstdarstellung of the "issue" of the
text, a critique of the illusions of the subject must be included in the very act of
"self-understanding in the face of the text." It is here that I see an essential
connection between the criticism of religion practiced by Marx, Nietzsche and Freud
and the self-understanding of faith. This critique of religion is, of course, constituted entirely outside of hermeneutics, as a critique of ideology, as a critique
of other-worldliness, as a critique of illusions. But for a text-centered hermeneutical understanding, this critique can simultaneously remain the recognition of an
external adversary, whom one does not attempt to retrieve and baptize by force, and
also become the instrument of an internal critique, which appropriately belongs to
the labor of distanciation which all self-understanding before the text requires.
Today, a "hermeneutics of suspicion" is an integral part of all appropriation of
meaning. And with it follows the "de-construction" of pre-judgements which impede
our letting the world of the text be.

The third and last consequence which I would like to draw from the hermeneutic of appropriation concerns the positive aspect of the distanciation from oneself which I see implied is all self-understanding before the text. The de-construction of illusions by the subject before the text is only the negative aspect of what
must be called "imagination." As we saw, it is "play" which liberates within the
vision of reality new possibilities otherwise caged by the spirit of the "serious."
"Play" also opens up in subjectivity the possibilities of metamorphosis which a

purely _moral_ vision of subjectivity cannot see. Imaginative variation, play, metamorphosis — all of these expressions seek to discern a fundamental phenomenon, namely, that it is in the _imagination_ that the new being is first formed in me. Note that I have said imagination and not will. This is because the power of letting oneself be grasped by new possibilities precedes the power of deciding and choosing. Imagination is that dimension of subjectivity which responds to the text as _Poem_. When the distanciation of imagination responds to the distanciation which the "issue" of the text unfolds in the heart of reality, a poetics of existence responds to a poetics of discourse.

TWO QUESTIONS TO PAUL RICOEUR

John A. Hutchison -- Claremont Graduate School


The purpose of this paper is to ask or to put two questions. I shall
also sketch possible answers, but since a question must be asked before
it is answered I am more concerned with the questions than the answers.
The two questions are these:

1. Can Ricoeur's use of symbolism be fruitfully conceived as a speech
   act?

2. Can interpretation or hermeneutics as understood by Ricoeur be
   fruitfully conceived as a speech act?

By speech act I mean this concept as developed and expounded in the main
line of Anglo-American linguistic philosophy from Ryle and Wittgenstein
to the present. Especially notable in this development have been the
contributions of John Austin and John Searle. Austin attempted a distinction between constative and performative utterances, the former
having the classic function of reporting facts and the latter of doing
or performing some act such as promising, demanding, etc. Thus the
sentence "I promise to do X" does not report an act but is the act of
promising. In the end this distinction between these two kinds of
utterance broke down, for "I report that..." or "I assert that such and
such is the case" is as much a doing or performance as "I warn that..."
or "I promise..." Nevertheless Austin had effectively made the point
that speaking is a form of doing. So too is the thinking that finds expression in words. He also called forceful attention to the different
kinds of doings or performances which take place in words, or by means
of words.

Austin's other main distinction, namely between illocutionary and perlocutionary speech acts (this is to say "in the words," in-locution,
and "through or by means of the words," per-locution) while sometimes
clear and distinct is at other times highly problematic. Thus, "I
promise...," "I warn..." are classic and clear illustrations of illo-
cution while persuading or convincing is perlocutionary. However,
"I argue..." or "I conclude..." might well be classified either way.
Yet once more, Austin's distinctions while in their intended use break
down, nevertheless do yield results. For every speech act has its
illocutionary and perlocutionary aspects, however their relations may
vary in particular cases.

Searle's analysis approaches speech acts as compounds which may be re-
solved into three kinds of elements. First and simplest of these
elements is the locutionary act which is defined as the simplest act
possessing meaning, a distinction being thus made between activity of
the vocal organs producing meaningless noise, and that which issues in
meaningful speech. (In passing, Searle pays insufficient attention to
this elemental fact of the emergence of meaning!)

19

A second level of meaning consists of what Searle calls the propositional act, which is itself a compound bringing together an act of
predicating with an act of reference or referring.  The act of referring as Searle states the matter picks out some aspect of the existent
world, thus presupposing the concept of existence; and predicating
attaches some quality or predicate to it.  Both of these acts proceed
upon the basis of presuppositions whose metaphysical or ontological
character is plain in even so cursory a sketch as the present one.

In a moment we shall point to expressive meaning as those speech acts
or aspects of speech acts which relate the works used to the self or
subject using them.  The traditional logical label for this aspect of
verbal meaning is "subjective intension."  Here we note that Searle
as well as Austin pass it over in total silence.  In terms of Searle's
analysis there is an expressive aspect of meaning at each of his three
levels.

The third level or element in the analysis of speech acts is called by
Searle illocutionary.  Here something is <u>done</u> with the locutionary and
propositional acts.  Thus, for example, promising, demanding, asking,
all add a clause beginning with "that such and such is the case," which
is shorthand for the propositional element.  Searle offers two lists of
illocutionary acts which differ with each other and neither of which
seems in any way exhaustive.  Searle's first list is as follows: requesting, asserting, questioning, thanking, advising, warning, and
greeting.  His second and shorter list includes the following:  requesting, asserting, questioning, warning and promising.  Surely neither list
is either complete or systematic.  Other kinds of illocutionary acts
come readily to mind.  What of "I comment...," "I believe that...," "I
believe in...," or "We teach..." (as said by the Chalcedon Fathers).
For this <u>adhoc</u>, indeed arbitrary, character there seems to me a very
good reason, namely that speech acts like other acts of free human
agents have an inexhaustible, unique and unpredictable quality.  We can
never know completely or in advance exactly what men will do in and
through the words they use.  Hence no list of illocutionary acts can
hope to be exhaustive or adequate.

As we turn from linguistic analysis to Ricoeur, we may note again the
almost total silence of the analysts concerning the symbolic or expressive symbolic function of language.  Surely this is a notable, gaping
omission for philosophers who claim a basis in common language, for the
daily language of human beings shows a significant component of expressive symbolism.  Poetry is not simply a specialized use of language but
an undeniable aspect or dimension of the language of daily communication.
We turn then to Ricoeur's discussions of this category as a corrective.

Symbolism is intimated in the concept of the language of avowal in
<u>Fallible Man</u>, and it emerges as a basic category of Ricoeur's philosophy
in <u>The Symbolism of Evil</u>.  It becomes even more important in <u>Freud and
Philosophy</u>, and in several of the papers in <u>The Conflict of Interpreta-
tions</u>.  Speaking in most general terms, Ricoeur seems more concerned to
use the category or concept of symbolism in his exposition of moral evil,
or in his Christian meditations on Freud (which incidentally must send
Freud spinning in his grave!) than he is concerned to theorize about the
nature of symbols or expressive symbolism.  In the judgment of one reader,
his use seems both substantially adequate and highly illuminating.

However, if we turn from practice to theory, questions arise. There is a
problematic passage in Freud and Philosophy in which Ricoeur says, "I
have decided to define, i.e., limit the notions of symbol and interpretation through one another. Thus a symbol is a double meaning linguistic
expression that requires interpretation, and interpretation is a work of
understanding that aims at deciphering symbols." (p. 9)

As a definition this won't do, for we cannot in a single argument define
a in terms of b, and then b in terms of a. However, common language
philosophy will provide an easy solution for this predicament. It is
namely to assert the primacy of common language, then to derive symbol as
a secondary language. In its turn, interpretation or the hermeneutical
act becomes the task of translating symbols back into common language.
All this seems so simple that I am tempted to believe that Ricoeur was
simply presupposing it in the passage just quoted.

There is another more substantial issue in this quotation, namely the
definition of symbol as a derivative language. In context it is offered
as a middle way between the too broad definition of symbol by Cassirer,
and the too narrow definition of analogy. However, in terms of Ricoeur's
definition, Freudian language (with which his book primarily deals) is
symbolic; but equally so, the Morse code or any of the world's spy codes
are symbols or symbolic in character. For they are derivative or second-
order languages. But in this case Ricoeur needs to add the adjective, expressive, for such second-order languages as the symbolism of evil, for
Freudian symbolism, and in general for poetic and religious symbolism.
Particularly is this true for the symbols which are so eloquently depicted
in the last section of Freud and Philosophy.

In this connection, which is to say, on the nature of expressive symbolism,
I have found two or three other philosophers helpful in the explication
of expressive symbols as these are employed or used by Ricoeur. They are
Suzanne Langer with her concept of "presentational forms," and Philip
Wheelwright and his expressive or depth symbols as set forth in The Burning Fountain and Metaphor and Reality. Indeed the latter bears striking
similarity to Ricoeur's treatment of the same issue. Wheelwright's exposition of expressive symbols not only describes in detail their use in
poetry, religion, and daily communication, but notes the logical relation
of expression to reference or referential use. If reference consists, as
Searle and others have made clear, the relation of words to the objective
world, expression consists of their relation to the selves or subjects
using the words. If we give both expression and reference affirmative
and negative values, then four possibilities emerge, namely $E_a$-R, $E_a$R,
-$E_a$R, and -$E_a$-R. All four possibilities find exemplification in the
actual languages of human beings. In a word Wheelwright's work might be
characterized as a detailed and factual exposition of Ricoeur's language
of avowal. Taken together the work of these two philosophers goes far to
redress the neglect of this area of language on the part of linguistic
analysts.

On the issue of the area or domain of expressive symbolism I raise in
passing a question concerning Ricoeur's Symbolism of Evil, which argues
that while good may be characterized non-symbolically, evil demands and
receives symbolic characterization. I question that this is the correct
place at which to draw this line, and propose that the line would better
de drawn between theoretical and practical reason, which is to say,
between the reasoning of the detached observer and the reasoning of the

participant in action. Gilbert Ryle has drawn a similar distinction between "engaged" and "unengaged" thinking. In these terms, un-engaged thinking concerning both good and evil takes place in non-symbolic terms, while engaged thinking (might we call it thinking on the playing field of human action?) takes place in symbolic terms. In Ricoeur's terms the language of avowal takes place in symbolic, or more specifically expressive-symbolic terms.

I return to the question: Can expressive symbolism be characterized as a speech act? In a trivial and tautological sense, any and all oral (and also graphic) activity is activity. But the more significant question is whether any fruitful results accrue from this particular equation. The answer I would wish to sketch is: Yes, but only if the categories of free action are expanded by contact with Ricoeur's analysis in Freedom and Nature. Here again, I seek to expand and correct linguistic philosophy by contact with Ricoeur.

Linguistic philosophy has frequently made its case by selection of over-simple illustrations or models. The classic illustration is the analysis of "I raise my arm" as a free action--an analysis which does not get far beyond Aristotle's distinction between the voluntary and invol-untary, and which does little to illuminate the complicated patterns of voluntary action in which men are actually involved.

In this situation, I specifically recall Ricoeur's threefold analysis of free action as involving (1) choice or decision, (2) movement and (3) assent to necessity. For the analysis of expressive language as a free act we need to draw upon all of these elements, and especially the third. The poet, for example, engages in free action as he composes his poem, but he is subject to many kinds of contraints. At times poets tell us that their poems are literally torn from them. Similar constraints are observable in the primary language of religious experience, as may be illustrated by the words of the Biblical prophet Amos: "The Lord took me from behind the plow and said, Go speak to my people Israel." Another similar but fuller illustration is to be had from the language of Isaiah's vision in Chapter VI of the Biblical book of Isaiah. In general terms, what is needed is detailed description of the speech activity of expres-sive symbolism as it actually occurs in the living experience of human beings. If Ricoeur's theory lags behind his practice, he has nevertheless provided us with invaluable examples of the latter.

Having now used all of my time on the first of my two questions, I turn all too briefly to the second, namely whether interpretation or hermeneutic activity can fruitfully be conceived as a speech act. Instead of analysis or exposition I propose a metaphor in terms of which exposition and analysis may proceed. Hermeneutics may be viewed as an expedition for the exploration of unknown or little known territory. The exploration party establishes its base, usually near the frontier of known land. From this base it sets out into the new territory, periodically returning to base with reports of its findings, and also for re-supply and re-direction. So the work of exploration goes forward. To interpret my metaphor, common language (and the community of experience for which it speaks) is the base from which the explorers of the hermeneutical movement set out, and to which they periodically return with reports and for fresh supplies and new directions. The new territories which they explore are any and all of the derivative languages and symbol systems which human beings have brought into being. It is also necessary to add: also the forms of human experience embodied in these languages and symbol systems. For Paul Ricoeur this includes notably the distinctive forms of experience in history and in religious faith.

True, my metaphor is a plea for a common language approach and interpretation of the hermeneutical movement--a suggestion that is likely to prove controversial to both parties. I can only plead that both parties stand to gain. Linguistic analysis will stand to gain from the wider scope and greater imaginative depth of the hermeneutical movement and hermeneutics from the greater rigor and clarity of analysis of Anglo-American analytic philosophy.

To summarize, it seems to me possible that the convergence of these two widely different philosophical ways of studying language may provide fruitful new leads for the study of language generally and religious language in particular.

# REFLECTIONS ON THE CONDITION OF THEOLOGY TODAY

Charles W. Kegley -- California State College, Bakersfield

Less than a year ago, I ventured the judgment that the "queen of the sciences, "Theology, is in very bad health.[1] There was a surprisingly large response to this statement from various parts of the country and from persons holding widely divergent theological positions or none at all. There was nearly unanimous agreement that the judgment was basically correct.

Obviously part of the difficulty with any attempt at assessing the status and prospects of theology is the confusing diversity of conceptions of what theology is or what it ought to be. In this case, as in so many others, the saying "the adjective rules the noun" holds, for whatever the assessment turns out to be, much depends on whether one is talking about biblical, dogmatic, or natural theology, to use three traditional adjectives. Even these presumably well-chewed over terms provoke argument and disagreement. Biblical theology ranges from such old fashioned efforts as George B. Stevens' 53 chapter book, The Theology of the New Testament, to very restricted studies of a single problem such as personal survival.

Dogmatic theology clearly began as an effort to interpret the official teachings of a particular church, e.g., Roman Catholic, Presbyterian, Lutheran, Anglican, but it would appear that very few people consider this a job worth doing any more.

If it is undertaken from the standpoint of such a well-defined system as Roman Catholic doctrine and dogma the work is likely to be either boring -- because so well-worn -- or radical and therefore an invitation to censorship precisely because it is innovative and different. The case of Hans Küng is especially instructive because of the way in which, after years of down-playing his theological writing, the Vatican finally said, in effect: "You may write such unorthodox theology, but you must not teach it in the classroom." Today, dogmatic theology is also taking the route of ecumenical effort. Thus, theologians of various persuasions explore their areas of agreement and disagreement. The results are likely to be perceived as amusing rather than as sustained efforts to discover "the truth." The recent appearance of the Common Catechism: A Book of Christian Faith, provoked one reviewer to point out that the "result of such a massive study" was neither a "common" theology nor a catechism but an overly cautious discussion of religion in general, Christian doctrine only secondarily. Clearly, we have come a long way from what theology was presumed for almost 17 centuries to be about.

Finally, "natural" theology is a breed which is quite difficult to evaluate. In some cases it is even difficult to identify. Most students of philosophy and theology have wrestled with such a classic as Kant's Religion Within the Bounds of Reason Alone, and any student of the history of Christian thought is supposed to be ready to discuss the "rationalistic" interpretations of Locke, Hume on miracles, the efforts of Rousseau and others to create a "natural religion" and the like. But it was not until the first quarter of the twentieth century -- Douglas Clyde Macintosh's pioneering Theology As An Empirical Science was published in 1927 -- that an impressive if not influential stream of books appeared. To these the labels "natural theology," "rational theology," "philosophical theology," might with almost equal propriety be attached.

Probably the most famous and continuous effort at producing natural theology is the famous Gifford Lectures, which, since the beginning of this
century, have sought to serve the "promoting, advancing, teaching, and
diffusing" of the study of "natural theology" which was conceived by
Lord Gifford as a science. Rarely has there been a more revealing and
amusing confrontation of natural vs. revealed theology than in the Gifford Lectures of Karl Barth in 1937-38. At that point in the history of
theology Barth stated that he could "not see how it is possible for it
/the science of natural theology_7 to exist and that surely he as a theologian of the Reformed Church is "subject to an ordinance which would keep
me away from 'Natural Theology'."[2] One might have thought that under
these circumstances he would have politely declined the invitation to
deliver the Gifford Lectures. Not Karl Barth. He not only accepted the
invitation but used the Lectures as an occasion for showing, at least to
his own satisfaction, why all forms of natural theology are to be avoided
and why "the teaching of the Reformation," as he understood it, is on the
contrary to be promoted, advanced, and diffused."

What is the situation as we enter the closing quarter of the
twentieth century? Two facts are especially striking. One is that this
century is distinctive in having produced the most remarkable collection
of brilliant theologians and the most comprehensive systems of theology
in the entire history of western thought. In what other period does one
encounter so dizzying a collection of contemporaries as Karl Barth, Emil
Brunner, Reinhold Niebuhr, Anders Nygren, Paul Tillich, Henry Nelson Wie-
man, and Rudolf Bultmann?[3] Nor do these seven exhaust the gallaxy of
stars, for during the same period Nikolai Berdayaev produced a full-
blown system of thought written from the standpoint of Russian Orthodoxy.

The second striking fact is that, apparently exhausted by such
heroic creativity, theological endeavors in the years immediately following the reign of these men have not only been rather trivial by comparison
but they have also moved away from the aims of comprehensiveness and in-
novativeness which characterized the preceeding decades. What has happened, and why it occurred are questions both intriguing to contemplate
and difficult to answer. The following observations do no more than identify certain features of the theological scene and suggest some reasons
why one finds theology in such a generally depressing and sick condition.

Recalling our earlier three-fold division of theology, the first
point to be noted is that both biblical and dogmatic theology have suffer-
ed from a change in the whole intellectual and religious climate. On the
one hand, biblical scholars have apparently performed their tasks so well
that, given the fruits of the higher criticism and the meticulous techniques of exegesis, few if any scholars would take the time to wrestle
with over-all summaries of biblical theology. Saying this of present-day
biblical theology is not intended to ignore the earlier and outstanding
work on Old Testament theology done by Walter Eichardt and Gerhard von
Rad. Particular issues, specific questions elicit articles in journals,
but not comprehensive statements of "the faith." On the other hand, the
present age is either uninterested in or incapable of producing "systematic" theology, i.e. rational and comprehensive statements of what, for
want of a better phrase, we might call the Christian philosophy of life.
The alternative is seen in specialized treatments, for example, the theology of hope and the theology of play. Now no one disputes that hope
occupies a central place in theology. Theologians have pondered for

for centuries questions concerning the nature, grounds, and fruit of hope in one's view of human existence. But two points are also pretty much beyond dispute. One is that "hope" is not anymore, and may be somewhat less important a concept    than say, "love" or "faith" in Christian theology. The other point is that theologies of hope are inclined to tell us more about our contemporary and near-universal sense of hopelessness and of absurdity than they are about the central concerns and affirmations of a comprehensive theology.

As for a theology of play, one is forced to say that (1) it fails to meet one of the prerequisites of any theology, namely, to offer a serious and systematic interpretation of all human existence; (2) it distorts the meaning of the very scriptures it purports to interpret. It does the latter to such a degree as to make a near burlesque of the content of theology. To the defender of theologies of play, who say that this is unfair and grossly exaggerated, I call attention to Jurgen Moltmann's embarrassed efforts to reply to his American counterparts in "play" theology. In effect he throws up his hands in despair, not knowing how to relate to them and what they have said. In the end he says that play theology comes close to faddism and snobbism.4

I have elsewhere called attention to a parallelism which is instructive, namely, between the situation in theology and in art in the past decade. This relation between artist and theologian is twofold. First, in the spheres of art and of religion there has been a drive to identify with life -- life as it really is. So the artist presents us with urinals or with a picture of a pile of logs as a work of art. Similarly, the theologian of play has played games with life and with words, telling us about "....the resurrection of the flesh."5 Is this anything short of the trivializing of art and of theology? One who has a sense of what art and theology have been and can be must pray either for their recovery or for their quiet death if this is all they have to say. The other instructive point about the artist vis-a-vis the theologian is that many artists in fact now perceive themselves as performing the function formerly served by the theologian. That is, with the death of God and the triumph of secularism and the vacuum of theology, -- among other features of contemporary culture -- the artist aims to provide the faith or meaning for which contemporary man is searching.

I have said nothing about the present status and prospects of the third kind of theology which was variously described as natural, rational, and philosophical. On this question generalizations and observations, although dangerous as always, may be permitted if only for brevity's sake.

First, there simply has not been much natural theology in the traditional sense. This is due, in part at least, to the mood and blick of our times. A curious conjunction has occurred. On the one hand, religious and theological issues have become the property of philosophers and teachers of "religious studies" in colleges and universities but what these writers have to say is severely critical and negative, not, as in a previous generation, constructive and affirmative. The drive has been to show the absurdity of most if not all God-talk. The consequence has been to lead even especially university-related schools, theological schools, to restrict themselves to high-powered literary and historical studies which shine with a kind of antiseptic and scientific objectivity but which studiously avoid the philosophical and theological issues which,

characteristically, concern the meaning and truth-claims of a religion.
Unless one argues from the dubious premise that in silence there is (an
ostrich-like) safety, theology in general and philosophical natural theology in particular can only be the losers.  It is a sign of the present
times that they are losers -- if they are -- by being ignored.

There is an additional feature of the present scene which is
closely related to the above point.  It may be expressed with combined
humor and irony by quoting the editor of a prestigeous journal of theology and religion who said, "Everybody wants to write about religion and
theology, but nobody wants to practice or defend them; they all want to
criticize it."  Now leaving aside the question -- though it is a serious
one and deserves scrutiny in another context -- of whether theology normally grows out of religious convictions and experience, the fact is that
theology, like religious ethics, is sick at present for two reasons.
One is the temporary lack of intellectual vigor of the entire religious
community and of theologians in particular; the other is the unending
criticism to which theology and all matters religious have been subjected by philosophers.  As to the former, there is abundant evidence, from
the records of colleges and universities as well as from sociological
and psychological studies, that the best brains have not gone into the
professional thought and life of religion but into other professions.
Paraphrasing the Old Testament Prophet, God is getting the runts not the
prize animals offered to his honor.  This phenomenon cannot fail to have
a debilitating effect upon theology for obvious reasons.  Of course there
are sterling exceptions, but theology cannot thrive and may not even survive on exceptions.  Further, there is simply no denying the fact that
in spite of the dazzling outward show of vitality -- new church edifices,
economic support, books on religion, etc. -- in the Western world secularism not religion is the winner.  Even sales reports on books on religion can be misleading because overall organized religion discloses a
clear trend of decline, i.e. in the closing of parochial schools and seminaries, the collapse of "foreign missions" departments, and the like.
Philosophy and the sciences are among the determinative voices of today's
culture, not theology.  And theology is not likely to regain its prestige
and influence unless it produces a quality of intellectual leadership
which many would say is conspicuously lacking of late.

As for the criticism to which theological ideas have been subjected, no college or university professor who knows either his books or
his students can be unaware of the way in which what appear to be the
wolves of philosophy and the sciences have attacked the sheep of theology
and religion.  Theological interpretations of the nature of man, of God
and the "proofs" for his existence, of life after death -- all have been
subjected to scrutiny in such a way that the whole theological enterprise
is perceived by the student as being outdated, misguided, and worst of all
simply false.  Of course scrutiny does not necessarily result in condem-
nation and rejection, but the content of most texts in philosophy of religion, and the way in which the courses are taught, leads the students
to conclude that in this case it does.  It would be reckless to predict
when and by what means theology can regain a position of respect if not
prestige.  To be sure, there are other factors at work to make the prospects for theology less bleak.  If there are philosophers whose critical
efforts are destructive, there are others whose imagination and vigor are
capable of not merely giving support to theological inquiry but point the
way to fresh and meaningful ways of undertaking the theological task.
For example, although it is too early to judge, the process philosophers
and theologians may be able to develop a terminology and way of viewing

theological issues that is as viable, and surely more scientifically
valid, than the historic Aristotelian-Thomastic stance. The case of
Charles Hartshorne and others in fact tells us that the philosopher not
only outshines the theologian in originality and brilliance, but that he
or she often makes the most constructive contributions to problems which
have traditionally been considered theological. Again, though it is
shockingly "left"for most theologians, there are resources in the humanistic tradition which remain unexplored. Yet another possibility is suggested by such juxtaposed studies as psychology and ontology. For the
reductionist behavioristic interpretations of man have carried their
logic to such a point that sheer accuracy of accounting for man -- what
he is capable of being and creating -- demands a fresh and corrected interpretation of his nature and destiny. Yet again: though there may be
a "logic without ontology," the persistent questions of ontology and
metaphysics are proving enormously interesting and important. The fact
that previous answers were inadequate or plainly false does not mean
that the questions are misguided or irrelevant. It may rather mean that
they call for new answers to the most important and ultimate questions
man can ask.

Finally, I am increasingly impressed by the ambiguity and confusion surrounding the fact-value disputes in all the academic disciplines.
Surely religion in general and theology as its rational interpreter has
always claimed that it had the answer to the basic question, What is of
value? whether that question be addressed to the ends and goals of man
or to the status of value in the cosmic process. This may not be the
issue with which the theologian of tomorrow ought to begin, but it certainly is central to his task and it has implications for almost every
other major field of inquiry.


[1]"God Is Not Dead, But Theology Is Dying," Intellect, Vol 103
#2361 December, 1974, pp. 177-181.

[2]Barth, Karl, The Knowledge of God and the Service of God According to
the Teaching of the Reformation. (New York, Charles Scribner's Sons,
1939)

[3]All of these theologians, except Karl Barth who declined to write a
"Reply to His Critics," are the subjects of volumes in THE LIBRARY
OF LIVING THEOLOGY, edited by the author and Robert Bretall.

[4]Moltmann, J., et al The Theology of Play (New York: Harper & Row, 1972)

[5]Sam Keen. "Godsong," in The Theology of Play, J. Moltmann et al
New York: Harper & Row, 1972 p. 97.

THEOLOGY WILL CONTINUE TO PROVE UNNECESSARY UNTIL IT ASKS ITSELF ANEW

THE QUESTION:   "WHAT IS IT TO BE RELIGIOUS?"

By

Thomas A. Idinopulos
Miami University (Ohio)


Responding to the invitation to discuss the status and
prospects of theology is like agreeing to draw a map of chaos:   One
could hardly know where one is if one doesn't know where one has been.
This paper seeks nothing more than to identify some sign posts.

I believe that the fundamental challenge to theologians
today is to achieve clarity about their discipline, which means
determining the proper object of their inquiry.   In this respect I
agree wholeheartedly with Peter Berger when he observes that the
fundamental cognitive problem of theology will not be solved by ex-
hortations to political commitment or by more sermons urging involvement and liberation.   (Peter Berger, A Rumor of Angels, Anchor Books,
1970, p. 12).   Yet the characteristic pattern of American Protestant
thought from the late '50's, after the Korean War, to the present
day, has been a retreat from cognitive questions, and a movement
towards expressing a theological language of moral consciousness and
action.   I discern this pattern in the writings of Joseph Fletcher,
Thomas J. J. Altizer, William Hamilton, Paul Van Buren, Harvey Cox, and
in two who are not American, but who have had a significant influence
on Americans -- Dietrich Bonhoeffer and John A. T. Robinson.

These authors obviously share a keen appreciation for relating theological ideas -- indeed to relate the theologian himself
as a person -- to the issues and crises of the day.   But this would
be meaningless without a way of expressing the relationship.   None of
these thinkers follows Tillich's method of correlating existential
questions with theological answers, for each distrusts Tillich's habit
of identifying through the principle of correlation the religious
factor or component of every cultural situation.   They pursue a curious
method of declaring social and moral and political values to be autonomous, and then announcing that as Christian theologians they have
been freed in their thinking by scripture or revelation or Jesus to
understand and advocate what is humanly essential in these values.
Anyone familiar with theological history will recognize the roots of
this practice in the polemic against religious idolatry in the writings
of the early Barth, and in the reduction of religion to a moral content, or ideal by Kant and Ritschl.   This double movement of repudiating
religion by translating it into a moral ideal was present much earlier
in American theology, as early as the rational liberalism and social
darwinism of the beginning of this century.   But fresh impetus for the
reduction of religion to morality was received when the writings of
Dietrich Bonhoeffer were read in earnest by American theological students
after the second world war.   Bonhoeffer in his thought and life confirmed what they had already learned from Barth, and what they as
American Protestant Christians had been predisposed to believe -- that
religion was not only inferior to morality but an actual obstacle to

31

the moral act.

In what follows I should like to (1) outline the Barthian and the Kantian-Ritschlian principles; (2) show the influence of both these principles on the theologians mentioned above; (3) propose an alternative to the characteristic style of American Protestant theology, by suggesting a way of analyzing the "religious senisibility" as the appropriate object of inquiry for theology.

## II

The proof of the remarkable achievement of Karl Barth is that the radical turn which he introduced to theology over fifty years ago continues to exercise a profound influence on American Protestant theology. The crucial implication of Barth's early writings is that theology is not just another form of scholarship -- some sort of specialized study of ethics, history and religion with the aim of answering the perennial questions about man's origins and destiny. Barth argued that if the uniqueness of God's scriptural revelation was to be respected, then the Christian theologian must stop thinking of himself as a philosopher seeking religious universals in human experience. He announced boldly and clearly that the theologian is less thinker than listener: not one who arrogantly seeks to penetrate with reason the mystery of divine being, but one who humbly awaits God's own Word addressed to him through the patriarchs, prophets and gospel writers. For if the theologian, no less than his fellow human, stands under the judgement of sin, in need of forgiveness, he knows nothing of God; rather, it is God himself who gives knowledge of himself to man through scriptures. The irreducible uniqueness of revelation Barth took as a theological sword to cut away with one powerful and clean stroke the contamination heaped on God's truth by theologians and churchmen who had confused grace with culture, faith with piety. This repudiation of the religious pretenses of Christian culture continues today as one of the most vibrant themes in American theological writing.

To understand the tendency of American theologians to replace religion with ethics one has to go back of Barth to the even more awesome figure of Immanuel Kant, especially in his influence on Ritschl and the developing tradition of liberal European and American Protestantism. The publication in the late eighteenth century of Kant's three Critiques had a powerful impact in compelling a new appreciation of the limits of human reason, and by implication a new understanding of the knowledge of God. The essence of Kant's critiques of reason was the dualism consisting of a sensually and mathematically knowable phenomenal realm and a metaphysically or speculatively unknowable noumenal realm. Herewith Kant denied any cognitive structure linking God and man, making it impossible for anyone to suppose that philosophical reflection could in itself discover the essential truths about God and God's creation. But what was forbidden to metaphysical or speculative reason was vouchsafed to moral or practical reason. The essential truths of the reality of God, the immortality of the soul, and the freedom of the will is accessible to man directly, through the inherent intuitive powers of his moral reason. The basis of man's moral knowledge of God is the recognition of his duty to obey divine law. Herewith Kant laid the basis of a vigorous, new understanding of the relation of religion and morality. Religion is to function as the watchdog of morality: through its dogmas and ceremonies to inspire man

to do his duty; to reward man with the promise of eternal life if
he does his duty well. If religion functions properly, divine law is
obeyed, God is honored, with the result that man lives in a just,
orderly society.

Karl Barth rejected Kant's belief in man's practical or
morally intuitive knowledge of God, because of his own predisposition
to regard scripture as the exclusive medium of the knowledge of God.
However, Kant's practice of translating what was noblest and finest
in Christian dogma and ritual into an ideal or essence accessible to
man independently through his moral reason -- this collapsing of
religion into morality had made its impact on European Protestantism
well before Barth, and it found its way to America long before Barth's
"dialectical theology" made its own way here. The contribution of
Ritschl to European thought and subsequently to American was to have
follwoed out the implications of the Kantian reduction by constructing
a theology based on the life and teaching of Jesus and the essential
human focus of the moral wisdom of God. The Kantian-Ritschlian
principle, no less than the Barthian, continues in present-day American
Protestant thinking.

### III

If one senses as I do a profound uncertainty today over the
purpose of theology, even over its worthwhileness, it is due in great
part to the practice of employing both Barth's repudiation of religion
on behalf of a unique revelation, and the Kantian-Ritschlian reduction
of religion to morality. The result is confusion and sterility:
the elimination of any distinct or necessary subject-matter, with the
consequence that any available object of attention can be and is
seized -- politics, literature, social relations, behavioral problems,
medical health. For where the theologian is uncertain about his
subject matter, he cannot help but doubt his methods of study. The result is a rather empty theological tract in which the author seizes
the social issue of the day, identifies and discusses the relevant
value, whether it be moral or political or whatever, and then mustering
all the theological acumen at his command, he delivers what is in effect
a homily, matching-up social issue and human value with a biblical
theme that is intended to reinforce the issue and confirm the value,
all the while invoking words like "prophetic,""revelatory," "incar-
national," and "secular," as if they constituted insights in themselves.

The authors and works I now wish to discuss are not in my
judgement the worst examples of confusion and sterility, but they
are the most guilty, by virtue of their success in capturing a reading
public, of promoting confusion and sterility in the American theological
student.

Dietrich Bonhoeffer, in the cryptic remarks he made in his
letters from a Nazi prison about the role of Christian theology in a
world of secular events and institutions, gave a new impetus to the
double movement of repudiating religion and translating it into its
ethical residue. One can look very hard in Bonhoeffer's letter, or in
his formal writings, and not find much in the way of an argument for
what he came to call "religionless Christianity;" but it hardly mattered
to the American theologians who proved eager to fasten on the arresting
phrases that Bonhoeffer offered: "Christ    for us;" "the religious

a priori;" "God the problem solver;" "world come of age;" "Christian
maturity."

John A. T. Robinson's Honest to God, 1963, as widely read in
America as in its author's native Britain, was an effort to take
Bonhoeffer's vague theme of Christian secular maturity (which Robinson
rendered as "honesty") and place it within the wider theological framework set forth by Tillich, Bultmann, and Bonhoeffer. In Robinson's
thinking what this new theological honesty resulted in was an utter
dismissal of the power, mystery and complexity of the New Testament's
proclamation of the Kingdom, in a trivialized call for emulating the
love of Jesus. Robinson put it this way, "Life in Christ Jesus, in
the new being, in the Spirit, means having no absolutes but his love,
being totally uncommitted in every other respect but totally committed
in this" (p. 114).

Joseph Fletcher's Situation Ethics, (1966), no less than
Robinson's Honest to God, was an effort to carry through Bonhoeffer's
call for a Christian secular maturity, with one difference -- it was
a calculated effort to capture an American audience, particularly the
college-age youth. One sees this in Fletcher's heavy-handed rejection
of the role of tradition and norm in ethical decision and responsibility.
The subtitle of the book was The New Morality, but the book had very
little to do with moral thinking or ethics. It had a lot to do with
persuading readers that the good proclaimed by Jesus in the New Testament consisted of the purity of a loving heart coupled with a sophistication about social and political contexts of experience. Fletcher's
effort was in the peculiar American theological tradition of reducing
the complex question of morality into a humanly manageable dictum
about the essentiality of love. Fletcher's chapter titles are revealing:
"Love only is always Good;" "Love is the only norm;" "Love justifies
its means;" "Love decides there and then."

The American death-of-God theologians, Thomas J. J. Altizer
and William Hamilton, also practiced the double-movement of repudiating
religion while translating it into a moral residue. Altizer owes much
more to Barth's polemic against religion than to Nietzche's critique
of Christian culture, when he declares that the repressive God of
traditional Christian faith has died in Jesus' Cross, which Cross has
liberated human beings to live freely in a secular or "Godless"
universe. William Hamilton shares the belief that in Jesus' Cross, the
repressive God of the Christian religion has died to free man to accept
the challenge of living fully human lives in the world. But his
thought takes a less mystical turn than Altizer's by urging a social
programme, influenced in great part by Bonhoeffer. He calls for social
action and for the end of religious or pious self-concern. "The
academy and the temple can, for now, no longer be trusted as theological
guides. Not only our action but our thought belongs with the world of
the city, which in our time means power, culture, art, sex, money,
the Jew, the Negro, beauty, ugliness, poverty and indifference." And
elsewhere he writes, "To mark the end of solitariness as a theological
posture, of obsessive senses of sin, of crying out to God, absent or
present, is to mark the end, in Protestant cirlces at least, of the
existentialist mood." (Radical Theology and the Death of God, 1966,
pp. 44-45)

God did not die for Paul Van Buren in his widely discussed
The Secular Meaning of the Gospel, (1963), but the language of religion

which speaks of God has died. And it has not died bacause people have stopped using it in the forms of worship -- myth, ritual, prayer, dogma; but rather because when judged by empirical criteria of meaning developed by contempoary analytical philosophy, theological as well as religious language about God is technically meaningless, hence dead. No less than the other authors mentioned here, Van Buren proceeds to examine religious or theological terms for their ethical content which he commends as meaningful. What this comes to mean is the now familiar identification of Christian existence in a secular world with the figure of Jesus as an ethical ideal. Van Buren speaks of the contagion of Jesus' freedom, which grasps human beings and commits them to a similar sense of living out of and for freedom.

IV

If we can believe the statistic published recently in The Christian Cenutry that The Secular City (1965) has sold 900,000 copies in 14 languages, then no one has done more than its author, Harvey Cox, in shaping the contemporary American Protestant theological style. In Cox's writing any conception of theology as an intellectual discipline is abandoned, joyously abandoned I should say. In his collection of essays, published under the title On Not Leaving It to the Snake (1969), Cox announces the purpose of theology "is to serve the prophetic community. For this reason the place of theology is that jagged edge where the faithful company grapples with the swiftest currents of the age. Any 'theology' which occurs somewhere else or for some other reason scarcely deserves the name." (p. 13) Strong, clear words these, but not becuase their author is sure what theology should do; much surer is he what the theologian should do. The theologian must look for a justification to exist in the world. And since Cox seems to believe that thinking about "God" and "religion" are dead ends in the present secular age, the theologian had better look hard or close up shop and find something else to do. Fortunately, Harvey Cox himself has found something to do and he commends it to all of us. In The Secular City he had no hesitation in telling us that joining a picket line in support of labor or marching in a civil rights march on behalf of voting rights for blacks is what a theologian should do. And more recently he has told us to join the revolutionary Latin Americans in their struggle against capitalist imperialism. He doesn't tell us to send money to Rabbi Korff to contribute to Nixon's legal defense'fund. Though he never quite tells us how he got that way, Cox's secular theologian serving the "prophetic community" turns out to be a young American, college educated, political liberal. He is terribly earnest, but I have my doubts as to how "prophetic" he would be. For if one leaves for a moment social issues which can be neatly categorized as "liberal" and "conservative," in order to confront the profound ambiguity of values represented, let us say, in the issue of legalized abortion, then I doubt that Cox's theologian would have anything to say that would serve the "prophetic community."

If, as seems clear, "prophecy" is one slogan word, "rev-olution" is another. The Secular City, as most of Cox's works, could be read as an ode to revolutionary change. The theologian must not only act, he must act in a revolutionary way, or at least, act to support the revolutionary actions of others. Cox admires Dietrich Bonhoeffer and Martin Luther King. And though he doesn't say so, I doubt that he would admire ex-Greek premier George Papadopoulos who

introduced some radical reforms in Greek society while torturing many
of its citizens; nor would he admire the Shah of Iran who raised the
price of oil, helped wreck the economies of Europe, and loves to talk
grandiloquently of a new Persian Empire.  They, too, are revolution-
aries; but they wouldn't qualify under Cox's understanding of revolution.
The reason is that the word "revolution" like the word "prophetic"
is an empty word in Cox's writing, not used to descrive an empirical
content, but used rather to trigger certain impulses.

We see the same rhetorical style at work in some carefully
chosen words Cox uses to promote another one of his interests.
Sloth, he says, not pride is the real sin of the Christian.  Using a
carefully contrived sexual image, he writes that "Sloth describes our
flaccid unwillingness to delight in the banquet of earth or to share
the full measure of life's pain and responsibility."  The image
conjured up by the word "flaccid" is ineffectuality, limpness.  By contrast what Cox promotes through this image is his view of the theologian
as an erect revolutionary penis, engorged with red blood, confident
with an American male's confidence that every problem can be tackled,
every problem penetrated.  Would that it were so.  But, of course,
it isn't so.  If our problems could be solved by moral earnestness,
masculine energy and secular hope, then indeed the Kingdom would have
arrived.  But they can't be solved.  Would that the collective penis
of man remain forever erect and effective, never tire and appear flaccid.
But it won't stay erect for very long.  The world isn't built that
way; nor is man.  If we take seriously the studies about work and the
working man in America, a different picture emerges of the preponder-
ant majority of Americans.  Human beings grow old in America, well
before they want to, and when they do, there is little for them to do,
which causes them to become very anxious and go to an early grave.
Human beings make few moral decisions in their lives, not because they
lack conscience or courage, but because the movement of modern life
removes the little basis left for moral decision.  The increasing
organization of society (ironically which Cox lauded in The Secular
City) makes choice less and less possible, and therefore responsibility
a much less prized value.  The overwhelming numbers of human beings
do not pursue lives of moral insight and action Cox so admires in Martin
Luther King and Dietrich Bonhoeffer.  He seems aware of this himself
when he qualifies his hero worship to ask, ". . . does this emphasis
on such exceptional people overlook the millions of unknown saints
who quietly do their daily task with compassion and dedication?"  And
he replies, "It would not, for there are such people and they are
saints also."  (On Not Leaving It to the Snake, Introduction, xiv).
This is pure nonsense.  It reminds me of the pulpit minister who is
forever trumpeting the virtues of Jesus or Moses or Abe Lincoln,
exhorting his parishioners to be like them, knowing full well, as
they do, they can't be like heroes -- all the while ignoring who
his parishioners really are, what their lives are really like.  The
preponderance of human beings not just in America, but throughout the
world, do not do their daily tasks with compassion and dedication;
they do them out of frustration, with resentment, driven by anxiety and
need, sustained in their lives to whatever degree one can be sustained
by small pleasures.  William James once noted that the ordinary human
being lives a life of quiet desperation.  If one thinks long and hard
enough about this, it will tell him something about the religious life
of man, and by implication what a theologian should be about.

V

   While the framework through which these authors developed
their theological proposals was both the Barthian polemic against
religion and the Kantian-Ritschlian reduction of religion to morality,
any further reflection on their works will reveal even more subtle
patterns of influence.  The enormous success which their works enjoyed
and continue to enjoy can be attributed in great part to their un-
questioned ability to capture in an exciting, arresting way a mood
developing amongst the theological public, as well as the educated
church laity, in the late '50's, since the end of the Korean War,
particularly in America.  It is a mood characterized by a distrust
of philosophy as socially irrelevant abstractions; by indifference to
history as archaic traditions forming a non-usable past; by rejection
of religion as pious self-concern and psychological dependency; and
further by the espousal of the biblical portraits of Jesus in his life
and teachings, as a humanistic, social ideal.  The question now becomes
what is the theologian to think about if he removes from himself the
resources of philosophy, history and religion, and has only the historic Jesus to turn to as a norm?  The answer, of course, is that he
has very little to think about.  The tendency in American Protestant
theology since the late '50's has been the progressive elimination of
a subject matter, with the resultant confusion over what constitutes
an appropriate method of theological thinking.  For if one doesn't
know what to think about, one can hardly be expected to understand how
to think about it.  The appeal to Jesus, in this regard, is little
more than a desperate effort to secure an anchor against the shifting
tides of contemporary culture which threaten to wash everything away
into an ocean of undifferentiated secularity.

   The successes of a Fletcher, an Altizer, and a Cox is due
not only to their ability to capture the developing theological mood,
but also to their ability to sustain, even to promote it.  Where theology
in the past twenty-five years has gradually eliminated its subject
matter in religion, and consequently become dubious about philosophy
and history as resources of inquire, the contemporary theologian has
turned stylist.  Language and manipulation of language has become the
essence of theology.  What matters is not what is said, but how it is
said.  The formulation of ideas, the discussion of events, the analysis
of issues -- these conventional acts of inquiry prove much less
important than acts of expressiveness, where words function to stimulate,
engage, move the reader.  Consider such phrases as "honest to God,"
"the new morality," "situation ethics," "the death of God," "the secular
city,""the politics of God."  These are rhetorical keys around which
their authors develop a language for stimulating and justifying
commitment to conceivable issue or action.  Thus the theological style
or rhetoric of such books as Altizer's The Gospel of Christian Atheism
or Cox's The Secular City has as its aim neither a description nor an
account of the humanly experienced world, but rather the engagement
of the reader at the point of the author's own enthusiasms and commitments.  The style is, of course, the pulpit style of preaching.  When
Bonhoeffer speaks in his prison letters of "religionless Christianity"
and "the world come of age," we don't hear the voice of a man struggling
to understand the meaning of religion in a secularized culture, but
rather the voice of a man who has come to realize that he is justified
in advocating a type of action he once had doubts about.  Words like
"maturity," "secular," responsible" are used not descriptively but
affectively -- to inspire and affirm commitment.  Fletcher, Robinson

and Van Buren, no less than Cox and Altizer and Bonhoeffer regard
theology not so much as thinking but as doing -- as the recommendation
of action, accompanied by a rhetoricaly style that openly or tacitly
justifies the recommendation.

What this means, of course, is that any recommendation
or commitment or action can inspire some sort of theological language
style. In recent years we have seen an explosion of theological
styles: "theology of hope," "theology of play," "black theology,"
"theology of liberation," "feminist theology," "gay theology,"
"theology of death," "story theology," "theology of the occult,"
"Jesus theology," the "theology of bioethics." When theology becomes
a style, what is lost is not only a subject-matter, but a method --
a loss of confidence about how to think about whatever theology should
think about. (Parenthetically, I should say that the lack of confidence about method produces in reaction that excessive formalism
and conceptualism noticeable in theologians who pursue interminably
methodological questions in the philosophies of Whitehead or Heidegger
or Wittgenstein or Husserl or Polanyi. For uncertainty about subject
matter inevitably means a preoccupation with method at the expense of
empirical investigation.)

This in sum is the depressing state of chaos in which American Protestant theology is to be found today. For when anything
goes, nothing really goes, nothing really is taken seriously, nothing
is actually necessary -- least of all theology itself.

## VI

Theology will continue to prove unnecessary until it abandons
the double-movement of repudiating religion by reducing it to an
ethical residue. For the repudiation of religion fails to recognize
the power of religion in human life to structure or order the
experience of the world, without which order there would be no possibility of living sanely in the world. The reduction of religion to
morality fails to recognize the depth of the human personality, beneath
conscious thought and action, at the level of feeling. Religion
is the response man makes to his sense that his life is cast into
a deep and mysterious and powerful relationship, through which he
lives out his life on earth in joy and suffering. Amongst the thinkers
who have come to an understanding of religion as I have described it --
as integral to the human sensibility, I should like to mention here
Richard L. Rubenstein (After Auschwitz, 1966); Peter Berger (A Rumor
of Angels, 1970); Bernard Meland (Faith and Culture, 1955); Langdon
Gilkey (Naming the Whirlwind: The Renewal of God-Language, 1969).

These thinkers have a clearer understanding than most that
man's religious life is a complex matter, composed of two vital
dimensions, as John Dewey saw some time ago in A Complex Faith when
he distinguished between "the religious" and "religions." There is
an elemental level of experience in which man encounters the world
through feeling at the conscious and unconscious levels of wonder
expectancy and trust, and negatively as anxiety, fear and doubt.
But there is also a formal level of experiencing in which man responds
to his elemental feelings through gestures, rituals, myths, beliefs
and other symbolic forms developed through his cultural imagination.
Richard Rubenstein understands this when he writes, "Today we understand that irrational phenomena in religion, as in other spheres of

human activity, are meaningful, purposeful, and goal-directed. They
express some of the deepest and most important feelings we experience
as human beings." (p. 229)   The Jewish rite of celebrating the coming-
to-age of a boy (Bar Mitzvah) is an example of that necessary "irrational"
phenomenon of which Rubenstein speaks.  He amplifies his point:

> "We have been far more successful in mastering the physical world
> than in dealing with emotional crises arising out of the developing
> personalities of individuals in our culture.  In such really
> important aspects of human experience as birth, adolescence,
> mating, guilt and death, our fundamental experiences tend to
> remain the same as those of primitive men.  If anything, we are
> at a disadvantage in our secular culture.  Primitive men never
> left the individual to face the crises of life unaided by meaning-
> ful myths and rituals as we do.  The Bar Mitzvah ceremony is
> significant because it confirms the young man in his growing
> identity at a most appropriate time and in a setting of the
> greatest possible significance." (p. 235)

Rubenstein's tendency to interpret religion functionally
as satisfaction of emotional needs suggests a one-sided view of
religion as a psychological device for overcoming personality crises.
Religion is no less an ontological experience, than it is a psychological one.  It is the perception of the wider, deeper context in
which human life is cast.  We experience this context in the feeling
of wonder, a sense of the thisness of life.  One supposes it is the
feeling at the root of Tillich's statement that philosophy begins
with the question, Why is there something, not nothing?  At the
elemental level of feeling, what a person experiences is not only
that there is something, but that he is related to this something as
the primordial sustaining ground of his being and of all other being.
In this perception it is inescapable that he will feel a sense of kinship with all other beings.  Bernard Meland has argued that when
expressed constructively man's perception of a ground to all reality
is the perception of a "more-than-human" dimension of experience." (p.45)
Insofar as we are related to a common ground, we are related to all
other beings, and related to ourselves.  Thus we are not alone.  There
is continuity to our lives in the world; hence there is the possibility of confidence that we can live out our lives in the world,
even live them out heroically, despite the inevitable experiences of
tragedy.  The biblical myths of creation and redemption are a dramatic
and true symbolization of this elemental perception of the deep and
transcending order of life in relation to which man has his
existence.

Peter Berger is another theologian who has a firm understanding of the elemental relgious sensibility and the formal meaning
of religious myths and rituals.  When he speaks of "signals of transcendence" he refers to human experiences of a common, ordinary sort
that provide a perception of a transcending reality upon which human
life rests.  The experiences he identifies are order, play, hope,
humor and damnation.  Order is understood by Berger very much like
Meland understands wonder, expectancy and trust:  to structure human
experience.  Insofar as we have a deep, unconscious sense that we
enjoy a place in the world, we are confident of a purpose to our
lives; and insofar as we have a purpose, life is essentially meaningful,
despite events of meaninglessness that befall us.  It should be added
that both Berger and Meland appear to be influenced by Schleirmacher

in the grasp of the signifcance of order in the religious sensibility.

In the same way Langdon Gilkey shows a sound understanding of the complex character of the religious sensibility when he writes in his essay "Dissolution and Reconstruction in Theology:"

". . . where our ordinary experience becomes peculiarly 'human' experience, taking on not only the rational, moral, communal and personal form we call human but also the burden of anxiety and inordinate self-concern that is uniquely ours, there man seems to touch a depth more ultimate than himself, to depend on it and to live from it. Thus our ordinary experience as it is lived from day to day takes its shape from these depths and the power to live creatively and meaningfully derives from this level of experience, as do the crippling despair and meaninglessness that are also human. Our most crucial experiences of inward serenity, joy and meaning, and the consequent outflow of love from such a newly filled creatureliness, arise in the answers which reveal the wonder, power, beauty and goodness of life. Correspondingly, our deepest anxieties, and the most destructive crises in the affairs of men appear when we find no answers at this level of experience, when all our acts are either trivial or idolatrous." (Frontline Theology, Dean Peerman, ed., 1967, pp. 34-35.)

It is important to state at this point that none of these authors is suggesting, nor am I, that man is homo religiosus in the debased sense of possessing a proclivity for an objective being called "the Holy." This, in my judgement, is the supposition of romantic, psychological misinterpretations of man's religious sensibility. Our authors place their most important stress on religion as a value and meaning experienced within what is ordinary or natural. We are able to identify a dimension of meaning called the Holy precisely because we can and do experience "holiness" within the structures of our common experience. Those who misinterpret Rudolph Otto by holding that religion creates the Holy because religion is the distinct "area" of its encounter by man, pay little attention to the multitude of religious expressions that suggest the presence of the Holy in virtually all natural experience. Religion does not create the Holy; it confirms it.

I stated earlier that the relationship between the elemental level of man's religious sensibility and the formal level of his religious myths and rituals is an organic one. The religious symbol is not merely a cognitive disclosure of the truth of the religious depth or feeling, it is an active, intimate and necessary response to it. In this regard, I view Tillich's effort to understand the relationship between life and religion according to the principle of the correlation of life's "questions" with religion's "answers," to be overly abstract, hence a somewhat distorted way of understanding the relationship. The influence of Tillich on Rubenstein and Gilkey distorts their otherwise incisive accounts, persuading them to believe that religion has an essential function -- to "answer" human questions. Certainly, at the highly conceptual or theological level of religion, questions are answered. But this is hardly the level at which religion is lived, or lived very deeply. I believe it is closer to the truth to say that religion does not answer the questions of life; rather religion, in its intimate relation to man's elemental sensibility, makes life possible by giving man a mode through which he can express his encounter with the complex depths and mysterious powers of his everyday existence.

The task of theology today is not radically different from what it has always been: to understand the religious existence of human beings. With respect to Judaism and Christianity this must involve the effort to understand the myths, rituals, doctrines, institutions affecting Jews and Christians in relationship to their elemental experiences as human beings joined to all other human beings in a common world. Theology can and must accept whatever help it can get from other disciplines of knowledge. For if religion is the traditional and public expression of the religious, it is no less true that the religious is not confined to religion, and further that religion itself is a complex cultural phenomenon affecting potentially every area of man's experience. Hence every cognitive inquiry is potentially relevant to understanding religion and the religious.

I part company with those who would argue that the essential task of theology is to clarify the claims of Christian faith with the aim of determining the validity of these claims. The question of truth is both a legitimate and an ultimate question; but in my judgement it must follow the more essential question of understanding. And when truth is thus seen to follow understanding, it will be appreciated that in matters religious, as in so many other matters, truth is an extraordinarily difficult attainment.

The two levels of the religious sensibility -- elemental and symbolic -- are organically related. This means that the dissolution or corruption of man's religious life from the "acids of modernity" is a complicated matter. Secularization may indeed threaten the traditional forms through which man expresses his elemental experience; but secularity cannot in itself prevent man from experiencing reality at the primary, psychic level, the level of his elemental religious sensibility. Moreover, insofar as secularity does in fact threaten the traditional means by which man responds expressively to his encounter with reality in wonder, suffering, joy, trust, guilt and death, secularity has the power to damage man in a fundamental, irreparable way. Secularization may indeed free man from the dominance and tutelage of religious superstitions, systems and powers, as theologians from Bonhoeffer to Cox have observed; but in threatening the vital and necessary forms of man's religious sensibility, secularity enslaves man in turn to an empty, hence destructive condition of living. In concluding, perhaps I can be forgiven for quoting some words of my own written on another occasion.

"If secularization threatens historic religious institutions and practices, it thereby threatens the means by which countless human beings give symbolic voice to their deepest feelings about the mysterious and ultimate meanings of living and dying. In fostering pragmatic and utilitarian attitudes, secularization reaches down to the basic sensibility of man and threatens every mode of its expression. We may very well have reached the time when art, music, literature, and architecture, along with religion and other symbolic means of man's spiritual self-expression, may be judged irrelevant to the contemporary culture; or, far worse, they may be made to conform to the measure of 'things' and 'services.' In the minds of many theologians, this would be the ultimate irony for

man living in a world he is persuaded to think has come of age."
(<u>The Erosion of Faith: An Inquiry into the Contemporary Crisis in Religious Thought</u>, 1971, pp. 240-241.)

THE PRESENT STATE OF THE DISCIPLINE OF
SYSTEMATIC THEOLOGY -- A PRELIMINARY REPORT

Thor Hall -- University of Tennessee at Chattanooga

This paper is in the manner of an introductory statement. It is a progress report on a project which has been under way for the last 18 months. Those of you who identify yourselves as systematic theologians should already have heard about it; you should have received our questionnaires last year.

I shall divide the present report into two parts: the first describes the project, outlines the procedures followed, and projects the phases remaining as we move toward completion; the second summarizes the responses we have received to one of the questions we asked -- one which haunts everyone who is involved in systematic theology, "How would you describe the current state of the discipline?" In the conclusion I shall offer a general estimate of the possibilities and potentialities systematic theologians find themselves working with as they attempt to reconstruct their discipline and move into the future. At the Symposium in Chicago I shall be able to provide more details on these and other facets of the inquiry.

Part I

Our project was designed to meet two specific needs, one represented by the general uncertainty which prevails at the present regarding the place and purpose of the discipline; the other related to the ongoing work of those of us who identify ourselves as systematic theologians.

The first of these needs -- the principal of the two -- is obvious to anyone who is engaged in the study of theology. The consensus is clearly that theology, and systematic theology in particular, is presently "between times," "in the doldrums." The great masters of the mid-century are all gone, and no one has arisen to assume the leading role. Present practitioners seem to be floundering, not clear about their mandates, not confident about methods, not certain about future directions.

There is, however, a great deal of theological experimentation going on -- attempts at rethinking and reformulation which are creative, suggestive, and potentially significant. It is important, obviously, for those who are involved in the discipline to take stock, to see where we need to go. This is precisely what the present study intends to do.

The second need to which it addresses itself -- the more practical dimension of the study -- has to do with the actual work we do, as teachers and scholars. Our individual methodologies, theoretical as well as practical, need to be checked against those of our colleagues; and our subject areas need to be correlated with those of the entire community of scholars, both so that we may relate to what others are doing and so that we may discover any areas left unattended. A complete overview of the work that goes on among us is clearly a desideratum of high priority, and this gives our project added justification.

The objectives of this project are as follows: We aim

43

44

1. to identify all professional systematic theologians
   who presently contribute to the discipline by way
   of teaching, research and writing (primarily scholars
   in seminaries, universities, colleges and institutes,
   Protestant and Catholic);

2. to obtain relevant information about their background
   and current activities (training, employment, curric-
   ular contributions, major sources, emphases, publications, and active research projects);

3. to prepare and publish a Directory of Systematic Theology (in cooperation with the CSR, the Scholars Press,
   a university press, or a commerical publisher);

4. to undertake an analytical summation of the material,
   including the prevalent viewpoints, methodologies,
   subjects and emphases among those presently active in
   the discipline (to be published in the form of a book
   or a series of articles entitled Systemic Theology
   Today).

The project is divided into two parts, Part I focusing on the
United States and Canada; Part II on Europe (Britain, the Continent,
Scandinavia); with the possibility of a supplement on the Third World
(Asia, Africa, South America) being added later.

Each part of the study involves three major phases: a) data
gathering, b) editing and computerization, c) analysis and publication.

Part I, Phase a) (gathering the data on active systematic theo-
gians in the U.S. and Canada) was initiated in January 1974, funded by
a grant from the Faculty Research Committee of the University of Tennessee at Chattanooga. Contact had earlier been established with the
Council on the Study of Religion, whose Research Committee encouraged
the undertaking with the understanding that it might later be incorporated in the so-called Scholars Inventory Project for which the CSR was
seeking funds from the National Endowment for the Humanities.

The CSR project was not funded, however, though the Council
was encouraged to submit a new application to NEH for special funding
for a feasibility study.

Recently we were granted another year's funding from the UTC
Faculty Research Committee, and further applications are being made to
certain foundations for a sizeable grant in support of intensified efforts, including additional staff.

Our first task was to build a roster of all active systematic
theologians in the U.S. and Canada. This turned out to be a long and
tedious job, requiring a great deal of plain detective work. In building
a roster of all active theologians in the United States and Canada, we
focused first on the seminaries and theological schools. From the Association of American Theological Schools we obtained a list of member institutions, and proceeded to write each school, requesting a copy of
their current catalogue. As these came in we began to build a card file
of all faculty members who were listed as having primary responsibilities

in theology, primarily systematic theology, but including those also whose responsibilities are in correlary disciplines (philosophical theology, dogmatics, history of doctrine, moral theology).

We went next to the Directory of Religious Studies Programs in North American Universities and Colleges, writing the heads of all departments that listed "theology" or "systematic theology" as an area of specialization, and requesting the names of all faculty members involved in such programs.

Thirdly, we contacted the Executive Office of the Council on the Study of Religion, requesting permission to utilize their membership records to identify those members that are active in systematic theology, whose names we had not already identified. We received the inventory questionnaires for all the members in CSR affiliated societies who listed theology and philosophy of religion as their areas of interest, which we then collated with our own roster. A note was also published in the CSR Bulletin, requesting anyone professionally involved in the discipline of systematic theology, who had not already been contacted, to write us. As a result of all these efforts a card file of 1,230 names and addresses was assembled.

The next task was to develop an appropriate research instrument. Since we were interested in analyzing the actual profile of the discipline at the present, our questionnaire needed to include certain general items (name, current position, year of birth, years of teaching, years in current position, membership in professional societies, religious affiliation), as well as inquiries concerning academic career, areas of teaching responsibilities and research interests, publications and active research projects. In addition we included certain evaluative questions ("Which of the major systematic theologians of the past do you consider closest to your own position"; "How would you describe your own theological method"; "What are the most important emphases in your own work"; "How would you describe the current state of the discipline of systematic theology"; and "What in your view is the main task facing the systematic theologian in the foreseeable future").

We estimate at this time that we have the information requested from approximately 90% of all active systematic theologians in North America. After computerizing the data gathered, analysis and the preparation of reports is possible. We hope to have the manuscript for the Directory finished in the Fall of 1975; and the writing of the analytical report entitled Systematic Theology Today is scheduled for the Spring of 1976. In the meantime, if we receive sufficient funding, we shall begin the data gathering for Part II of the study, dealing with Europe, during this summer. This will proceed parallel with the concluding phases of Part I during the Fall and Spring of the 1975-76 academic year, with the editing and computerization, analysis and publication of Part II scheduled for the Fall of 1976 and Spring of 1977.

### Part II

I shall now proceed to summarize the responses we have received to the question, "How Would You Describe the Current State of the Discipline of Systematic Theology?" But before I do, let me submit a few of the comments people have made in regard to the project itself. One colleague was obviously annoyed at being asked to fill out another question-

naire. He said: "I can't think of anything the world needs less than
a directory of systematic theology; and I feel sufficiently compiled,
stamped out, listed, numbered, and categorized for one lifetime."

But that response was fourtunately not typical. Many have
wished us success with the undertaking. Several have congratulated us
on the project, though a number of people have also warned us -- openly
or more diplomatically -- that the plan is obviously a very ambitious
one. The prevailing opinion is that it is "a much needed task", "a
valuable project", "an interesting and helpful undertaking", "an excellent idea", "a great boon to all of us in the profession." One colleague wrote:

> "I hope your directory and your analyses are successful....
> I think one of the great problems of theology today is
> the lack of communication among theologians about basic
> issues. Even in..., a rather ecumenical institution,
> it seems to me that theologians often ignore the insights
> and contributions of some of their colleagues, whether...
> they are in 'systematics' or some other discipline. If
> this state of affairs is also true at the national level,
> as I presume, then communication is the greatest need that
> theology faces today."

I take this last comment -- that communication is the greatest
need of theology today -- as the kind of exaggeration which is legitimate only in the narrowest of contexts. The material I am about to sum-
merize shows clearly that our discipline is up against problems far more
serious than that. But perhaps a summary of these more serious problems
will help alleviate the more obvious ones, also.

The responses to the question, "How Would You Describe the Current State of the Discipline of Systematic Theology?", ranged very widely.
Some were short and concise, others more belabored and detailed. Many
were strongly negative, many strongly positive. A great many people
deplore the developments of the last couple of decades, as they perceive
them, but there are many also who look upon the very same developments
with appreciation and great optimism. There is a certain amount of nostalgia at work among systematic theologians, nostalgia coupled with a
sense of loss; but there is also a sense of hope among us, hope projecting itself toward a future envisioned as more significant than any past
period in the history of the discipline.

Let us look at some details, organized around the several major
impressions we have received in perusing our material.

A first impression is that the discipline of systematic theology is in need of redefinition. Several respondents indicated that there
is much equivocation among us, between those who hold a broader definition
(one which considers systematic theology an integrating discipline, utilizing the insignts of the entire spectrum of theological disciplines,
from philosophical theology and biblical theology, through dogmatic
theology and historical theology, to moral theology and practical theology, including preaching) and those who follow a narrower definition
(one which delimits the role of the systematician generally in the area
of dogmatics or doctrinal analysis). The broader definition is obviously difficult to maintain; it requires that the systematician is informed

of and has a stake in everything that is going on in philosophical, biblical, dogmatic, historical, and practical studies, and this is of course
quite problematic -- as is the implication that systematic theology is
somehow the queen of the theological sciences, and that the other disciplines are in some way subsumed under its inclusive umbrella.  But the
narrower definition causes problems also, especially in the area of interdisciplinary relationships, and particularly in the relation of systematic to biblical theology.  This unhappy situation must clearly be overcome.  One of our respondents described the problems of isolation he
faces as a moral theologian.  Another lamented the fact that in his institution systematic theology is getting a steadily smaller piece of the
pie, while the practical disciplines receive constantly increasing emphasis.  Still another expressed satisfaction that in his school systematic theology now receives increased attention as against the history of
doctrine.

Perhaps there is time for another attempt at what Philip Schaff
called "theological propadeutic," i.e. a basic analysis of the nature
and interrelationships of theological disciplines.  Such an analysis is
greatly needed in the case of systematic theology, obviously.  The end
result would perhaps not have to be quite as drastic as that suggested
by Seward Hiltner -- he urges us to ditch the phrase; it was something
the Germans hung on us in the first place.  Perhaps all we need to do is
walk over the common territory once again with our friends and neighbors
in the theological community, determining in good faith what is what.

A second impression which we glean from our material is that
systematic theology is now in serious upheaval.  Not yet a life-time removed from the publication of several significant 20th century systematic
theologies (it is sufficient to mention the names of Barth, Brunner, Tillich, and Aulen), we find now a generation of theologians rather like
the children in the market place described in Matthew 11: 16-17: "One
group shouts to the other, 'We played wedding music for you, but you would
not dance!  (The other responding) We sang funeral songs, but you would
not cry!'"  From left and right come generally negative expressions: the
discipline is "chaotic," "confused," "fragmented," "in disarray"; its
status is "sad," "not good," "poor," "very poor," "abominable," "indescribable"; systematic theology is "neglected," "disoriented," "drifting,"
"stagnating," "in the shadows," "bankrupt," "sick," "dead."

If we should attempt to systematize the reasons for this disturbing state of affairs, they are often expressed in terms of direct op-
posites such as "systematic theology is unwilling to cut its old moorings"
and "the discipline is totally at sea, drifting with every wind of the
weather."  The first part of this dialectic is expressed in criticisms
such as these: the discipline is "altogether too academic," "confined
within safe theological circles," "preoccupied with scholarly games of
intellectual analysis and theological one-upmanship"; it is "stuffy and
jargon-filled," "wooden and irrelevant," "archaic and outmoded," "preoccupied with non-issues."  What has happened, some suggest, is that the
discipline has become "too dominated by philosophical form," "married to
classical philosophical traditions which isolate it from the contemporary
mind."  Others suggest that it has been "captured by ideology," "dicho-
tomized from the realities of life," "separated from the concerns of the
church as well as the secular world."  These critics would like to see a
discipline which "justifies its existence on a practical plane," which
is "situational or contextual," "interdisciplinary" (recognizing the

contributions of psychology, sociology, and anthropology), "more respectful of the varieties of contemporary personal religious experience."

But the other side of the dialectic has equally elequent pro-
ponents: systematic theology is here considered "in a state of confusion,"
"dominated by passing fads," "given to binges of fancy" -- "weird, slov-
enly, and juvenile ideas tossed off on a boat trip, teddy-bear precious,
banal." From this perspective, the fantastic pluralism of new theological positions is usually criticized as "fragmentation," "disarray,"
signifying a "loss of unifying vision" or "uncertainty about directions."
This is considered the result of several things: "the loss of metaphysical bases." "demythologization-demetaphysicalization-demysteriorization,"
"extreme subjectivity," "lack of anchoring in Christian tradition," "loss
of a common language," "differing presuppositions," "cultural and psychological upheavals," "uncritical acceptance of contemporary intellectual
fashions." What we have, then, in this view, is a discipline in which
there is no discipline; "everyone is doing his own thing," producing "an
agglomeration of little schools," "overly ambitious to be original" or
"to say something new or different in the contemporary situation," and
therefore completely "relativistic," "inclined toward eclecticism and syn-
cretism."

The upheavals in the discipline are thus considerable, whether
one takes a more traditional or a more progressive point of view. But
the discipline is not therefore given up. A third impression which we
receive loud and clear from our material is that the present state of affairs contains some promise for the future. There are some who speak of
"a loss of confidence," "a state of limbo," "anxiety," "retreat," "quies-
cence," "apathy," "vacuum," and "waiting." But there are those also who
describe the situation as "constructive turmoil," "ferment," "seismic
shifts," "seed time," "pregnancy." Some even manage to be somewhat euph-
oric about the future, seeing the discipline is "open," "healthy," "developing," "full of exciting possibilities," "more alive than 35 years ago."

What is the basis for such hopefulness? Let me summarize the
material by reference to several major viewpoints. One strong note which
is struck repeatedly by our respondents is the presence of "a host of
good people" in the discipline, "a number of very gifted people at work
on a staggering diversity of concerns." The consensus among these respondents is that this staggering diversity is a sign of life; theology is
once again "exciting," "vigorous," "dynamic"; theologians (at least some)
are considered (at least in their own opinion) "bright," "fertile," "promising," "progressive." The situation, in short, is "challenging."

A second note of optimism relates to the work now being done.
Many recognize that theology is presently "issue oriented," "working at
individual problems," "concentrated in essay form" or "monographic insights," each theologian working with "his own little pieces of ivory,"
"the ground at his own feet." Many think this is the kind of period we
are in; it is "not a time for complete systems," only for "examination,"
"reflection," "analysis" -- or what one respondent calls "inadvertent systematics." One characteristic feature of this ongoing work is its "poly-
logical" nature -- it is beyond both the monological and the dialogical
stage. characterized more by discourse and interchange than by synthesis
and irenic singularity. New directions are being explored; many methods
are being tested; different models are being suggested -- theologies "not
for the whole world, but for smaller units," "theologies for specialized

groups."

A third basis for optimism is the reassessment now going on on the level of assumptions and presuppositions, i.e. on the level of basic methodology. Many of our respondents regret what they call "this preoccupation with methodology," but many feel that the discipline can only go futher if it is willing to go deeper into these kinds of questions. And they see signs of such willingness, "a desire to lay a secure intellectual basis for theological work," "to find a common level of discourse," "to undertake a radical questioning of basic assumptions." This entails "a deeper study of philosophy" and of "the relationship between philosophy and theology" and "theology and culture." It involves "looking for a workable metaphysic," "a more explicit and critical metaphysical grounding." But it includes also concern for "modern scriptural parameters," "rediscovery of its innermost realities," and "reassessment of the role of theology within the community of faith."

Fourth, and more specifically, the current optimism based on methodological advances emphasizes the importance of "the profound sense of historicity" which characterizes much of our contemporary rethinking, i.e. the "realization of the historical nature of theology" and "the experiential character of revelation." Also, much emphasis is given the new-found interdisciplinary contacts between systematic theology and other theological and academic disciplines. In the estimation of our respondents, systematic theology is clearly "moving out of its own closed world," "realizing its natural closeness to the other disciplines in the university," and "becoming less defensive than in the past."

Finally, the impression that the discipline of systematic theology shows some promise for the future is supported by a number of responses indicating a certain desire for convergence and synthesis; some see this as a "need," others describe it as a "hunger," and others again speak of "a possibility for some revival." Systematicians are obviously aware of where they are in the evolution of things -- they are quite conscious of their responsibility to engage in "creative dialogue with contemporary culture," "a translation of tradition into forms that are congruent with present culture," "a search for sound and effective responses to current needs and demands," and "finding a point of contact with the contemporary world of thought," "the midsets of post-modern man," or "the realities of the social, political, and economic dynamics of contemporary life." As one respondent puts it, "systematic theology is coming alive in ecologically creative processes of thought and action." This may continue to take many forms; we are in a period of "paradigm changes," emergence of "heuristic perspectives" and "new systematic images." But certain distinct approaches are clearly more exciting than others -- though there is nothing even approaching consensus regarding their significance.

A number of respondents indicate that they consider "process thought" the most promising framework for systematic work in the immediate future. Others mention the new possibilities in linguistic analysis (particularly the analysis of myth and symbol) and in hermeneutic (especially the focus on narrative and story). Some find long-term significance in the new eschatology (a la the theology of hope) and in the categories of liberation and political utopianism.

If, finally, we should ask who among the active theologians at the present are considered most promising as systematicians, Pannenberg

and Moltmann clearly outrank the rest of us. Others considered highly
significant are Kaufman, Ogden and Gilkey. Honorable mention is given
Macquarrie and Pittenger. Among Roman Catholics, the highest ranking
goes to Lonergan and Rahner (though the latter obviously has despaired
of systematic synthesis). Among younger emergent lights, Catholics
usually name Tracy and Dulles. Evangelical theologians assuming leadership at the present are Thielicke, Braaten, Weber and Ramm.

I shall close this initial report here. Much work remains to
be done in summarizing and analyzing the material we have gathered. It
is our hope that this study will assist us all in the further development
of our work, individually and corporately.

THE STATUS AND PROSPECTS FOR THEOLOGY
Paul van Buren -- Temple University

Our topic is the status and prospects for theology. My subjective and
personal response to this is that, because I am almost fully engaged in administrative
work, the status is stagnant, but, since I shall be able to return to theological work
full-time next June, the prospects are dazzling! When I pause to consider the matter
more generally and objectively, I think that the terms I would use would be "churning"
for the status, and "exciting" for the prospects. That is to say, I think we are maneuvering around in the face of certain recent developments, and that some of these are
coming to a head in a way that will open the door into a genuinely new state of theological work. I want to isolate two quite minor and the one major development that
open the way for new theological work, and then to define some of the major tasks that
lie ahead for theology and which lead me to be excited by the prospects. In the course
of doing this I shall only suggest some of the ways in which I think the task may be
carried out.

The first development worth mentioning is that the doctrine of God has once
again come back into the center of theological debate. Whatever else may be said about
what was written in the 1960's on the subject of God, it has at least opened the subject
up for fresh consideration. Death-of-God types, process theologians, theological futur-
ists, and many others have combined to make it more possible to reconsider, to put into
question and to explore alternatives to classical formulations of the central doctrine of
Christian faith. That sort of loosening-up process is all to the good, although its
service has been largely negative. I don't think much of the attempts we have made to
move on to something positive. Nevertheless, a widening concensus that all is not well
with the very center of traditional theology is a precondition to getting down to the
task of something positive that may yet lie ahead. I look upon the backing and filling
of yesterday and today, then, as a hopeful sign for tomorrow.

Perhaps a more important development has been the growing disenchantment of
theologians with the promises and possibilities of western civilization generally, and,
especially for American theologians, with the American dream in particular. The culture
religion which has been the prevailing tendency of Christianity becomes a bit easier to
identify and to resist as the character and consequences of our way of life and system
of political economics comes daily more sharply into focus. The evident failure of
America and its allies to offer to Southeast Asians any alternative to a Marxist-inspired
vision of a new social order suggests to more and more people that in fact we have no
alternative. All we have to offer is a larger automobile, and even we are discovering
that only a quarter of the population benefits from that, while on another level, the
whole population's very existence is threatened by it.

As disenchantment with the American myth spreads, the more possible it becomes
to think of Christianity not as a cultural support of the establishment, but as a counter-
culture. The increasingly convincing evidence that we the people have been lied to and
are still being lied to by our highest officials is not at first sight a matter of theological import, yet I believe it is or may be a help in loosening the stranglehold which
the values, standards and canons of our civilization have had upon Christians, especially
in this country. The rise of an increasingly interesting Marxist-Christian dialogue is
evidently a piece of this. So too is the challenge of fellow Christians from the Third
World, especially from Latin America, pressing to see whether there are any Christians
in North America who will side with them against governments supported by the interests
that control our government and determine its policy. All of this makes for a situation
which invites new thinking, which opens a window on a new view of Christian faith and
the Christian's role in a society such as ours. Twenty-five years ago such matters were
called "non-theological factors" in the ecumenical movement. That we are no longer so
sure that they are non-theological is a sign that theology is beginning to stir and is
far from dead.

It might be objected that these remarks do not take into account the danger of theology falling victim to a ghetto mentality. Whether that is a danger I leave open, but reference to the ghetto brings me to the really important development, the one single factor which more than any other opens up prospects for theology that may turn out to be genuinely revolutionary. I refer of course to the revitalization of the ghetto, or better, to the resurgence or renaissance of Judaism, centered in the birth and continuance of the state of Israel. Since that is what has happened to the ghetto, we shall have to think again about ghetto theology.

The renewal of Judaism in our time, as a historical development having historic consequences for theology, has its beginnings, of course, in the birth of the state of Israel. The birth and the survival of this tiny state has been of such profound and obvious importance for Jews of all persuasions, be they religious or secular, whether feeling called to move to Israel or choosing to remain in the Diaspora, that the points need little elaboration. Jews as well as others have not been and are not now of one mind about the policies of the Israeli government, but they are few indeed who do not feel some sense of identification with Israel or have not some commitment to it. The birth and survival of this small country in less than hospitable surroundings have played an incalculable role in strengthening the sense of identity of Jews.

From this strengthening has followed a second development: Jews have begun slowly to speak of the unspeakable, to look in the face the valley of dry bones out of which this exceeding great host has arisen. There was nothing inevitable about this further development. On the contrary, it might seem more probable that the silence would have continued. Certainly one wouldn't have expected the Gentiles to open that book. No, if the silence was to be broken, it had to be the Jews who made the first move, although doing so for them was an agonizing, even a traumatic experience, like breaking a solemn oath. Another people might have succeeded in forgetting the past and looking only to the future, but the Jews are a historical people and it is part of their identity to remember. So it has happened that the memory began to stammer and speak, and the Holocaust became a subject of reflection.

Reflection? That puts the matter in too Waspish a way, as anyone would know who has read any of the testimony at the Eichmann trial, for example. It would be more accurate to say that the Holocaust became a subject for tears, for stammering, for screams of anguish. However we put it, what matters is that it came out into the open, accompanied by all its stench. It is now there before us, unavoidably on the agenda of any who dare to pick it up. And this has to be said in the present tense, for this stage of the development is not finished. Therein lie the prospects for theology.

Confronted by the existence of the state of Israel and the Holocaust out of which it was born, Christians - or at least some of them - found themselves having to speak of Judaism in somewhat different tones. This is the next stage of the development, which I am not as concerned to lay out in chronological sequence as I am to develop in its logical bearing on the prospects for theology. From both Catholics and Protestants, one began to hear voices calling into question the long sanctioned anti-Judaism of the churches, although it would be more accurate to say that it was anti-Semitism that was deplored. The fruits of Christian anti-Semitism were all too evident in the death factories, but perhaps more importantly, the Jewish presence, which has been there all along, was now all too unavoidably evident in the form of Israel. Christian speakers were beginning to speak with an awareness that Jews were among their hearers, that they were speaking in the hearing of those who had survived a Holocaust planned and carried out by baptised Christians. I think it is worth noting that what has been said by Christians speaking to this issue has been spoken to the Gentiles first, and then also to the Jews, not yet recapturing the Pauline order of the Jew first, and then the Gentile. But at least, and that is part of the status of theology at the present, the Jew has come into the picture as one of those who hears what the theologian is saying. The Jew has always been there. What makes this present status new and interesting is that the theologians seem to have become aware of the fact.

This brings us to the final aspect of this development of the renewal of Judaism which sets the stage for considering the prospects for theology. Having begun by taking the Jews into account in a way not known before in the history of Christianity, at least a few Christians have begun to realize that a reconsideration of what Christians have been saying about Judaism and of Christian Jewish relations must lead to a reconsideration of Christianity itself. The groundwork for this was laid by the 1960's by Marcel Simon in France with his Verus Israel and Salo Baron in America with his Social and Religious History of the Jews. (The earlier work of Leo Baeck should of course be mentioned, and Ben Zion Bokser's Judaism and the Christian Predicament provides a guide to other sources, as well as an honest delineation of the issues.) The first steps of the reconsideration seem to be those of Roy Eckhardt in his Elder and Younger Brothers. More recently Rosemary Ruether's Faith and Fratricide (1974) and F. H. Littell's The Crucifixion of the Jews (1975) have brought us to the point of no return. Theology can shut its eyes and pretend that the Holocaust never happened and that Israel doesn't exist. Theology has shown itself capable of such blindness before! But if there are prospects for serious theology, for a theology not hopelessly blind to matters that pertain to the heart of its task, then the time has come for a reconsideration of the whole theological and Christian enterprise of the most radical sort.

I use the word radical in its etymological sense: going to the roots. A reconsideration of theology in the light of the Holocaust, the founding and survival of the state of Israel and the consequent renewal of Judaism, can be nothing less than radical because the more carefully we look into the matter, the more unavoidable becomes the agonizing conviction that anti-Semitism, or anti-Judaism, far from being an accidental excreseence, is rooted in the very heart of Christian faith, beginning with the apostolic witness to Jesus as the Christ of Israel's God. The roots of Hitler's final solution are to be found, I must fearfully confess, in the proclamation of the very Kerygma of the earliest Christians. I try hard to say to myself that that first-century quarrel among Jews about the real meaning of Judaism, or (to use other terms) that clash within Israel as to what God's plan for Israel was, which is, after all, what we have in the so-called New Testament, was a family quarrel that the Gentiles were bound to misunderstand. There are things which you can say about your own family, about your brothers or cousins, which, were I to say, would be hardly the same thing. When words that Jews say to fellow Jews are then said by Gentiles, the result is hardly faithful to what was originally said. Yes, the meaning of words is always a function of their context and of the speakers. So perhaps, I try to tell myself, the Kerygma and quarrels of the earliest Jews whom Gentiles called Christians, the real message of the New Testament, is in order, and it was those Gentile early Fathers who distorted that message into a religion which we call Christianity, including its anti-Judaism. Once you get to the Fathers, there is no evading the centrality of their anti-Judaism. Dr. David Efroymson, one of our recent graduates, concluded his dissertation on "Tertullian's Anti-Judaism and its Role in his Theology" with the words: "The road from here to Auschwitz is long and it is not direct, but you can get there from here."

I must confess, however, that I am not winning the argument with myself that this is all there is to it. The anti-Judaism lies deeper than that, in the very roots of the earliest Christian confession itself. Helpful as it will be in the work ahead to remember that the writings of the so-called New Testament, or most of them, are the work of Jews, written by Jews, for Jews, and not to be understood as anything but that, that is not going to settle the matter. The task for theology is a harder and more painful one than that, and if we do not take the easy way out, then we shall have to see that we do not get "off the hook" so easily. Radical reconstruction is what lies ahead, and if I am only five percent right in what I am saying, then the prospects for theology are indeed exciting. It will, however, be the excitement of a revolution that will be extremely painful, that will tear the veil of the temple from top to bottom, and no doubt it will take years to accomplish. If such were to happen, then such a change would leave the 16th century reconstruction looking like a minor ripple in the unbroken history of Christianity before it came to its senses.

I have defined the status, that is, the present situation of theology as coming face to face with the fact that anti-Judaism is not an unfortunate aberration of Christian faith but is rooted in the New Testament itself. Baeck, Bokser, Ruether and many others are right about that, I believe, whatever we may think of their various proposals about what to do about it. If we can agree with Barth that anti-Judaism is an attack upon revelation and so upon God, then the status of theology is that of crisis. It has come face to face with the fact that it stands in an essential self-contradiction. And yet I have said that the prospects for theology are exciting. I say that because I think that in fear and trembling, there may be an alternative to calling the whole enterprise to a halt as misguided from the beginning. Misguided in important respects it may have been, but that does not exclude the possibility of a better guiding, of going back and reconstructing the heart of Christianity from the ground up. So I do think there is a choice, that there are alternatives. There can be either no more theology, or there can be radically reconstructed theology. Any intermediate position is possible only to one who has not seen the renewal of Judaism, who can manage to shut his eyes to the Holocaust and the existence of the state of Israel. But there remains the choice for reconstruction. In order to help win support for this painful and difficult work, I want to address briefly four major areas and suggest lines along which demolition and reconstruction might proceed. These are the doctrine of God in his relationship to the world, the interpretation of Easter, the claim that Jesus is the messiah, and the relationship of the apostolic literature to the Scriptures, or, as we have been accustomed to put it, of the New Testament to the Old Testament.

The God of Abraham, Isaac and Jacob, the God of the Exodus and Sinai, is the God who has committed and compromised himself for good in his relationship to the people Israel. If we grant that, as the Jew Paul could still write in Romans 11, then we must go on to say that God's decision stands in the face of the crucifixion of Jesus, the destruction of Jerusalem by the Romans, the rise and spread of a movement begun by Jews who came to be called Christians, the turning of that movement against his people, the Jews, up to and including those Christians setting up and carrying out the work of Auschwitz, Theresienstadt, Dachau and other centers for the man's attempt at a final solution to God's commitment. If God is free to make that continuing commitment to his people, and yet allow all this to take place, or at least to have not acted so as to prevent it, then Christians have to come off their high horse and admit that they do not understand God. He is too free to fit their neat theories. He certainly cannot be the omnipotent, omniscient God of Christian theology. He cannot be the God of the theism that theology has presumed to present to the world.

Any reassessment and reconstruction of Christianity that, thanks to the existence of the state of Israel and the horror of the Holocaust, finally begins to recognize that Judaism exists, has endured against all odds, and is the root from which Christianity lives and the trunk into which it has been grafted, would have to be one that went to the heart of the matter and reconsidered the God whose commitment to Israel is the starting point for theology. But that committment to Israel is a free act by which God has compromised his own freedom. Whatever God is, he is one who has compromised himself in such a way that he will not cease to be the God of this people. If we say, as the weight of the theological tradition has said, that that self-compromise of God was nullified with the events of Good Friday and Easter and confirmed in the destruction of Jerusalem in 70 C.E., then we are saying that the God of Christianity is another God than that of Abraham, Isaac, Jacob and Jesus. In which case, so-called orthodox Christianity is not just a heretical position: it is full-blown apostasy, from the Gospel according to Matthew down to and including today.

We Gentile Christians have had a great deal to say about the crucifixion of Jesus. We have developed all sorts of theories which explain it. We have presumed to understand it, as the early fathers of Christian theology claimed to understand the destruction of Jerusalem. It might be observed that such a careful and thoughtful student of the modern history of God's people as Uriel Tal reiterates that we lack the ontological tools to understand the Holocaust. That sort of recognition that God's

freedom is a mystery, that we do not understand God and his relationship to this world
is something that would have to be central in any reconsideration of Christianity in
the light of the events of this century.

But if we are speaking of the God of Abraham, then perhaps, like Abraham, we
may dare to bargain a bit, or risk a few further thoughts on God's mysterious freedom.
My grounds for moving further have to do with a point I shall return to later. Jesus
proclaimed the immanent messianic age, the reign of God, in which the sick would be
healed, justice would be done, love would reign supreme, and even death would be overcome.
Those who believed him believed also that at least in his case, this new situation had
arrived, beginning with Easter. But the writings of the early Christians which we have
preserved to us reflect a clear awareness that the messianic age had not come. And after
1900 years, we can hardly deny that what Jesus promised has still not come! Could it be
that in his freedom, the God of Abraham, Isaac and Jacob has decided that he will do no
more, that he will stay his hand until we have done our work to usher in the era of peace
and freedom that he wills? He has, after all, given us the Torah! Halakah has been set
before us. He waits! Could that be it? Then how radically would we have to reconstruct
our ideas of providence, of faith, of justification, and of the whole construction we
have made of the works/faith relationship!

Christian theology has committed itself to speaking of God as the God of Abraham
and Sinai. What we have failed to admit is that this God, by His own free, sovereign
choice, is and remains the God of this people. Whatever else has happened along the way,
be it Egypt, Babylon, the destruction of Jerusalem, the ghetto and Christian pogroms,
Crusades and finally Asuchwitz, The God of theology is the God of Abraham and his de-
scendants. If we let go of that so-called Jewish particularism, or, otherwise said, the
electing God, then we have no grounds for saying anything at all.

The God of the Exodus, if Gerhard Von Rad's exegetical work is still worth anything, is the God who, because he was understood to have created this people as a people,
was also and in consequence seen as the God who had created the whole environment, the
world. But as Creator, God qualifies his freedom. He binds himself to the consequences
of his own act. This may or may not be the best of all possible worlds, in some logical
sense of possibility. It is in fact this world, the world, so Israel understood, that
God had created. But the other side of the coin is that God is the one who has cast the
die for this actual world, who has bound himself by his act, whose freedom, by his own
choice, is now limited by what he has done. There is then a reciprocity between him and
this actual state of affairs that we call the world. I do not conclude from this that
God is not free, but rather that God's freedom is not the abstract and theoretical freedom that Christianity-endorsed theism has made it out to be. It must be, rather, genuine
freedom, a freedom that can risk concrete and particular consequences, that can choose
for particularity and fact, over against universality and abstraction.

I do not mean to imply that any of these more or less logical consequences of
the call of Abraham or the giving of Torah are binding or correct. I mean only to indicate that if theology is to rethink its foundations in the light of the reality of Judaism,
then it will need to make room for the idea that God's freedom may be a freedom to compromise or qualify that freedom. If by committing himself to Israel and the covenant,
God is no longer, by his own decision, free to do what he wants with human history, if
by creating a world and thus granting to it its own development and life, God can no
longer make it totally subservient to his merest whim, then that is the mystery of God's
freedom that theology must accept. Having said that, I must, to be honest, add that I
do not presume to understand the mystery of God's freedom, and that these can be only
suggestions of lines along which theology might work. I would point out, however, that
these lines are sufficiently new for theology, that the prospects for theology along
these lines are as exciting as those which the early Fathers developed and which may now
have to be worked out afresh from the ground up.

A second area for demolition and new construction is the interpretation of
Easter. Easter has been interpreted by the Christian tradition as God's mighty act
whereby death has been overcome and the victory of God's plan has been revealed for the
whole world. Being Gentiles and so not so burdened by the call to remember as the Jews,
Christians have simply forgotten the utter difference between the kingdom which Jesus
proclaimed and the fact that nothing else has happened as a result of Easter. The Jewish
authors of the apostolic community were accutely aware of the gap and they agonized over
the delay. For them it followed as night upon day that since Jesus was the Messiah, the
messianic age must come and come soon. Since it didn't, they went on to devise sub-
stitutions. The promised kingdom was spiritualized into another world, so that a coming
of the risen Messiah to this world to redeem it was translated into believers going at death
into a heavenly, spiritual realm to be with the Christ. Easter was seen as the transformation of the defeated preacher of God's kingdom on earth - and where else would it
make sense to locate the kingdom of a God who had compromised himself to the extent of
creating this world? - into the spiritualized pioneer who opened the way into another
world. No longer need men long for the kingdom; it was there, running parallel, if invisible, above this realm. No longer had men to struggle for righteousness on earth; the
realm of righteousness that mattered was elsewhere, and this world was reduced to a practice field for the great game to be played out in that a-historical realm of eternity.

This perfidious shift having been accomplished, then why not proclaim Easter
as the absolute, total triumph? What it hadn't accomplished (e.g. any affect on the
suffering, injustice and deaths of men and women on earth, including specifically those
slaughtered by the Romans in Jerusalem in the year 70 and those slaughtered in Europe at
the hands of baptized Germans from 1941 to 1945) was simply scaled down in value as being
of only transient concern. After all, with eternal life won, why care about actual human
life? If a righteousness of faith by grace was available, what matter that simple human
righteousness be trampled by tyranny and corruption? Souls were being saved; what matter
that their bodies were decaying? The more triumphalist the interpretation of Easter, the
more Christianity betrayed the world which it had claimed that God loved.

Matters need not have so developed. Although there are passages enough in the
apostolic writing to feed that triumphalism, there are plenty more to offer grounds for
a new departure. Central to any serious reconstruction will be the recognition that
Easter was not the great triumph, not the ultimate victory, but at most a tantalizing
hint of what might yet be but definitely was not yet. What there was in the way of
victory was his alone, however much the rest of us may wish to share in it. For the
rest of us, we remain in a world still awaiting the messianic age, still groaning, along
with the environment and with the Spirit (N.B.!) for liberation, according to Romans 8.

Moreover, reconstruction will have to come to terms with the highly ambiguous
character of Jesus's victory. He was seen, but he also disappeared. It was really him,
the crucified one, the stories insist, yet the disciples were clearly afraid it might
have been only a ghost of some sort. What sort of victory was it that could not be
realized in a full and open return to the land of the living? Like the other restorations
of Israel's history, this one too is ambiguous. The Exodus from slavery in Egypt was
into suffering in the wilderness for forty years. The return from Babylon was followed
by subjugation to foreign powers. And in our own day, we can hardly hide our eyes from
the ambiguity of the phenomenon of Israel as a nation state, threatened by war after war.
So Easter is in good company and we had better learn how to interpret it within and as
a part of Israel's continuing history.

I do not think that this reconstruction will require doing violence to the
apostolic writings. Rather, it will challenge the selectivity in reading those writings
during the past 18 centuries which could pass so lightly over those sections which express
the anguished waiting, the sense of near despair at the delay, the recognition that as the
early community was reading its own tradition and consulting its own memory, something
was wrong, something was outstanding, unaccomplished. And then, with all the time since
then driving the point home and making the issue unavoidable, we shall have to ask about

the meaning of Easter in the light of the fact that nothing more happened. If we dare to think that God was speaking to men in what happened on Easter, on what grounds will we be able to deny that he has been speaking to us by means of this long period of delay? Could it be that Easter followed by the delay adds up to a word of God that says the next move is up to us? I think we may find that the apostolic writings can also be read in this way. Behold, the duck becomes a rabbit, and without having to invent the perverted theory of a Church and a New Covenant which displace God's people and his Covenant of Sinai.

Along with the reconstruction of the interpretation of Easter, inevitably, will go a reconstruction of the confession that Jesus is the Messiah. And now we arrive at the point at which the fat would seem to be in the fire. For if we allow the question whether Jesus was a false messiah, then at the same time we open the question whether Jesus is rightly confessed as Kurios and Logos. Before our questions become too wild here, let us see what help we can gain from two sources. The first is the apostle Paul, especially the part of his letter to the Romans found in Chapter 11, and then, with that, the old Christ-ological principle that Jesus is not defined by his titles, but is, rather, the one who provides new content to ancient titles. On the basis of the second point, we should pose the question in this way: what are we saying about the Messiah when we confess Jesus as the Messiah? And to get at that question I think that Christiological reconstruction will do well if it spends a great deal of time thinking about Romans 11.

If there is one recurring theme in Romans 11, it is that in all that has taken place in the history of Jesus, his life, his death and his resurrection, together with all that had happened in the next generation or so, especially the entry of Gentiles into this new, highly irregular branch of Israel that Paul called the ekklesia, there is no question of God rejecting his people, or of the Jewish people falling away from God's plan for them, or of there being any other future for all the Jews than the kingdom of God's promise. Again and again Paul returns to this theme, as the basso continuo against which he plays the counterpoint of the strange new fact of Gentiles having a part in Judaism's destiny.

I am sensitive to Leo Baeck's thesis that Paul was a Romantic, yet I think we must also add that there was a strange pragmatic streak in Paul. I mean, damn it, there the Gentiles were, worshiping Israel's God! Put the pragmatism and the romanticism to-gether, and you get Paul's conclusion: that Jesus and the message about him was God's way of opening Judaism's role out to the rest of mankind. The word had been spoken before, "a light for the Gentiles." Now it was happening: Gentiles were beginning to see the light, to count themselves as stones raised up to be sons of Abraham, strangers who had been adopted as younger brothers into the tribe of Israel, branches of wild trees grafted into the true tree that was Judaism. There is no question about where Paul saw the center of the action. Israel, or to be more concrete, the Jews, were where it "was at", for Paul. But he was convinced that something new was happening on Judaism's frontier toward the world: God had set something in process whereby there was an opening to the world, a new missionary force for Judaism. Let Judaism stand in the center, serving God by the light of Torah; then let there be a new force - call it Judaism's mercenaries, hanger's on who help in a small way to serve the covenant - the sect of Judaism, the foreign service arm of Israel, who work to open the way for all mankind to come to worship Israel's God, or, better said, in the light of Torah and the Prophets, to join Israel in the calling to do justice, love mercy, and walk humbly in the way of the Lord.

Is that what the Messiah was called to be? That is hardly how Judaism had thought of the Messiah. As the one who was to usher in the kingdom, Jesus was not the Messiah. But if we follow Paul's lead, then an unexpected role of relating the covenant to the whole of human history was indeed inaugurated with the history of Jesus. Perhaps we can conclude that in the accepted terms of Judaism, Jesus was not the Messiah. We have still to wait for that day - or better, not wait, but work for that day. And yet, Jesus could yet prove to be God's annointed, the one in whom the word of Abraham's God is made audible to the nations, made fresh, we could say. Whether he in fact is God's word and God's annointed depends to some extent on whether we carry through with the program of Romans 11. The whole great Christological development of the second through the fifth centuries of our common era need by no means be thrown out the window. That would be to settle for a liberal, tolerant evasion of the hard issues. On the contrary, just those classical questions need to be taken up again with Romans 11, the Holocaust, and the continued vital tradition and existence of Judaism as essential parts of the puzzle. Clearly, theology has before it a prospect of immense work and great possibilities!

The fourth area which I would single out as crucial for demolition and re- construction is the relationship between the New Testament and the Old Testament, or as I am convinced we must learn to call them, in conformity with the early Christian community, the apostolic writings and the Scriptures. My suggestions is simply this: that we must learn to put the Scriptures first, and to learn to read critically the apostolic writings in the light of Scriptures. Rather than using the apostolic writ- ings as a critical screen through which we sift the Scriptures - and it can hardly be denied that this is the Christian tradition, only beginning to be brought into ques- tion in this century - we need to learn to return to the Scriptures as the norm and critical screen through which we read the apostolic writings.

This fourth proposal follows inevitably from the general tenor of the first three. Together all four add up to an attempt to call a halt to a continuation of a tradition and a direction that is rooted in the apostolic writings themselves, blossom- ing especially in the Gospel according to Matthew, finding sharp, systematic expression especially in Tertullian and Chrysostom, gaining a pattern in anti-Jewish regulations, practices and theories, and finally coming to its full flower at Auschwitz. To turn away from that tradition would be no small task and not one that we could hope to ac- complish in one generation. Nevertheless, if we see it as something which must be done, then a part of that work must be done by theologians. That will require that theology reconsider, indeed reorder its approach to its previous norms or standards, especially its Scriptural norms. For if we are to set out to affirm the one history of God's one people, then the apostolic writings must be set within the larger context of the Scriptures to which they look back and on which they feed, and the other writings and traditions of Israel which came later, the Talmud and traditions of the Rabbis, even down to our own day.

The Christian theological tradition has used the apostolic writings as a guide for picking and choosing what to emphasize and what to ignore in the Scriptures. The prospect for a theology that would acknowledge the Holocaust and the existence of the state of Israel as further steps in the history of God's people, would have to re- verse this process. The apostolic writings, like Talmud, will have to be seen as commentary on Torah, or as steps along the way of Israel's understanding and misunder- standing, but always wrestling with, the one who gave Israel that new name at Jabbok and his Commandment at Sinai.

I trust it is now clear why I said that the prospects for theology are revo- lutionary and exciting. An almost insuperable job lies before us and theologians have no need to feel that all the important work has already been done. On the contrary, the real work has barely begun! For what is at stake is a recognition that the whole past of our theology has been that more nearly of a Pagan-Christian tradition, not a Judeo-Christian tradition. As we set out on this task, we should have no illusions that Judaism itself is a ready-made answer to the dilemma of Christianity. I am not proposing that we all simply convert to Judaism. Judaism is itself partly a product of and a reaction to the anti-Jewish character of traditional Christianity. How a people can remain a people and still tolerate an opening to the Gentiles is a problem which the early course of Christianity foreclosed and which would have to be reopened. Where we will end up with this I have no idea. What I am convinced of, however, is that there is a commanding voice coming out of Auschwitz for Christians as well as for Jews. Jews have heard that voice and responded in part by building the state of Israel. For us, the command is that we accept a judgment on something false lying close to the very heart of our tradition, and that like Abraham, we have to set out on a journey of radical reconstruction not knowing the final destination. If theology does not hear

that voice of command to go, if it shuts its ears to the voice of Auschwitz, then I
see no reason to bother ourselves or anyone else with a discussion of the prospects
for theology.

Our present situation makes me think of the start of an off-shore ocean
race. The uninitiated looking on would probably find the scene utterly confusing,
which is one of the reasons, I suppose, why the uninitiated don't bother to watch.
Each boat seems to be just doing its own thing, going around in circles, heading in
opposite directions, even carrying radically different combinations of sails. And
then, suddenly it all comes together and you see that each boat was maneuvering so
as to hit the line going full speed with spinnakers breaking out just as the gun  is
fired. Those who know what the game is could tell you that all that milling around
is carefully timed and planned, for good starts don't just happen. So it seems to me
that much of the milling around of present theology is not as random as it might seem.
Increasing numbers of theologians are clearly starting to worry about the Holocaust.
A few have even taken notice of Israel. The Jewishness of Jesus and Paul have been
heard of for some time now, and the fact that anit-Judaism is rooted in the New Testament is hardly to be denied. When I put all that together, I think I have grounds
for seeing that something is being planned and prepared. Unlike off-shore racers,
we do not know where we are heading, but we do know where the starting line is, and
I believe the gun is about to go off. And for this particular start, for the most
obvious reasons, we had better time it and hit it ourselves, for we can hardly expect
German theology to lead the way.

FIVE OBSERVATIONS IN SEARCH OF A METHOD

TO JUSTIFY RELIGIOUS ACTIVITY

T. R. Martland

SUNY at Albany


If Kierkegaard's suggestion has any validity, and his Abraham is the paradigm of a religious person, so much so that "only he who is troubled finds rest, only he who descends into the nether-world rescues the beloved, only he who draws the knife obtains Isaac,"[1] then part of what characterizes the religious person is his openness to, or respect for, that which he encounters. The religious person's willingness to stretch his understanding to newly encountered dimensions of experience marks him. For Abraham this meant he had to stretch his understanding to include a God which demanded that he draw the knife on his son Isaac. In contrast the more common practice would have been for him to cut down this challenging new dimension in order to fit his previously established understanding of God as He who gave him Isaac as comfort in his old age.

I will cite two contrasting examples to support this generalization that Abraham's willingness to strike out against the previously established, constitutes a religious paradigm. Though both are from chuan 12 of the Ch'an Buddhist text The Transmission of the Lamp, and though both involve conversations with the same religious master, Chên Tsun-su, it is only in the second example that we find Abraham's sense of openness to the new to which we refer. The first example has to do with a monk who has come to visit Chên Tsun-su. Upon his arrival the master asked, "Where do you come from?" The monk answered, "Liu-yang." Chên Tsun-su asked, "What did the Ch'an master in Liu-yang say about the meaning of Ch'an?" The monk answered, "You can go anywhere, but you cannot find the road." Chên Tsun-su then asked, "Is that what the old master there really said?" The monk answered, "Yes, it is." Now it is here in this reply, "Yes, it is." that the traveling monk reveals his lack of religious sensitivity. The structures and limitations of previous understandings dominate. The monk can not let go of these in order to enter into the religious exchange with the old master, and so the conversation is over. Appropriately, the master thereupon picked up his staff and gave the monk a blow, saying, "This fellow remembers only words."

But now consider the second example, the religious one, one in which both disputants do reveal an openness and a stretching of their understanding to newly encountered dimensions. This time Chên Tsun-su meets an Abbot and asks of him, "When one understands, a drop of water on the tip of a hair contains the great sea, and the great earth is contained in a speck of dust. What do you have to say about this? The abbot wisely answered, "Whom are you asking?" Chen Tsun-su said, "I am asking you." The Abbot's back sliding reply was "Why don't you listen to me?" Whereupon Chen Tsun-su's quick response was, "Is it you or I who does not listen to the other's words?"[2]

I

I now wish to use this intentionally narrow but directed analysis of religion to make five observations which are relevant to any
attempt to justify religious activity.

1. If the religious person, i.e., Abraham and now the possibly enlightened Abbot, is willing to stretch his understanding to
what he encounters, then we can not say that religiously speaking he is
in safe possession of a fixed conceptual framework which necessarily entails certain conclusions. In fact the very opposite seems to be the
case. When the religious person asserts that God has chosen the Jews
for no reason, or that God has created the world ex nihilo, or that God
makes things good simply by declaring them to be good, he is acknowledging the perpetual imcompleteness of conceptual understanding. He
may be making a confession of faith, but he is also making a confession
of intellectual and psychical incompleteness and dependence. Religious
openness to newly encountered dimensions is an acceptance of this fact
and a means of passing out of or through seeing things from this old
incomplete way of understanding or experiencing things to understanding
or experiencing them in a new way, from a new context. Our examples
from The Transmission of the Lamp suggest that the new experience may
be akin to getting the point of a pun; suddenly 'seeing' an unsuspected
relationship between what previously were two unrelated or incongruous
ideas.

What this means is that there is no a priori standard or
structure of meaning or purpose from which or against which the philosopher can check religious activity. I mean before it has had its say.
The problem with the monk in conversation with Chên Tsun-su was that he
held on too tightly to his prior standards of meaning and therefore he
never entered into the religious domain. The philosopher never can ask
the religious person "Why?" or "What purpose does your religious activity serve?" if by this question he means some clearly defined pre-
arranged understanding which the religious person wishes to defend.
Vedantic Hinduism is so sensitive to this observation of ours that it
goes so far as to assert that the Lord Isvara himself does things without a purpose. We are told that he is the lonely cosmic dancer who
creates the worlds out of sheer joy, in play (līlā) or, simply, for the
sake of sport. This is to say, there is no analytic prior necessity or
purpose; he did what he did, he created the world... just for the fun
of it.

Malinowski also points to this religious characteristic when
he observes that "while in the magical act the underlying idea and aim
is always clear, straightforward, and definite, in the religious cere-
mony there is no purpose directed toward a subsequent event."[3] This
observation may well account for the priority religions usually give
to worship as over against doctrine or creed, and for religion's resistance to all insistences that a final stand be made somewhere so that
philosophers can put a particular religious claim to a decisive test.
If they must argue it would go something like this; though it is
reasonable to ask for such a decisive stand, data still is coming in,
and since the religious person must remain open to it, it is wise for
religion to preserve the option of a possible abandon later on and to
make room for discoveries revealed as the understanding so advances.

2. If an openness to the new which he encounters marks the religious person and this openness brings about new ways of seeing things because the old ways are incomplete, then religion must be that kind of activity which intervenes in the world. This is to say, its standards follow from its activity, not vice versa. It is through religious activity that the religious person comes into possession of whatever standards or purposes he may have. The activity is intrinsically related to the end result. For instance, it was only through the open participation in a dialogue with the master Chẽn Tsun-su that the Abbot came to see things the way he did. The dialogue itself counted. It made a difference, so much so that without it there was no enlightenment.

Religion isn't alone here in assuming a kind of coalescence between its activity and its fulfillment. In a conversation with Samuel Johnson, Boswell learns that sometimes a judge's decision or ruling in certain cases of law can be of this kind. By this I mean the decision, like catching the point of a pun or like the Abbot's possible enlightenment, also goes beyond that which the premises themselves entail, it too intervenes in the world: that is, it too makes that kind of difference without which there isn't a difference. Boswell first asks: "But what do you think of supporting a cause which you know to be bad?" In his typical manner Johnson replies:

"Sir, you do not know it to be good or bad till the Judge determines it. I have said that you are to state facts fairly; so that your thinking, or what you call knowing, a cause to be bad, must be from reasoning, must be from your supposing your arguments to be weak and inconclusive. But Sir, that is not enough. An argument which does not convince yourself may convince the Judge to whom you urge it; and if it does convince him, why, then, Sir, you are wrong and he is right. It is his business to judge; and you are not to be confident in your own opinion that a cause is bad, but to say all that you can for your client, and then hear the Judge's opinion."[4]

Perhaps it is this idea of the essential relatedness between the religious act and religious knowledge or experience that accounts for and explains Augustine's assertion that "The knowledge of Christ is not one thing and Christ himself another. He is both the light and the source of light, wisdom itself, and the source of wisdom, knowledge itself and the source of knowledge."[5] It may also account for the Christian theologian's insistence on an ex opere operato interpretation of his church's sacramental activity: that is, the interpretation that the sacramental activity itself is automatically one with its signified and realized grace. He would want to say the sacraments are effecting activities as well as labeling activities, that religious activity is a reconciling or saving activity and that the works of God are inseparable from the truth of God. In those terms we used earlier, we would want to say there is a stretching toward the new experience (of grace) but notice, the stretching itself makes the difference (it is grace).

3. That religious people come into their new understanding by being religious and by no other means, suggests the necessity of a kind of experiential confirmation of religious claims as against the

more familiar experimental method of confirmation.  It seems that philosophical inquiry into the validity of religious activity can garner
its relevant criteria only by being in touch with, or sensitive to,
that activity itself and thereby to the new understanding for which it
is responsible.

The necessary prerequisite is that the inquirer adopt a prior
provisional receptivity to the religious activity and to its findings
so that he can begin to work.  This is not the same thing as unqualified commitment but it is fraught with the danger of so becoming.  Even
so, the obligation stands.  It is only by standing within the flow of
religious activity that man is in a position to receive the religious
experience, much less to measure it as it comes along.  Here is the
basis for the often heard claim that religious language is not for the
world but for the church, and for the popularity in religious thought
for variations on Anselm's theme that one does not understand in order
to believe, but on the contrary, one believes in order to understand:
neque enim quaero intelligere ut credam, sed credo ut intelligam.

We shall point up some of the almost unbearable complications
which stem from an experiential method of confirming prior claims such
as this.  Let us contrast say, the psychiatrist's laboratory procedures
with those of the physician's.  Like religion, the former relies upon
experience whereas the latter relies upon experiments.  First notice,
however, that both the psychiatrist and the physician begin with an
analysis.  Both people, like the religious person, want to recognize
patterns of understanding where possible, dare even create them when
necessary, that is, when the facts are not reliable or available.  At
each moment of their analysis they want to be able to supply a hypothesis which is coherent with the rest of their analysis, one which
contains a suggestion of what action should be taken and a meaningful
prediction of what will happen.  But from here on their methodologies
differ.  Whereas all three must wait for the future to determine
whether the hypothesis is valid, only the physician's answer comes, at
least in theory, from a fixed understanding or meaning related to a
fixed situation.  The religious person and psychiatrist find that their
answer comes from an ever expanding situation.  The physician can verify
his analysis if his hypothesis works, i.e., if the patient takes the
prescription and it solves the patient's particular problem.  That is
the end of the matter.  However, things are not so simple for the psychiatrist.  He finds that even though he tries to verify his analysis
in the same general manner, his analysis, if acted upon, creates a new
situation which demands a new analysis which he now must subject to
that new situation.  This in turn contributes still newer data or understanding which again creates still newer analyses and situations.  In
other words he is doomed to function in an incomplete, forever open,
situation.  Like religious activity his analysis intervenes, and like
religious activity some sort of provisional receptivity to the continually new situation, bordering on unqualified commitment, validates
it.

4.  If an openness to that which he encounters marks the religious person, and it is through this openness that he comes into his
new understanding, then insofar as the religious activity is still
on-going and new discoveries are incoming, it is impossible to establish any kind of final criteria against which future religious activity

can measure itself. There is no possibility of a conclusive verification. Nothing can count decisively against the validity of a religious claim or a religious activity because of the open endedness of the future, because of the discoveries which the religious person may yet uncover.

Now this does not mean that we fold up our critical tent and go home. It does suggest however that in our now required experiential sensitivity to the impact of what turns out to be an on-going cumulation or funding of selectively relevant material we should at best look for that kind of procedure which is akin to that made say when we decide that a certain dirt road is passable or that it isn't. Although our decision, strong or not so strong, is made all at once, yes it is passable, or no it isn't, the funding of the relevant material has been going on in terms of weighing the pros and cons over an indefinite length of time and from different perspectives. There isn't an 'arguing' from premise to conclusion and it is difficult to think of it as linear, unless we are willing to paint that imaginary line with a wide brush.

John Wisdom reminds us of the appropriateness of our previously mentioned parallel with law. He points out that in those cases in the courts of law which settle not questions of fact but whether somebody "did or did not exercise reasonable care, whether a ledger is or is not a document, whether a certain body was or was not a public authority," there is "a presenting and representing of those features of the case which severally co-operate in favor of the conclusion, in favor of saying what the reasoner wishes said, in favor of calling the situation by the name by which he wishes to call it."[6] Here too, it is a matter of selectivity cumulating independent and inconclusive premises and weighing with provisional receptivity, one mass effect against another. This of course does not rule out an appeal to observables. It is just that the observables only become observables by dint of the cumulating process which establishes the basis for selective observation. It also assumes a willingness to look at the process from this particular cumulation, and with a contextual consistency of expectation that has grown out of the cumulated premises.

5. If a pre-arranged purpose does not stimulate religious activity, but it is that kind of activity which intervenes in the world and thereby brings about a new situation which men, standing apart, can not foretell, then we must look to that new situation and not to the past for our means of verification. Specifically, we must ask whether this or that religious intervention does provide a new situation, meaning thereby, a situation by or through which later generations come to understand their challenges and experiences. The question that we must ask is twofold; first, does this resultant religious stretching of the religious person's understanding suggest ends, purposes or insights which men can not, or at least will not, grasp otherwise, and second, are these ends, purposes or insights fruitful in suggesting new systematic correlations which men find to be in agreement with still newer observations?

Quite frankly, I wish to suggest here that if religion is defined as that kind of activity which stretches the religious person's understanding to newly encountered dimensions, then we must judge it not only by its ability to do just that, but also by the quality of the

new understanding it produces. Religion must be heuristically valuable
in bringing about future understandings. It must help provide the new
parameters with which mankind expands into unknown territory.

We should not think this demand strange when we consider the
development of thought in other fields. Some hundred years after
Saccheri's geometrical exploration into alternatives to Euclid's postulate or parallels, mathematicians, with the help of Lobaschevsky and
Bolyai declared quite in harmony with this our fifth observation, that
Saccheri's findings were now acceptable in the same way Euclid's postulates were to be acceptable, namely because they were fruitful in
suggesting a wide range of new and interesting ideas. And can we not
point out also that contemporary scientists accept the undulatory
theory of light and the four dimensional continuum because each allows
them not only to describe their physical experiences in a simple and
practical way but also because each helps them to find new theories
which continue to be in agreement with still newer observations? In
other words are not both acceptable because they do what the caloric
theory of heat or "art Deco" for example fail to do. Each one suggests
further system correlations within experience beyond those which scientists originally drew their assertion or model.

Northrop Frye, in his essay entitled "Lord Byron", provides
us with a less prosaic example from literature. It is our last. He
suggests that what makes Byron's work valid is that it has released,
produced or created, a new sensitivity, a new cultural force, which
lives today in such writers as Melville, Conrad, Hemingway, Housman,
Thomas Wolfe, D. H. Lawrence and Auden; writers whom he notes, "have
little in common except that they all Byronize." Frye's point is that
they all have responded to the "Byronic hero" in some way or other,
that is, to the outcast from society who in his loneliness can make no
judgment or commitment, and thereby assume no responsibility for his
life or for his actions. Obviously Byron has stretched his and our
understanding, and for the moment we must say the stretching is fruitful, so much so that this newly encountered understanding of man's
plight has come to be the most modern of ailments; ontological boredom,
that sense of inner emptiness which we recognize in the _ennui_ of
Baudelaire, Sartre's _nausee_ or simply existential _angst_.

II

This completes our five observations in search of a method
to justify religious activity. They are related. If it is true that
(1), religion has no a priori standard against which an inquirer can
check its validity, or as a religious person may want to put it, its
goal is nothing at all, or the identity of yes and no, or perhaps even
an emptiness, and, if it is also true, as we next observed, that, (2)
it is only through his religious activity that the religious person
comes into possession of whatever standards he may have, or as a religious person may want to put it, the whole universe comes along with
his activity, then it must be true as we next observed, that (3) the
philosopher also must be willing to go along, if it is the validity of
religious activity he wishes to consider. In effect this means he
must be willing to consider an experiential confirmation that, as we
next noted, (4) though closing out the possibility of a conclusive
verification, nevertheless does insist, (5) upon religion providing

insights which men find fruitful in suggesting new systems of thought which in their turn prove to be fruitful for suggesting still newer ideas and/or observations.  Gregory of Nyssa prepares us for the former, when commenting on Ecclesiastes, he declares that "To find God is to seek Him without cease.  For seeking is not one thing and finding another; the profit of the quest is the quest itself." (Migne, PG XLIV, 720C).  The Taittiriya Upanishad insists on the latter when it declares that "Who denies God, denies himself.  Who affirms God affirms himself." (2.6)

Footnotes

1 Soren Kierkegaard, _Fear and Trembling_ (London:  Oxford University Press, 1939), p. 23.

2 Translated by Chang Chung-Youan in his _Original Teachings of Ch'an Buddhism_ (New York:  Pantheon Books, 1969), pp. 108, 109.  I would have liked to have cited as my example of religious openness the following more famous dialogue between the Emperor Wu of Liang and Bodhidharma.  It is also found in the _Records_, Wu comments: "Since my enthronement I have built many monastaries.  I have had many holy writings copied.  I have invested numerous monks and nuns."  "How much merit Have I gained?"
Bodhidharma: "None."
Wu:  "Why so?"
Bodhidharma: "Those are inferior deeds.  They may conduce to favorable births in the heavens or on earth, but are of the world and follow their objects like shadows.  They may seem to exist, but are nonentities.  Whereas the true deed of merit is of pure wisdom, perfect and mysterious, in its nature beyond the grasp of man's intelligence, and not to be sought by way of material acts."
Wu:  "What then is the Noble Truth in its highest sense?"
Bodhidharma: "It is empty.  There is nothing noble about it."
Wu:  "And who is this monk now facing me?"
Bodhidharma: "I do not know."
But alas, D. T. Suzuki differs with my interpretation of the significance of Emperor Wu's last question and so I lose my courage.  See his essay "History of Zen Buddhism from Bodhidharma to Enō (Hui-Neng)," reprinted in _The Essentials of Zen Buddhism_, edited by Bernard Phillips (London:  Rider & Company, 1963), pp. 95-149, especially page 117.

3 Bronislaw Malinowski, _Magic, Science and Religion_ (Garden City:  Doubleday Anchor, 1948), p. 38.

4 James Boswell, _The Life of Samuel Johnson LLD_, Modern Library (New York), p. 333.

5 Augustine, _In Joannis Evangelium Tractatus_ 21,5.

6 John Wisdom, _Philosophy and Psycho-Analysis_ (New York:  Philosophical Library, 1964), p. 15.

LANGUAGE, TRUTH AND COMMITMENT:
A STRATEGY FOR LOCATING THE GROUNDS OF RELIGIOUS HOPE
By Charles L. Lloyd
Southern Methodist University

Is it possible for us to hope, not just wish but really
hope, that we might honestly and comprehensively be glad to be who we
are (or shall become)? The question is important because it inquires
into the potential limits and the possible grounds, if any, of our
self esteem or respect. It raises questions of value, truth, and personal identity in an unlimited form which suggests a religious setting.
And while the notion of self and the value to be placed on it vary a-
mong religious traditions, the relation between one's present or possible identity and some ultimate criterion of value is a frequently recurring, basic issue in all of them. Therefore, I propose that we
adopt this hope as at least one criterion of the religious life and
that we proceed from that adoption to infer other basic features of
that life. In particular, I propose we take faith to be that set of
convictions and commitments which purports to justify some form of
that hope. Given these definitions, the problem for the paper is that
of determining the truth conditions of religious faith.

The difficulty of the question appears most forecefully in a
dilemma. On the one hand, our identity determines our standard of
value. If that which is truly good is in fact foreign to us, how
could we miss it? What else might we mean by the Good than that value,
process, or state of affairs which perfects all that we hold essential
to our identity? Never to affirm this standard as the measure of our
hope would be tantamount to withdrawing from a contest for which our
entire lives had been a preparation. No doubt, convictions which are
never subject to criticism are naive at best, but principles of criticism are self defeating if they succeed finally in devouring the very
activities whose integrity they were developed to secure. Perhaps it
is just such an outcome as this that one might have in mind by calling
life absurd. But then one wonders what point is served by calling it
absurd. It is more reasonable to assume that every serious claim to
truth implies a conception of human identity and value which is equally serious. Therefore, if the first is a genuine measure of conviction, the second will be a genuine measure of hope.

On the other hand, we are at least somewhat aware of the
dangers of self deception. These have, for good reason, long been a
topic of concern to religious leaders. One needs mention here only
the names of Augustine and Luther, to say nothing of countless others
in the western tradition or of such introspective adepts as Sufi
Shaykhs, Yoga Swamis, or Zen Roshis. Long before Marx or Freud these
men were well acquainted with the subtle, pervasive, and dishonest
strategies by which men and women often maintain their equanimity and
self esteem. They too knew that we often construct our experience by
denying certain dominant features of our own "consciousness", by distorting our perceptions of the "world", and by projecting our unre-

solved conflicts, guilt, and aggression onto others. And they were
quite as convinced as any secular critic that a life composed of these
strategies was a lie, that a faith dependent on them was a fake, and
that a hope which sprang from them was a delusion. This is not to
say, of course, that they were thereby immune to these strategies. Nor
is it to say that a religious tradition which provoked such insights
was thereby protected from the errors which were there perceived. I
simply mean to suggest that the strategies of self deception are sufficiently well known, sufficiently pervasive, and sufficiently related
to the means by which we undertake to secure those values which we
deem essential to our identity, to call into question the entire process. The basic task for paper may now be restated as follows. Can
we devise some means whereby the value commitments which are implied
by our existence can be made compatible with that process of criticism
and reflection which is also implied by our existence. For the sake
of brevity, I shall refer to this as the problem of commitment and
of truth.

Perhaps it is obvious that the above problem especially pertains to religion. Nevertheless, it is important to specify that feature of the religious life which subjects it to this concern. The
heart of the matter is that the believer aspires to a state in which
his religious vocation is coextensive with his personal identity.
Therefore he assumes the problem of commitment and truth in its most
thoroughgoing form. What his religion offers him is a definition of
his situation which will account for his deepest fears, his most persistent frustrations, and his highest hopes. He is invited to overcome the hazards of existence, so defined, and to share in the unqualified good which is proposed but if and only if he allows his life,
his attitudes, and his practices to be shaped by the transforming
means of that religious tradition. This commitment is both comprehensive in extent and total in degree. Only he who endures to the end
will be saved (purified, reborn, perfected, enlightened). Thus, in
monotheistic religions faith is viewed as that fundamental relation of
the believer to God by means of which the divine sovereignty moves towards an omnipresent perfection in the life of believers like that
which it has in all original acts of deity itself. Whatever is self,
will be God's. Whatever cannot be God's, must not be self. Naturally, the terms of this transaction change as one moves from one type of
religion to another. Nevertheless, whether one describes his condition as being defined by the providence of God or the system of
Varnashrama Dharma or the five relationships of Li or the steps of the
Noble Eightfold Path, the stake hazarded is always the same; it is
one's identity as a human being.

It is just this type of commitment which raises the question
of truth in its most acute form. This identity is not something given.
It does not arise from that naive (and healthy) confidence with which
a child receives the customs of his family and locality as the conditions of human life as such. It must be chosen with at least some
sense of the options which it excludes. Furthermore, it cannot be

construed simply as a mood, attitude, or other form of non-cognitive
stance.  Although religious traditions usually include options in
which dogmatic pronouncements or creedal affirmations are of secondary
importance (if that), their prescriptions for religious action, whether simple or complex, always include a diagnosis of the human situation which is taken to be true and an image of human destiny which
is taken to be good.  Whoever undertakes the path of religious action
without at least implicitly agreeing with those judgments has imitated
rather than achieved the religious life.  Therefore, it is essential to
faith to be concerned for truth.  But this concern brings the vision of
faith into some relation with a realm of experience which is shared by
those who are not of faith.  This realm, perhaps, must be overcome, but
it cannot be avoided or denied.  It must be transformed.  Therefore,
with regard to the question of truth, the believer is not given a free
ticket to call false what he previously had good reason to call true.
The transformation which faith achieves must assume and honor even
while resetting the context of the criteria of truth.  Yet how is this
possible for the central act of faith itself?  Is there any room here
for an extraneous principle of criticism - one which might legitimately
demur to the movement of faith on the grounds of its lack of truth?
The answer must be negative for it is faith which establishes the
criteria of judgment.[1]  But then what can we mean by the truth of faith?
This is the essence of the problem, a recurring issue in all philosophical inquiries into religious truth.  It is against this background
that we can best appreciate the work done by recent critics of religious meaning and truth.

The moral power of the critics' case arises from the intimate connection between human integrity and truth.[2]  The fundamental
(though not unique) feature of the modern, empiricist critic's case is
the claim that this integrity can be secured if and only if all human
commitments are subject to a criticism which is in turn based on experience and on principles which are independent of the commitments
which they criticise.  This case has been forcefully presented in the
recent literature of the subject by Roger Trigg.[3]  Only those commitments are rational, he insists, which can account for their contents
by reference to criteria which do not depend for their authority on
that commitment.  His argument in support of this claim begins with
the observation that any description of someone as committed is incomplete without a statement of what that person is committed to.  The
concept of commitment necessarily implies not only a psychological
orientation but also a conceptual content which can be stated as a set
of beliefs.

What I am committed to determines the nature of my commitment.  If
my beliefs change, my commitment must.  A man cannot be called a
committed Christian if he holds no distinctively Christian beliefs.[4]

How then, shall we assess these beliefs?  Trigg claims that
they must be supported by evidence and reasoning sufficient to make

them credible on their own terms - i.e., without reference to the commitment which the believer associates with them. Any other point of view, he asserts, will imply a license to believe anything at all and to call it true.[5] The support for this assertion, he continues, is to be found in the conception of language as such. If language is to be something more than a complex symptom of various behavioral dispositions, in short, if it is to have explicit meaning, it must somehow refer to something other than itself.[6] Furthermore, this reference may be more or less adequate, and in this fact lies the essential connection between the concept of language and that of truth. Consequently, commitments are subject to criticism on the basis of their contents. If the beliefs which compose them are not justified by reality, the reference to which is essential to language as such, they must be rejected. Therefore, with regard to matters of truth, faith has no autonomy. Its only proper, internal order is that which is fully vindicable by reference to a reality which, to the extent that it is known, will be known to have the same intelligible form, whether or not one approaches it in faith.

The above argument is fundamental to the critic's case but not sufficient, for it allows the following rejoinder. Granted that language as such requires some procedure of assessment which we normally associate with the concept of truth, is it the case that any unit of language is determined in its meaning simply by its reference to a nonlinguistic entity in isolation from its connection with other elements of language? This is surely false. Within each natural language there are various, relatively autonomous forms of explicit meaning, each of which has its own rules for what it will recognize as significant. For instance, the concept "empirical regularity" determines what will or will not count as a scientific law as much as the notion of "touchdown" determines what will or will not count as a significant crossing of a white chalk line on a grassy field. Any attempt to derive these conceptions directly from experience would be misguided, for they are not hypotheses seeking confirmation but rules determining what will count as being significant for some activity. Furthermore, these rules are not lightly abandoned. The dedicated fan (and the dedicated scientist) will accept a good bit of frustration without changing the "rules of the game" in any fundamental way. Each will test a variety of "plays" before he gives up the game altogether. Consequently, Trigg's simple model of checking beliefs by comparing them to "reality" must be complicated by at least one additional set of considerations. Furthermore, the choice of set is crucial, for it is probably here that one will choose either to complicate while retaining the model of extra-linguistic comparison or to abandon it altogether.

Modern, empiricist, critics of religion have chosen to retain it. And the distinctive form of their critique arises from the principle by which they clarify and limit the reference range of "reality". It is the well known verificationist principle of propositional meaning. In its weaker and more common form, it states that a

claim may proport to describe reality it and only if there are at
least some empirical observations relevant to the determination of its
truth or falsity.[7] Given this rule, the above example of "empirical
regularity" is relevant to claims about reality whereas "touchdown" is
not. Although activity oriented to both of these terms is, or at
least can be, intelligible, only that activity oriented to the first
can be described as a quest for truth.

Without crossing again this much traveled terrain, we should
notice two points at which the above position touches the quest for
religious truth as here defined. First, we cannot ignore it. It is
not sufficient simply to show that the verificationist principle itself, in either its strong or its weak sense, is open to question.
Its lack of self evidence does not entail either its falsity or its
irrelevance. When it is cast in the form of a persuasive definition,
it presents a challenge to defenders of religion that is both logically unexceptional and practically most demanding.[8] For instance, if
by such phrases as "creator of heaven and earth," "A very present help
in trouble," "the father of our lord, Jesus Christ," "the resurrection
of the dead," and many others, if by these we imply no limit to any
future empirical state of affairs, just what do we mean when we use
them? I do not suggest that this question has no answer. It is
clear, however, that we must either pose an answer to it or specify
some limit to experience which is subject to empirical test. In either case, the consequences for much of what passes as religious faith
(certainly as Christian faith) are likely to be both profound and controversial. The second major point to note is the consequence of the
above position for the relation of questions of truth to those of self
identity. Since the criteria of truth are now found in matters that
are common to all (i.e., deduction and intersubjective testability)
rather than in what is comprehensively adequate to determine the special character of each of us, questions of distinctly personal identity are excluded from those of truth or reality. To the extent that
such matters are a suitable subject of scientific inquiry, they must
be recast in casual (i.e., neurophysiological, behavioral) terms.
Ethical, aesthetic, or religious patterns of meaning are not themselves candidates for truth. They may, like football and other games,
be interesting, coherent, useful, perhaps even important - but not
true.[9]

For all its achievements, the consequences of the above approach are sufficiently disturbing to warrant a second look at the alternatives. Granted that the notion of language entails the notion of
its assessment, how else might that assessment be conceived? Since
the above position is based on a referential theory of truth, we might
reasonably look to its classical alternative, the coherence theory.
Needless to say, it has problems of its own. Nevertheless, given the
question with which this paper began, it has one significant virtue.
In suggesting that reality and language and thus intelligence are
somehow mutually implicating entities, it renders unnecessary that
separation of truth from personal existence which is forbidden by our

opening question. If one apprehends the real in roughly that same way that one grasps the point of a story or poem or game, then his knowledge of the real need not imply an encounter with something outside of the very structures whose point it is. And if, furthermore, it is just such cultural structures as these which most nearly portray the distinctive identity of any one personal existence, then one might at least undertake to answer questions regarding the reality or unreality of various attempts to give that existence an intelligible, comprehensive form. In what follows we shall pursue the conditions of such an assessment and the conception of language, truth, reality, and religious commitment which they require.

The function of the concept of truth is neither to designate some ideal set of propositions nor to denote some state of affairs (whether real or ideal) termed "reality". Its function is to reward an activity. Its role with regard to that activity is precisely on par with the blue ribbon one gives to the athlete who wins the race or scores the goal or hits the bulls-eye.[10] The meaning of the reward will be a function both of the structure and of the purpose or value of the activity within which it operates. Note that this model allows us both to describe the conditions of the reward (the rules of the game or structure) and to assess the activity of game-playing itself without supposing that the game somehow "stands for" something other than itself. One may enjoy, be proficient in or approve of one game rather than another. Nevertheless, the standard of comparison governing these distinctions is not some entity or value to which one gains access by means other than the procedures outlined by the games themselves. (One may, to be sure, value games for extrisic reasons - e.g., money. In this case, however, they are not valued as _games_.) Even if one decides to do something other than play a game, he declines not because of a judgment that reality is insufficiently "gamey" but because he seeks a value other than that which is provided by that activity. Consequently, this assessment does not involve the notion of reference, and even in the form of a rejection, it does not entail the denial of significance to the activity declined.

Clearly, the game that identifies truth as its highest award is language or some portion of it. The rules which determine its play are its grammatical and semantic (GS) structures. The play which is to be rewarded (or not) is the particular use of the counters governed by those structures. It is only in this use, this linguistic action, that language has determinate meaning and consequently, only this action which can be termed true or false. As suggested above the significance of the judgment will be a function both of the structure and of the value of this game being played. Taking the structure first, three features collectively distinguish GS structures from other structures. First, like the rules of courtesy, they are social. Their rules are inherently public (or capable of being made public). Second, the activity, which they govern, like all purposive activity, is intentional. The sounds or marks which constitute the physical presence of the language refer to something other than themselves.

Third, unlike the elements of purposive, pragmatic action, (which also is intentional) the connection between those sounds or marks and that to which they refer is arbitrary. They are valued not for themselves but for the entities which they intend.[11] The second major point to note is that these rule governed, intentional, arbitrarily selected sounds, signs, and motions are used. Whatever pleasure one may take in their production or in their reception as something other than language is secondary. This use, furthermore has two aspects which are distinguishable though not separable. It establishes for some individual a stable order of recognition, relation, and reflection that constitutes a complex entity in its own right. And it provides a common framework of of thought and action to the community whose language it is. Whatever linguistic action satisfies the above criteria, we call true. Insofar as the concept of truth has literal application, the standards of truth are identical with those of correct expression.

Needless to say, the above discussion omits a matter of fundamental importance. How does a procedure such as that just defined succeed (or fail)? If it is a creation of society, how does it serve the interests of that society? Clearly, it must do so. Language is tested all the time. Communication is successful not merely because a number of people respond to the same set of cues in systematically interrelated ways. This response must somehow secure their extra linguistic needs. If it did not do so, it would be maladaptive, and maladaptive structures of an importance approximating that which language has for the human species are either dropped or quickly lead to the disappearance of the species whose structures they are. It is this obvious feature of language use which is intended by the term "reality". Nevertheless, it is crucial to note that the designation of reality as the value which animates and justifies the use of language need not imply that we have any intelligible access to it other than the structures of language themselves. To understand the significance of reality for the assessment of language (and thus for the concept of Truth in its indirect application), one must first understand the forms and functions of language use. The following discussion will seek to account for this use by reference to three interacting and interdependent processes of language usage which I shall term "linguistic behavior," "linguistic action", and "linguistic identity."

In its most elementary form, that of linguistic behavior, language use can be accounted for entirely in terms of behavior. It is called "linguistic" only because it appears in the forms that are in other uses distinctively so. It is at this level that attention to an infant's first moves towards language are especially significant. On first encounter, the "world" of experience is, apparently, so ill formed, so vaguely outlined as to be no world at all. In this "booming, buzzing confusion" the complex response we call language is probably no more or less arbitrarily chosen than the complex response we call "hand and eye coordination." Both make use of and organize fragmentary behaviors that are either instinctive or virtually unavoidable. And both can be understood in terms of explicit conditioning or reinforcement. At this level, one does not use language; one is used by it. Language use is simply a feature of that gradually clarifying encounter with other beings in a gradually expanding world that one accepts without question. (Note that these are encounters in a world, not with one.) One adopts them not because they accord with reality but because they are the (unrecognized) preconditions of their being any reality to know. This usage is, to be sure, governed by social conventions rather than, for instance, biological "laws". But this distinction has no significance for a child whose experience can no more envisiage society than it can biology (taken as a field of study rather than as a collection of certain contents). Habits of thought at this level are, if anything, less subject to examination than are the processes of digestion. They arise from the given interplay of various felt needs and social forms, neither of which are present in a form which would allow them to be an explicit subject of experience.

The move from linguistic behavior to linguistic action, although perhaps present from the beginning, manifests itself gradually throughout childhood and is fully evident at least by adolescence. At this stage of language use, the conventions which organize the various components of human experience in some society become evident as such (by whatever name). Consequently, it is then possible for some member of that society to use as well as be used by those conventions. A crucial factor in this new use is the individuals growing awareness of the various values which it is the function of these conventions to convey. Courtesy, for instance, is now seen as a form for showing respect to others. And respect, furthermore, comes to be sufficiently clear as a particular value given or received in social exchange to provide a basis for criticism of the very conventions through which one first came to know it. This is not to say, however, that respect is known as an entity which one might encounter outside of social conventions. It is available only and always in, with, and under the conventions by means of which it is displayed (or withheld). Nevertheless, the recognition that the rules of courtesy have a point or function other than their mere enactment, the quality of which can be experienced through a rule governed, social exchange, does provide one the possibility of assessing any particular set of rules for that exchange. It opens the forms of experience to a reality beyond them and thus transforms them from self justifying prescriptions into fruitful means for the creation of experienced value.

The above model, illustrated by the relation holding between the rules of courtesy and the substance of respect, can be applied to all elements of human awareness. In just this way one both learns and transcends the established forms of art, music, business, ethics, politics, and - science. Not even in science does one encounter reality free and unadorned by cultural form. The primary quality of linguistic usage which distinguishes it from other social forms is its universality. Unlike other social forms, science not only aspires to extend its GS structures to all human societies but actually has largely succeeded in doing so. It has arranged a fruitful marriage between the most nearly common form of experience (termed "empirical") and the most general form of tought (mathematics) by relating them both to the relatively uniform conditions of human action and survival. This extraordinary achievement dominates contemporary life, and it is no part of my intention to belittle it. Nevertheless, its newly displayed power gives neither scientists nor their philosophical advocates the authority to use the GS structures of science as the criteria of reality. The human force of scientific truth should be understood, as all truths are, in terms of the service provided by action oriented to a given human interest as it receives intelligible form by means of a given GS structure. The force of scientific truth is given it by its ability for providing us with the means of prediction and control of those phenomena which bear, more or less uniformly, on the physical existence of all members of the human species. Within this realm, its criteria define the conditions of true statements. Beyond it, they are irrelevant.

The point of the above argument has been to show that our conviction that there is an internal connection between the notion of language and that of truth does not require us to adopt the model of extra linguistic comparison. Language not only assesses; it is assessed - but not by reference to a reality which is available independently of language. Reality is not some comprehensive, uniform ideal structure to which it is the ultimate aim of all natural languages to conform. It is present in and through language as the set of values which it is the primary aim of all language in however many subordinate orders or interests to manifest and perfect. Therefore, insofar as it is actually available to our understanding, reality is constituted in experience by those linguistic actions which are authorized by the GS structures of our languages. These structures, in turn, are reinforced whenever they establish stable, public conditions for fruitful interaction. Reality, therefore, properly encompasses all values which are fruitful for life - for its continuance and well being.

It is unreasonable to restrict the accolade of truth (or its functional equivalents - e.g., beauty, goodness) to languages whose attention is given over merely to the uniform conditions of human action and survival - i.e., the sciences. Is it really so clear that at heart we desire only to survive? Some men and women, at least, have sacrificed their lives for values which they considered to be more important than survival. And even those of us who are deeply frightened by the prospect of injury, sickness, and death often aspire to a concern for other values which will, upon its maturity, enable us to withstand these hazzards with dignity if not serenity. The strength, the endurance, and the ubiquity of the values conveyed by the languages of obligation, friendship, beauty, - and religion - are such that I see no reason why they should not be recognized as playing their own, proper, independent role in that complex set of games animated by those values to which I have given the collective name of reality. It is necessary only that they be shown to be coherent, distinctive, and productive of human well being.

The above program leaves a basic issue unresolved. Even if one were to grant its account of the development and meaning of linguistic action, he might inquire by what right I have assigned a single term ("reality") to the many values which animate life. He might observe that it seems to authorize an arbitrary (because unruled) hopping from one language to another simply because one wants to and discovers (to his furtive delight?) all languages nestled together under the indiscriminately protective umbrella of reality. If this were true, the cost of this attempt to legitimize the epistemological status of art, ethics, and religion would be too great. It would introduce an instability into the realm of language which would render it incapable of providing that enduring public order which is its reason for being. Furthermore, one must note that we cannot, on this approach to the question, account for the integrity of linguistic action by reference to any GS structure, for these are altogether functions of the various needs of human life as it appears under specific conditions. They arise, as we have seen, in the course of our undertaking to clarify, differentiate, and render effective the needs which animate life. These needs, furthermore, are plural. Therefore, there is no reason why one set of needs should take a form that is systematically compatible with that of another. On the contrary, it is more probable that we learn to differentiate one set of needs from another by recognizing the differences in the linguistic action or behavior which the languages developed to serve them authorize. Therefore, the association of systematic coherence with reality is not an implication of language as such.

That functional unity which we aspire at least to approximate I shall refer to as "integrity". The process which yield this integrity constitutes that third level of language which I earlier termed "linguistic identity."[12] The role of linguistic identity is to establish a distinctive unity of and for one's experience and action. Although it operates through social forms, it is not primarily a social function. This must be stressed, because there is a social function closely parallel to it. In fact, one of the main functions of culture, taken broadly, is to provide a standard pattern of selection and subsrdination to guide its members in their life long passage along the intellectual smorgasbord which I have attempted to outline. This pattern is usually present in several variations, each of which constitutes a standard social role. These roles are, on the one hand, selectively distributed to all members of a society and, on the other, unified by some central set of images, stories, or practices which suggests that the whole arrangement is true, right, and beautiful. In traditional societies this process is so closely associated with religion as to be largely co-extensive with it.[13] Furthermore, to complicate the relations between this social function and linguistic identity even further, the standard pattern proposed by a society or some major portion of it usually will provide the imagery by means of

which an individual expresses (and therefore comprehends) the achievements of his venture into linguistic identity. Nevertheless, unless
that individual can give an account of this imagery which both accurately reflects its significance for his action and honestly describes
the value which this action, so animated, has come to have for him, he
has pretended rather than achieved linguistic identity.

Linguistic identity bears to linguistic action roughly the
same relation as the latter bears to linguistic behavior. In both
cases the individual brings into increasingly clear focus patterns and
values that previously were the presuppositions rather than the subject of his experience. In both cases this increase in awareness
brings with it both the possibility and at least part of the motiva-
tion for action that is creative and therefore, from the perspective
of the earlier level, unaccountable. In the case of linguistic identity, the forms are those of the standard selection of human values
and activities which are available to an individual in the social
roles of his experience. The value is that of human life overall.
This concern normally appears about the time of adolescence and develops unevenly throughout life. Nevertheless, its appearance and development are less functions of age than of self awareness. Whether
the occasion for it is a confrontation with death or with sex or with
some stringent obligation, the key element in this process is the a-
wareness of one's comprehensive responsibility for his life as a finite, valued, singular good. This awareness is customarily provoked
by changes in one's relations with others (e.g., puberty, marriage,
career selection, business failure, divorce, death of a loved one,
serious illness) so fundamental as to call into question both the accustomed structures and the justifying values which together compose
one's sense of identity.[14] In the discovery that one can respond to
these crises in such a way as to incorporate the new situation without a breech of continuity in his developing capacities for linguistic action, one becomes aware of that integrity which is distinctively his own. The willing use of this integrity as the criterion by
which one determines that selection and arrangement of certain linguistic resources to express the particular value of one's life is
linguistic identity. Consequently, one can identify linguistic identity as that process which creates the only world which can be known
in fact. I shall speak of "world" in this sense as "cosmos." The coherence of any cosmos is a direct function of the integrity which has
produced it.

We have come at last to the point where we may consider the
distinctiveness, the coherence, and the value of that activity which
I shall term "religion". I suggest that we understand as religious
any process of linguistic identity animated by the conviction that
the world created by one's comprehensive process of language use
(cosmos) is to be valued not merely as the distinctive sign of one
species' adaptive strategy but as the expression or vehicle of a transcendent value which is itself the justification of any structure
whatever. Stated more formally, this definition comes to this:

Religion is that human activity by means of which one comprehensively and continually orders, reorders, and enjoys all forms and
activities in his life in an unending quest for a comprehensive,
functional coherence (cosmos) by means of which he can act so as
to render his life good regardless of any circumstance which may
befall him.

Note that the primary difference between religion and linguistic identity is that the value of reality in the former, being transcendent,
is indefeasible. This should not be taken to imply that man "saves
himself," whatever that might mean. This activity can and does give
widely varying accounts both of the problems to be faced in the pursuit of indefeasible value and in the resources available to meet
those problems. It does mean, however, that it is the religious quest
which yields that explicit, complex, comprehensive image (cosmos) by
means of which we most clearly acknowledge our devotion to and our
confidence in that comprehensive value (reality) which, though the aim
of language, necessarily eludes it. The cosmos is altogether the creation of our quest for the comprehensively real. That is, apart from
an aim like that described above (whether one identifies it with religion or not), one would have neither need nor occasion to speak of the
world, of reality, or of being-as-such. The particular arenas of a-
wareness which arise in response to our organisms' specific, non-com-
prehensive needs (e.g., food, sex, security, approval, diversion)
would be sufficient. Whether or not language would be possible in
those terms is not clear. Nevertheless, they clearly preclude such
fields of inquiry as metaphysics, religion, and science (as distinguished from technology). This, however, is not our condition. The
cosmos is not something given; it is something sought. Of all conceivable things it is the one least likely simply to be "there" as the
intention of our thought. On the contrary, as the self-evident, seemingly given matrix of our intelligible action, the cosmos is the product of our quest for a distinctive value. Therefore, one who asserts
the reality of this cosmos does so not because he has "checked" the
latter against the former. He does so rather because he has found a
non-systematic, functional coherence of all his linguistic structures.
And this coherence, in turn, conveys in, with, and under all its elements a value which one could not have expected and cannot account for
which he recognizes (the believer will assert) as the good which is
distinctive of human being. That is, the judgment that any conceptual
world has cognitive value is dependent on the prior judgment that this
value which defines human being and authorizes a conceptual world has
more than merely adaptive significance. But this judgment is identical with religious faith as defined above. Therefore, so far is the
cosmos from standing in judgment on the essential movement of faith
that it is itself dependent on that movement. Truth, in the philosophically interesting sense, is dependent on ones commitment to the
distinctive integrity and value of human life.

There remains now only the task of relating the concepts
"cosmos" and "God". The difficulties of the concept "God" have long

been recognized. They have recently provoked a careful study by
Michael Durrant[15] in which he concludes that "God" lacks a coherent
use in religious language. It is, he points out, used both as a proper noun and as a predicate, and this, he argues, is impossible, for
the uses are incompatible. I would agree with that conclusion to the
extent that a single term cannot simultaneously be both a subject and
a preducate.[16] Nevertheless, the two uses may have a coherent, functional relationship, and it is just this that the position set forth
in this paper makes possible. On the terms of this discussion, it is
evident that "God" must stand within one's conceptual horizon (if it
is to be used at all) and yet point beyond it (to the reality which
transcends language even though it is pre-supposed by it). Even within one's conceptual horizon it will have a peculiar status. Because
its function is to stand for the non-systematic coherence of that
world, it cannot fall within any of the explicit GS structures which
compose it. This may seem to be an extraordinary conclusion, for its
consequence is that "God", to the extent that it appears within ones'
conceptual world, is not a suitable subject of knowledge. Or, to put
that claim in its inverse form, to the extent that "God" is a figure
within an explicit GS structure such that statements regarding deity
might be true or false, the "deity" referred to is not the subject of
a proper religious interest. In this sense "God cannot refer directly
to God. Nevertheless, we must remember that there are intelligible
relations other than that of reference. I suggest that the concept
"God" as it appears in the GS structures of theistic religions bears
an instrumental relation to the God which is the proper subject of religious interest. The meaning of "God" is to be found in 1) the network of action and thought prescribed by a religious tradition which
gives it an intelligible setting and 2) the achievement which this action makes possible. In brief, the action is that of worship (in this
realm D. F. Phillip's work is very much to the point),[17] and the
achievement is the construction of a redeemed world.[18]

This feature of the logic of "God" is suggested by the religious stores and forms of worship themselves. God plays a double
role in these that is not always appreciated. He is both a particular
figure within a story (e.g. The Garden of Eden, The Exodus) or a specific object of worship ("laudamus te", "Our Father who art in heaven,")
and the precondition of there being any story or any worship at all.
In the first role, he is seen in the story or as the particular object
of worship. In the second, he is approached by means of or through the
story or prayer. Seeking God in this role the believer does not merely
read the story; he contemplates it. One does not merely pray, he im-
plores the possibility of prayer. Recognizing the importance of this
double role in sacred story and action, Christian theologians have always held that the knowledge of faith was imperfect until it operated
in fact as the foundation of the believers self-knowledge. Any less
penetrating skill with or knowledge of religious forms was short of a
perfected faith. The significance of this "imperfection" has been
variously assessed, but the recognition of it has long been a common
feature of Christian reflection. Thus, one who seeks to understand

the believer's actions in worship or scriptural recital should attend
not merely to the content of those acts but also to the relation of
that content to the forms through which it is available.

I suggest that it is the structure of these forms as they are
used by the faithful which constitutes the intelligible form of God as
a religious entity. The believer gains this knowledge roughly as follows. He is asked to attend to certain stories in which a figure
identified as "God" is a crucial agent. He is, furthermore, asked to
take them seriously as images of fundamental truth.[19] The function of
these stories is twofold. First, they characterize the figure "God"
by displaying a certain dramatic consistency in his action. Second,
they manifest in their literary form a dramatic unity (as opposed to
systematic coherence) which provides a model for the world which is
being commended to the believer. Since the significance of the story
lies in its dramatic structure rather than in the particular events or
behaviors which carry that structure in the story itself, the believer
is not tied to its details. On the contrary, he is called to recreate
its structure in whatever behavioral, institutional, or technological
material his contemporary setting provides. Given these models, the
believer is then asked to address (through prayer etc.) a figure so
conceived in the expectation that a serious address of this sort will
have the effect of producing in the believer's life a fruitful integrity congruent with that of the religious stories, and that his life
will, in time, appear as one unified activity within a fully realized,
redeemed cosmos. Therefore, as a proper noun within the GS structures
of Christianity, the concept "God" is not so much known as used. As a
predicate which refers to the comprehensive function of religious action, he is known, but only "through a glass darkly," i.e., as the
transcendental precondition of the distinctive, valued cosmos which is
the experienced fruit of the life of faith.

We can now consider directly the grounds of the believer's
hope. One observation is clear. That hope cannot rest on proofs
which move from the world to God. These proofs may have religious
uses, but they cannot authorize the claim "God exists." In part, this
follows from the necessary transcendence of the religious object from
all GS structures. Even more, however, it arises from the circularity
of such arguments. They propose to move from the world to God, and
yet, apart from our willingness to assert some entity or state oper-
ating on the logical place of reality (e.g. God), arguments based on
the "world" have no subject matter. Apart from the religious quest,
no cosmos exists. Nevertheless, although the believer shares no cosmos
with the unbeliever, his claims are still intelligible to both, for
they are specifications of a basic human quest. On the one hand, as
an image of that ultimate value which authorizes all language, the
believer's cosmos is a completed instance of the human project to
produce a realm of intelligibility within which one can bring into
view and reflect upon the values implicit in human life. On the other
hand, as the particular vehicle by means of which some community expresses its fundamental quest for indefeasible value, the believer's

cosmos is an autonomous reality, the ultimate background of all systematic thought carried on within his religious community, which neither seeks nor needs any justification beyond the values which its structures render to those who live within it. As long as they find them to be good, they must rely on it as the measure of the real. As the activity which establishes that reality, religion creates an autonomous realm of meaning oriented to a comprehensive, indefeasible value. It presents the believer with a cosmos only on the condition that it conforms to the imperative implicit in religious activity as such. And this imperative is to transcend all contingency in the quest for value. Whether the believer withdraws from the wheel of birth and into the serenity of enlightenment of triumphs over the lures of the devil in the service of God's Kingdom, he cannot lose the one thing that he properly cares about - a life which, however short or painful, is worth living. As long as the religious man is faithful to his distinctive task, he cannot fail. He shall be glad and one and true.

## Footnotes

1. It is just this point that Barth makes when he insists that God remains the lord of our knowledge of him, the subject who denies the meaning of all the predicates applied to Him. (CD I/1, 178; I/2, 271f, 471f; II/1 129 ff). A similar point is made by Reinhold Niebuhr when he insists that the doctrine of justification by faith has, as its epistemological consequence, the claim that the truth of faith is to be found within the believers commitment and nowhere else (The Nature and Destiny of Man, I, 165).

2. This is a major theme of Van A. Harvey in The Historian and the Believer (New York: Macmillan Co., 1966) esp. chap. 4.

3. Reason and Commitment (Cambridge: The University Press, 1973).

4. Ibid., 45.

5. Ibid., 15, 43, passim.

6. Ibid., 153

7. Kai Nielsen Contemporary Critiques of Religion (New York: Herder and Herder, 1971), esp. 18-22.

8. Ibid. 65ff

9. This sort of question is put to believers by a variety of critics. In Religion and Secularization (New York: Macmillan and Co. Ltd., 1970) Vernon Pratt has argued that it is just the necessity of this question and the unlikelihood of its satisfactory answer that defines this as a secular age. pp. 22ff. See also Antony Flew "Theology and Falsification" (i) A. New Essays in Philo-

84

sophical Theology, eds. Antony Flew and Alasdair MacIntyre
(London: SCM Press Ltd., 1955) and Herbert Feigl, "Philosophy of
Science," Philosophy, Gen. ed. Richard Schlatter (Englewood
Cliffs, New Jersey: Prentice-Hall, Inc., 1964).

10. Cf. Gilbert Ryle, The Concept of Mind (New York: Barnes and Noble,
1949), 133f.

11. Cf. Charles Landesman, Discourse and Its Presuppositions (New
Haven: Yale University Press, 1972) esp. 28-57.

12. It by inserting a further stage between those of behavior and
action on the one hand and religion on the other that I most
notably differ from such philosophers of religion as Robert H.
King in The Meaning of God (Philadelphia: Fortress Press, 1973)
esp. chaps. 2 and 3.

13. Cf. Peter Berger, The Sacred Canopy (Garden City, New York:
Doubleday and Company, Inc., 1967) esp. part I.

14. Cf. John E. Smith, Experience and God (New York: Oxford University Press, 1968) pp. 46-67.

15. The Logical Status of "God" (London: The Macmillan Press Ltd.,
1973).

16. Ibid., pp. 1-28.

17. Cf. Faith and Philosophical Inquiry (London: Routledge and Kegan
Paul Ltd., 1970) and The Concept of Worship (London: Routledge
and Kegan Paul, 1969).

18. I do not imply by this claim that only this type of religious
action can yield this kind of achievement.

19. Contrary to what most believers have thought and many still think,
it is not necessary for the stories to be historically true in
order to be "fundamentally" true. They are indeed under constraints. But these constraints are only indirectly historical.

# THE STATUS OF RELIGIOUS BELIEFS

Frank B. Dilley
University of Delaware

In recent decades there has been much discussion as to whether it is possible for religious belief-systems to live in peaceful coexistence with naturalistic or empiricist doctrines of factual truth. The effort at rapprochement has taken two forms, the reduction of religious reference to the realm of practical commitments and attitudes, and the attempt to leave the realm of factual truth intact for the empiricist while staking out a realm of religious truth which is gained by methods other than scientific. While these approaches are radically different in some respects, they are united by the abandonment of any claim to challenge naturalism on the fields of reasoned metaphysical inquiry. Both agree that the path of reasoned inquiry leads to naturalism. One response is to accommodate religious meaning to a naturalistic framework while the other is to overthrow that framework on the basis of truths of revelation which must be accepted on authority. The attempt to develop a comprehensive metaphysical outlook which fits rational and scientific knowledge into a religious framework has been abandoned by both.

It should be quite evident that religious belief-systems cannot be grounded by scientific tests for factuality as interpreted by empiricists. The options, given empiricist readings of scientific method, are to justify an hypothesis in terms of direct appeal to sense experience or to justify an hypothesis about unobservables in terms of a prediction of observable events which cannot be predicted on any alternative hypothesis.

Plainly beliefs in supernatural beings cannot be justified in either of these ways, given the kind of world that we inhabit and the kinds of things that do occur in that world. It is possible to imagine alternative worlds, or sets of events which might (but do not) occur in this world, which would constitute validation of religious belief-claims. However in this world the gods do not appear in publicly verifiable form high in the sky, giving loud predictions and performing miracles in accordance with those predictions, hence religious belief-claims cannot be established by scientific criteria.

The direct test, observation, rules out validation of God-claims because God, by hypothesis, is not observable by ordinary sense experience. It is sometimes claimed that religious experiences give people access to the Divine, but given the rules of scientific method the claim that the objects of that experience have objective existence cannot be justified. Suppose that it could be shown that under conditions $c$ every observer has an experience of the divine (being, consciousness, bliss). Since the object of that experience cannot be located spatio-temporally, the lawful occurrence of religious experience would no more be acceptable as a demonstration of the existence of God than would the fact that everyone might experience pink elephants under conditions $d$. Presumably hallucinations are lawful and will occur uniformly when the proper causal conditions occur.

Religious experiences will be given a subjective interpretation in the absence of any locatable spatio-temporal object of that experience. There are after all, experiences which are demonstrably hallucinatory (optical illusions, pink elephants) and it is a rule of scientific inquiry that a solution which is more complicated should be rejected if an adequate simpler one is available.

Cornford and Lehrer say

> Given all this evidence, it is reasonable to conclude that many mysti-
> cal experiences have natural causes. We should be careful, however,
> about inferring from this that all mystical experiences can be given
> naturalistic, scientific explanations. Nevertheless, in the face of
> such evidence, there is little justification for holding that some
> mystical experiences are not scientifically explainable. We can con-
> clude, therefore, that there is no reason to postulate that some super-
> natural force is the cause of religious mystical experiences.[1]

Although in the preceding passage Cornford and Lehrer allow for the possibility
that there might actually be supernatural causes, they conclude that it would be
unjustifiable, methodologically, to postulate supernatural causes. Since there
are some cases where the experiences can be explained by naturalistic causes,
parsimony requires that naturalistic causes be provided for all the rest.

Religious believers claim that there are supernatural causes of all
events, and in addition many religious believers hold that there are events
which are caused by God in a special miraculous sense. Many religious believers
think that God has sent special messengers or takes human form himself or has
caused miraculous healing to occur as clear evidences of his existence for those
who will recognize the miracles. However most of these events are of the sort
to which naturalistic causes could be attributed. Others can be disregarded entirely as illusory because of lack of substantiating corroboration. Those corrob-
orated by large groups of people have to be weighed against the evidence of all
our other non-miraculous experiences (the Humean rule). By this test, given the
kinds of events that occur, no postulation of supernatural causes for the kinds
of events that are admitted as having occurred is ever warranted. These rules
are plainly biasing in that supernatural causes, if they did occur, would be
denied because of the method. To adopt the methodology is to prevent our ever
knowing about or recognizing the existence of whatever supernatural causes there
might be.

The prediction option cannot be exercised because any event of the
type that religious believers expect to occur can be given naturalistic explanation, as is proved by the fact that naturalists have given such explanations to
all the events that religious believers have claimed were divinely caused events
in the past. It is not as though we were faced with two theories of light, able
to devise experiments which would fit one theory but not the other, because
whatever occurs will be made to fit each of the theories. The one exception,
predictions about rebirth into an order of existence in direct communion with
God, is of no use now in this world since you must leave this world to have the
experience.

One of the ways in which critics attempt to discredit theism is to pose
the question, does theism say anything about the world other than that which non-
theisms say? If so, supposedly, there are grounds for taking theism seriously,
if not, then it can be dismissed as a live option for rational people. Renford
Bambrough asks the question: "Is it conceivable that God should exist and yet
that everything else should remain exactly the same as if he did not exist? Is
it conceivable that God should not exist, and yet that everything else should
remain the same as if he did exist?" [2] He goes on to claim that transcendentalist theology has given no adequate answer to this challenge.

If one takes the word "adequate" at its face value, one can only be baffled by the question, but once one comes to understand that the word is a portmanteau for "adequate to meet Bambrough's criteria" then the question makes sense, and his claim that transcendentalist theology gives no adequate answer is correct. It is correct because it is impossible for an answer to be given which would be adequate given modern naturalistic criteria for adequacy.

There are many answers which are adequate if the word is taken in a broader sense however. In the first place, a reading of St. Thomas Aquinas (and many others) makes it plain that many theists claim that there would be no value-ordered world at all if there were no God. If all things were contingent, if there were no first final cause, if there were no supreme instance of Beauty, etc., then there would be no value-ordered world at all. This constitutes a direct answer to Bambrough's question, for if God did not exist then almost nothing would be the same as it is in the present world.

There are other answers as well which could be given. If there were a world in which every good act were immediately followed by punishment of the good-doer and the cancellation of the good that was done, no one would suppose that that world had been created by God. Or if there were intelligent and good-wishing beings but those beings had no power whatsoever over the things that went on in their bodies, so that when they wished to hug their neighbors they strangled them instead, no one would think that that world was created by God. Or if the world had intelligent beings, but was a hedonistic paradise in which wishes for sensual pleasure were followed immediately by gratification like the world the fox and cat persuaded Pinocchio to seek, no one would suppose that there was a God. In all these cases a designer would be required, but not God.

It does not require much imagination to give other examples of what worlds not created by God might be like, hence it must be that Bambrough and Flew and other philosophers who ask this question have something special in mind. If what they have in mind is "In what respects would a world created by God be different from this one?" the theist response has to be that such a world would not be in basic respects different from this one. The present world is a very good illustration of what a world created by God would look like, once you learn to recognize what a world created by God looks like.

The Bambrough question is not neutral at all, it is as metaphysically loaded as the requirement that theological propositions be verifiable in terms of sense experience or that language in theistic propositions be used in the same literal sense as that used in speaking of finite things. No one can give an "adequate" answer to the loaded test without renouncing the religious belief-system he or she defends.

Thus even if religious believers win the argument that their belief-systems are empirically meaningful, there is no hope that they will win the battle for truth if naturalistically biased truth criteria are used as the test to distinguish truth from falsehood. This leaves only three options for the religious believer, to try to accommodate religion to a naturalistic world-view, to give up the quest for rational justification for religious belief but continue to believe, or to challenge the claim of naturalism that its view of reality and its methodology for evaluating truth claims are adequate to human experience. These options will now be taken up in order.

Occasionally one encounters the view that the verification criterion has been liberating to religion, even that it has helped religion to return to its proper sphere. According to Paul Schmidt, "the primary purpose of religious language is to produce certain attitudes in oneself and in others."[3] The advent of logical empiricism has enabled religion to recover its real meaning, for now religious statements can be seen to be attitudinal and all the overlay of secondary propositions which claim factuality can be skimmed off. (90) Religion thus is rescued from the detrimental effects of being understood to be factually true. "To say that God is omniscient," for example, "is to express the attitude of continuous search for the solution of problems and of action that awards a high place to knowledge." (92) Thus to transpose fact statements to attitude expressions is to recapture the proper role for religion.

Another advocate of religious accommodation to naturalism is John Herman Randall, Jr. Religion offers no descriptions of fact, no truths about this world or some other world not attainable by the methods of science, he says. Its function is to offer a set of symbols which will help us "see" something about our world. "A religious symbol unifies and sums up and brings to a focus men's long and intimate experience of their universe and of what it offers to human life."[4] These symbols "through concentrating the long experience of a people and the insights of its prophets and saints, seem to serve as instruments of revelation, of vision---and as a vision of the powers and possibilities in the world." (118) Religious symbols both strengthen practical commitments to certain values and present to man a vision of a world "purified and recast in the crucible of imaginative vision." (119) Religious genius, like poetic and artistic genius, opens up for us things we have not seen before, possibilities for using our eyes and ears and lives that we have not noticed before. Thus Randall in no way means to denigrate religion, but to remove it from competition with science as a source of factual knowledge and to liberate it for its proper task in the values realm.

Braithwaite gives more attention to the particular historical religions, but agrees also that religious assertions are "primarily declarations of adherence to a policy of action, declarations of a commitment to a way of life."[5] The believer's intention to follow that way of life is the criterion for the meaningfulness of his assertions in religion. Braithwaite gives particular attention to the value of particular stories connected with historical religions. These stories may be factual in part or purely fanciful, and need not be believed to be true in order to carry out the function for which they are valuable. He notes that "many people find it easier to resolve upon and carry through a course of action which is contrary to their natural inclinations if this policy is associated in their minds with certain stories." (27) These stories need not be consistent, and he suggests that inconsistency may well be a virtue if the various needed sides of the values problem can be presented. Stories of providence can provide confidence, while stories of the battle between light and darkness can serve as spurs to action, and both may be needed.

These philosophers are successful in providing accounts of religious assertions which are compatible with naturalistic and empiricist criteria for factual knowledge. As long as religion concerns something other than descriptions of fact it can be made compatible with the scientific world-view. The proposal is a radically revisionist theory of the nature of religious-belief systems. While it preserves an essential feature of religion, its concern with providing a path of life for believers to follow, a way of salvation, it denies both the existence of supernatural beings (and aspects to human beings) and any divine influence on the conduct of nature and human affairs. Clearly this theory does not describe how typical religious believers themselves look upon their belief-systems but is a proposal that religious believers from now on look at their belief-systems in this new way. This proposed revision of the nature of religious assertions has not been widely accepted by religious believers, as might be expected. Clearly most religious believers regard the claim that their statements about God provide information about the world and man as essential to their belief-system. Religious matters are not, for them, merely matters of ultimate concern but also of theory of reality.

The second option is to consider whether it might be possible to claim that religion provides an autonomous source of knowledge. It might be defensible to claim that there is a methodology and way of describing that is appropriate to scientific truth and a methodology and way of describing that is appropriate to religious truth, and that each kind of truth has a method of justification internal to the truth-system. You should do science parsimoniously, but it might be all right to be a bit more generous when you do religion. Neither type of activity should dictate to the other how truth questions should be answered.

There are two major forms of this approach, that suggested and later abandoned by Alasdair MacIntyre, which apparently offered a frankly supernaturalistic and neo-orthodox version of religion, and that offered by D.Z. Phillips, which entails drastic modifications in what religious believers have typically believed.

The movement which Kai Nielsen has styled "Wittgensteinian Fideism"[6] arose from a combination of a philosophical movement associated with the later writings of Wittgenstein, typified by the claims that language is basically all right as it stands and that each of the language-games which are played have their own standards of intelligibility and rationality, and a theological movement associated with the writings of Soren Kierkegaard and Karl Barth, who shared the belief that revelation is the sole source of religious truth. The common ground is the emancipation of religious language from any connection with science or rationality, hence agreement on the autonomy of basic language systems. The role of philosophy is neutral, to analyze and clarify the basic language-systems to keep them from interfering with each other, but not to bring an orderly combination out of them. Reconciliation is metaphysics, and metaphysics is a game which cannot be played. Religion, ethics, science are all autonomous and valid realms, to be protected from mutually interfering with one another.

Religiously this position is similar to that taken by the early Reformers except that the reformers were not fideists because they acknowledged and distinguished knowledge of God which man has from nature from saving knowledge which he obtains by revelation, while the new breed of fideists claims that man acquires no knowledge of God whatsoever through sense experience and the orderly reflection thereon. In the realms of empirical fact man draws an absolute blank when he tries even to think of God, let alone when he tries to show that there is one. Both religion in its claims to revealed truth, and science in its claims that the empirical world scientifically understood has no room for the hypothesis that there is a God, are to be accepted.

The fideistic claim is a repudiation not only of the efforts of philosophers to ground religious claims by reason, but also of traditional religious appeals to miracles, divine actions and the like as evidence for the truth of religion. The ties were broken not only with the classical proofs for God's existence but with all attempts to use God as an explanatory hypothesis for nature and history as a whole or for particular events or chains of events occurring in nature or history. For the new fideists arguments over religious belief as a whole system now become pure "Tis-Taint" arguments, as free from arbitrability by reason or science as matters of taste or feeling or morality. Religion as a whole appeals solely to religious authority, or at least will come to do so when the theologians are led out of the fly-bottle by proper philosophical analysis.

In presenting Wittgensteinian fideism my goal is not to show that it is incoherent, for this is not in question--it could be played--but to show that it fails to account for how religious belief-systems actually work. Theology has not been and is not now practiced in the manner described.

Religious assertions, Alasdair MacIntyre claims, are not hypotheses. To say that they are hypotheses would be to clash with the way they traditionally are held by believers, he claims. The system of religious belief rests upon authority. "The only apologia for a religion is to describe its content in detail: and then either a man will find himself brought to say 'My Lord and my God' or he will not."[7] It is "tis" or "taint." Elsewhere he says, "to ask for reasons or a justification of religious belief is not to have understood what religious belief is." (208)

What is true of religion is true also of science and morals. "Of science and morals it can also be said that one can justify particular theories or prescriptions, but that one cannot justify science as a whole in non-scientific, or morals as a whole in non-moral terms. Every field is defined by reference to certain ultimate criteria." (202) In religion that criterion is authority.

It is pointed out by MacIntyre that he does not mean to say that religion does not say things about the world, merely that what religion says cannot be justified by means of appeals to evidence or arguments drawn from the ordinary world. Of statements about God's love he says, "We do not offer evidence for these statements, we offer authority for them. We point to the state of the world as illustrative of doctrine, but never as evidence for it." (201) "Our ground for saying it is that we have the authority of Jesus Christ for saying it: our ground for accepting what he says is what the apostles say about him; our ground for accepting the apostles? Here the argument ends or becomes circular; we either find an ultimate criterion of religious authority, or we refer to the content of what authority says." (200)

But is it really the case that religious believers typically refer questions about religious belief to Jesus Christ as authority? Sometimes believers may say that they believe what they do because Jesus said so, but the statement bears inspection--do believers claim to trust Jesus as authority simply on the basis of his claims to embody authority or is it that they think that they have good reasons to think that his claims are valid? In other words, is belief in the authority of Jesus itself believed to be justified in terms of some other criterion? Official religion, at least, holds that belief in Jesus can itself be justified in terms of proofs and evidences.

If MacIntyre's theory were true we should expect not only that religious believers should never attempt to justify their belief that Jesus Christ is the authority who should be accepted, but also that the content of religious belief would never be modified unless the words of the authority plainly support such a modification. It is difficult to see how this latter would occur, short of the discovery of a new document which is certifiable as authentic.

In point of fact, however, religious believers, including those believers who were historically closest to Jesus, do not justify the content of their beliefs just by appealing to authority but make attempts to prove that Jesus is divine, and, secondly, they have significantly modified their beliefs under the pressures of changing secular views in metaphysical age after age. The religious game is just not played in the way that MacIntyre leads us to expect.

When John the Baptist's disciples asked Jesus if he was the one to come, he told them to look at the signs--the lame walk, the deaf hear and so on. Elijah offered to demonstrate that he spoke for God by challenging the priests of Baal to see whose sacrifice would be burnt supernaturally. The early followers of Jesus told their hearers that God had raised Jesus from the dead and that for this reason they should believe in Jesus and be saved. The Catholic church has always claimed that its miraculous universality and its freedom from error on matters of faith and morals show that it has supernatural backing. These rather typical religious claims are simply illustrations of the fact that advocates of religious belief-systems have typically maintained that there is evidence which justifies accepting the belief-system, evidence which is not just of the sort which is accessible to people who accept the belief-system but is accessible in principle to all. Moreover, they have often also offered philosophical arguments to support the religious world-view.

What is typical of advocates of religious belief-systems is not that they say "Jesus says he is divine, hence accept everything that he taught." They say instead, "God showed that Jesus was divine by raising him from the dead, by fulfilling prophecies made long ago, by the miraculous powers he manifested, therefore you can believe in him as divine and trust what he says." And people still offer arguments for religion in that way, perhaps naively, but still that is how the game is played.

The second thing to notice is that the content of religious belief is subject to changes that would be unexpected on the fideistic theory. If MacIntyre were correct, religious assertions should never change unless new discoveries about Jesus' teachings are made. However, the history of Christian thought is a history of changed understanding, Jesus' words are Platonized, Aristotelianized, Newtonianized, Whiteheadianized, and Wittgensteinianized, to pick only a few examples. Almost no one thinks of navigating the solar system by Jesus' cosmology, curing diseases by his theory of medicine, or of selling their possessions to be ready for the imminent end of history as Jesus advised. His cosmology, science and theory of history were all of them incorrect, many believers would say, or at least they say that the words must be "understood" in some fashion beyond their surface meaning, a claim hard to distinguish from changed understanding.

It probably is true that Christian believers attempt to believe all they can of what Jesus said, and that they perform wondrous feats of reinterpretation to make Jesus sound like Plato, Aristotle, Newton, Whitehead or Wittgenstein, as the case may be. On MacIntyre's theory this is difficult to explain, except as a muddle perhaps, whereas the phenomenon can easily be accounted for on other theories about the relation of religion to secular forms of knowledge. Believers need to have coherence in their beliefs about God, man and world. They want what their authority (justified) says and what their senses say to be consistent with each other. It is not enough that theology is played and that science is played, but the statements of each must be consistent with each other, hence they try to make Jesus' statements fit in with other truths.

Only a few would believe, I submit, that had Jesus said "2+2=5" believers would accept that as "gospel." Jesus apparently believed that Moses wrote the Pentateuch and presumably believed that history had the kind of time span consistent with the more recently proposed 4004 BC chronology, but religious believers do not generally accept such things as factual assertions even though Jesus apparently believed them. MacIntyre claims that historical events can be believed on religious authority. He says that "certain past events can be part of a religious belief, that is that they can be believed on authority" (207) in speaking of the empty tomb. Because this is so, he says, any newly discovered document claiming to establish that the resurrection did not take place would be rejected as forgery. Why do not believers accept all the things that Jesus said as factually true on the MacIntyre thesis? He gives no satisfactory account for how believers select which facts to believe, and he cannot without violating his fideistic theory about autonomy of languages.

Religious claims and scientific claims seem to conflict at times, but the fideistic theory seems not to permit using an answer from the religious realm to settle a science question or vice versa. Does this mean that religions should make no statements about scientific fact questions? No, MacIntyre says that certain fact statements are to be believed on religious authority, and that is consistent with his fideistic thesis that science and religion have autonomy. Should the outcome of apparent conflict be that a person should accept conflicting answers, one from science and one from religion? Religious authority says that the earth is young, while science says it is old. Should we alternate days or should one answer be believed in church and the other in school? If neither science nor theology can criticize the other it seems logical to say that both should stand in their proper spheres.

The trouble with the MacIntyre thesis is that religious believers do try to bring coherence into their whole system of beliefs, religious, moral and scientific. They do not believe on religious authority that Moses wrote the Pentateuch, or that creation took place 6000 years ago, no matter what religious figure says these things, even if they believe that the person who said them is divine. They search for coherence as though they thought that there is an overarching system of thought which may begin with religious teachings but which must be developed and tested in terms of its applicability to the whole of human experience. They believe that the games must not only be internally consistent but must be played consistently with each other, a belief no Wittgensteinian fideist can justify.

In elaboration of this point I shall discuss some passages written by D.Z.Phillips. While affirming also that each language is subject to its own criteria, Phillips is forced also to admit that religious language is subject to correction by other criteria, apparently. This seems to be the import of the following statements: "I have argued that religious reactions to various situations cannot be assessed according to some external criteria of adequacy. On the other hand, the connections between religious beliefs and such situations must not be fantastic. This in no way contradicts the earlier arguments, since whether the connections are fantastic is decided by criteria which are not in dispute."[8] Also, "When what is said by religious believers does violate the

facts or distort our apprehension of situations, no appeal to the fact that what
is said is said in the name of religion can justify or excuse the violation or
distortion." (98-99) He, like MacIntyre, believes that religious beliefs often
concern the world, his claim is merely that they are not justified by appeals to
the facts of the world.

It is natural to ask whether the foregoing passages maintain this distinction. If religion claims things which are fantastic, how can one reject
these things on the grounds that they constitute a violation or distortion of
the facts without by that very act of rejection showing that an alien criterion
has been used to judge religious claims? Suppose, to cite an example from Phillips,
that a boxer crosses himself before entering the ring because he thinks that this
will protect him from harm. He is committing a blunder, according to Phillips,
because he is violating well established views of causality. "We can say that
the people involved are reasoning wrongly, meaning by this that they contradict
what we already know. The activities are brought under a system where theory,
repeatability, explanatory force, etc., are important features, and they are
shown to be wanting, shown to be blunders." (102) But for Phillips to say this
is to impose an alien theory of causality. It is characteristic of some religious belief-systems to claim that in fact there is divine intervention in events.
Moses expected God to do certain things when he held out the rod, and Elijah expected fire from heaven to consume his sacrifice. To claim that God does things
in nature and history is to make a religious claim, it is part of the religious
way of viewing life.

The problem is that while Phillips in these passages is reporting a
fact, that religious claims about divine causality and scientific claims which
supply natural causes for these same events are conflicting explanations, his
thesis about the independence of languages cannot account for this fact. Many
religious believers have demythologized claims about divine activity because they
do not believe that such events happen. They believe instead that events are
caused by natural forces or by human agency because they have come to accept a
scientific view of the universe instead of that part of the religious view they
once held. But unless one wants to claim that the disappearance of belief in
the miraculous is based on religious reasons (and an argument of this sort could
be developed, however Phillips does not develop it as far as I can see), to reject the belief that crossing oneself protects one from harm is to subject religious beliefs to an alien criterion.

In short, Phillip's concession to the elimination of the fantastic is a
partial abandonment of Wittgensteinian fideism. It looks rather more like the
kind of theory which results when one practices, as I would advocate doing, the
once-honored activity of building philosophical systems which integrate systems
of language into comprehensive world views.

It has been my contention that two features of the way religious language develops support this latter way of structuring the problem and deny the
adequacy of Wittgensteinian fideism as a model for analyzing religious language.
In the first place, religious believers have always presented what they take to
be evidence in support of their views. They argue from extraordinary events,
unusual persons, historical movements, patterns of design, and they offer explanatory hypotheses for religious experience and of moral demands. Secondly, religious views have varied relative to changes in scientific and metaphysical
frameworks for interpreting ordinary events. For these two reasons it cannot be
successfully maintained either that religions do not seek justification for their

claims to truth or that religious beliefs are subject only to religious criteria for truth.

To put it differently, Phillips is right in maintaining the thesis that religious belief-systems cannot be justified by "alien" criteria. The truth of a religious belief-system is shown by religious experience and by no other type of appeal (assuming that a coherent metaphysics can be developed). This does not mean, however, that all the parts of the religious belief-system are justified only in terms of an appeal to religious experience or religious authority. Religious beliefs are justified also by the realities believers see, not just by the way they are told to see things by their religious community and in their religious language. They are heavily influenced by science in how they see the religious world, and the particular modifications in traditional belief that Phillips himself acknowledges is evidence of this.

Phillips rejects the efficacy of petitionary prayer, the belief that life goes on beyond death, the belief that God intervenes in the world, the idea that the last Judgment is an event, and the belief that all evil will be made right some day, in all these respects providing clear evidence of the intrusion of science upon his religion. Nielsen is right in noting that what Phillips advocates is "a radically reconstructed Christianity masquerading as a neutral conceptual analysis of Christian discourse."[9] He is wrong, however, in his claims that fideism is self-refuting.

My previous remarks are not meant as a refutation of the possibility of being a consistent fideist, merely as a refutation of attempts to represent fideism as typical of religious believers. What I have tried to show is not only that fideism is atypical of believers but also that it is not followed by either of the fideists selected for examination. Fideism could be played, however. A fideist could say of every belief that he has, this was revealed to me. He could reject scientific regularity and claim that God is cause of every event and that every event has a particular reason and serves a particular purpose. The eight ball will go in the side pocket if God sends it there, but not if He does not, no matter what the skill of the pool-shooter. This pair of objects when added to that pair could result in four objects or three objects or eighteen objects as God decides in the particular case. Whatever is true is true because God wills it and I know it is true only because God so reveals it. This is the kind of outlook that would result if every belief were derived from authority. It is plain that this is not the system expounded by either MacIntyre or Phillips, however I would contend that it _could_ be defended consistently.

This critique of Wittgensteinian theism is quite different than that offered by Kai Nielsen who desires to show that fideism is guilty of self-contradiction. In the paragraphs that follow I shall try to show that Nielsen misses two essential points about fideistic claims that renders his charge of self-contradiction incorrect.

Noting correctly that conceptual relativism is the position that "what is to count as knowledge, evidence, truth, a fact, an observation, making sense and the like is uniquely determined by the linguistic framework used and that linguistic frameworks can and do radically vary," and that "since our very conceptions of intelligibility, validity, knowledge and the like are a function of the linguistic system we use, it is impossible for us to attain a neutral Archimedean point in virtue of which we could evaluate the comparative adequacy of our own and other linguistic frameworks,"[10] Nielsen then incorrectly infers that the conceptual relativist cannot claim to be speaking of a reality to which his conceptual framework must correspond. Conceptual relativists are not, contra Nielsen, forced to jettison "metaphysical talk of a concept of reality which linguistic frameworks, forms of life, universes of discourse may or may not square with or correspond to." (98) A conceptual relativist believes both "there is an external world to which my ideas correctly correspond" and "the criteria by which my beliefs are established are conceptually relative." What he rejects is the contention that his claims to speak truth can be justified by appeals to "neutral" truth criteria, not the contention that his views correspond to external reality.

Nor must conceptual relativists deny that the views they hold are really true, as Nielsen apparently thinks they must. They do hold that truth is relative to criteria which are part of the belief system, but not that no systems have "legitimate claim to a superior reality or deeper truth or profounder insight than any other language game," (104) nor that "given the truth of conceptual relativism, there can be no such general statements about the nature of reality. We cannot succeed in making statements about reality überhaupt, but only about the realities of a particular situation." (105) A conceptual relativist would be baffled by the claim that to believe that his criteria give truth, but to acknowledge the fact that there are other people who believe equally strongly that their criteria are the ones which really yield truth, means that he must give up claims to be speaking real truths about the real world and must admit that conflicting views held by other people are equally valid.

Nielsen's "refutation" consists in claiming that the only legitimate outcome of conceptual relativism is scepticism. If conceptual relativism is taken seriously, only three options are open--to be "sceptics, Quixotic knights of faith committed to what in our own terms is plaintly irrational, or reductionists committed to a form of belief that is so transformed that it is in substance atheistic." (111) Since what is irrational ought not be believed, the only real answer is scepticism, he contends.

In brief, conceptual relativists of the type exemplified by Wittgensteinian fideists could bite the bullet and declare for both the claim that they have the whole truth and the claim that other people believe also that they have the whole truth but are mistaken. There is, from the point of view of fideism, nothing wrong or irrational about this stance.

The proposed refutation plays on the multiple meanings of the word "irrational". If one means that a rational justification is one which accords with some universally acknowledged conception of rationality, then the conceptual relativist had to deny that any position is ever rational because he is committed to a denial that there are universally acknowledged conceptions of rationality. Rationality in that sense is a myth. But if by rational is meant a criterion of truth for which a valid justification can be found in the conception of reality which is believed to be true, then conceptual relativists can believe that what they propose is rational. Moreover, there is nothing irrational in being a "Quixotic knight of faith" if one believes that the logic of religious belief is such that leaps of faith are the only means of access, as for example if one believes that because of the transcendence of God human knowledge of God must of its very nature be paradoxical. If the logic of what is believed requires this, then it is no argument for scepticism to show that it requires believers to be Quixotic knights of faith. Nielsen is judging by an "alien" criterion of rationality.

Even among less Quixotic conceptual relativists there are legitimate answers to Nielsen's complaint. There is no inconsistency in claiming that one's view is true but that it is perfectly possible that there be careful philosophers who do not ever come to see that that view is true because they have adopted points of view which lead them systematically into error.

These inadequacies aside, Nielsen is basically correct in his view of the live options for belief-systems. "Reductionist" attempts to reconcile religion with naturalism are in fact an abandonment of historical religion. "Christianity and Judaism as we know them commit us, if we are to be Jews or Christians, to the belief that in these religions there is an admittedly mysterious assertion of an belief in an ultimate order of fact which is different from anything skeptics can accept."11 He is also correct in his judgment that Wittgensteinian fideism is an inadequate path to the justification of religious beliefs, though not for the reasons he suggests. If religious belief-systems are to be defended it must still be in terms of a chastened warfare between empiricism and theology. Religious belief systems must be defended through the development of a comprehensive metaphysical theory grounded in religious experience which is not only adequate to all the known facts but also which can be defended as superior to the view of reality based on acceptance of the verification principle that Nielsen supports. It may have taken fifty years to establish that the attempts to dissolve metaphysics associated with Wittgenstein (in both early and later stages) and with Karl Barth rest upon a mistaken account of how religious and other language systems function, but there are signs of growing recognition that the battle has returned to the fields of yore. It is somewhat comforting to know that those philosophers who have argued the pros and cons of religious belief were, after all, really _arguing_ about something after all.

## FOOTNOTES

[1] James W. Cornford and Keith Lehrer, Philosophical Problems and Arguments: An Introduction. Second Edition. (Macmillan, 1974), p. 344.

[2] Renford Bambrough, Reason, Truth and God (Methuen, 1969) p. 52.

[3] Paul F. Schmidt, Religious Knowledge (Free Press, 1961), p. 77.

[4] John Herman Randall, Jr., The Role of Knowledge in Western Religion (Starr King Press, 1958), p. 117.

[5] R.B. Braithwaite, "An Empiricist's View of the Nature of Religious Belief," The Eddington Lecture (Cambridge University Press, 1955), p. 15.

[6] Kai Nielsen, "Wittgensteinian Fideism," Philosophy (July, 1967).

[7] Alasdair MacIntyre, "The Logical Status of Religious Beliefs," Metaphysical Beliefs (SCM Press, 1957), p. 205.

[8] D.Z. Phillips, Faith and Philosophical Inquiry (Schocken, 1971), p. 98.

[9] Kai Nielsen, Scepticism (Macmillan, 1973), p. 32.

[10] Kai Nielsen, Contemporary Critiques of Religion (Macmillan, 1971), p. 96.

[11] Nielsen, Scepticism, p. 39.

IMPLICATIONS OF NORTHROP'S DISTINCTIONS

FOR THE PHILOSOPHY OF RELIGION

Robert C. Smith
Trenton State College

The problem of locating an identity and mode of expression suitable for a secular technological environment is part of a common human quandry in the modern world. Almost three decades ago F. S. C. Northrop in The Meeting of East and West expressed the hope that East and West could be mutually benefitted through increased contact and appropriation of divergent epistemologies. At a time when East-West dialogues were minimal Northrop suggested that Westerners will increasingly go to the East to acquire modes of intuition and contemplation of things in their aesthetic immediacy. Easterners would come to Europe and America to acquire Western science and more theoretically grounded determinate economic, political, social, and religious values. They could "meet" not because they were saying the same thing but because they have been expressing different yet complementary things, both of which are required for an adequate conception of man's personal and social fulfillment. As Northrop puts it, "The Orient, for the most part, has investigated things in their aesthetic component; the Occident has investigated... things in their theoretic component."[1] This thought as expressed by Northrop is developed with cogency and originality. It has been given wide exposure and gained the tacit acceptance of a large number of scholars concerned with comparative studies in philosophy, religion, and world culture. Because of the importance of Northrop's theses, they are deserving of the most careful scrutiny.

The touchstone of Northrop's outlook is that "The true relation between intuitive, aesthetic, and religious feeling and scientific doctrine is one of mutual supplementation."[2] This theme is sustained through a host of chapters expounding no inconsiderable part of world culture -- Mexican, United States, British, German, Russian, Roman Catholic, and finally Oriental culture. In a discussion of twentieth century culture of the United States, Northrop says: "And for philosophy, there comes the additional demonstration that this purely factual, immediately apprehended component by itself -- which we shall henceforth term the aesthetic component of things -- is its own justification..."[3]

By virtually expounding a philosophy of culture and emergent world civilization Northrop maintains that divergent philosophical assumptions underly and perpetuate ideological conflict and misunderstanding. An important task of philosophy for him is to overcome limitations of past religious and cultural history in the search for balance and integrative wholeness. Only by such philosophical self-consciousness can cultural distortions resulting from constrictive onesidedness be overcome.

In a section titled "Intimations of New Values" he says: "A culture rooted in such a philosophy can build with confidence since the aesthetic component is immediately apprehensible and the theoretic component is scientifically verifiable."[4] The possibilities of the analysis are interesting to ponder. It is not clear whether in Northrop's mind cultural optimism is based more upon scientific verifiability or upon aesthetic realization. His recognition of the importance of the aesthetic component appears to be more of an awareness of the onesidedness of theoretic knowledge than of genuine affinity with Eastern modes of expression. For him the bankruptcy of Western religious expressions is symbolized by Grant Wood in "Daughters of Revolution" which "...made us look at our blankish Protestant souls with all their rigid ethical virtues, but devoid of a hearty, human spontaneous expression of feeling, compassion, and the emotions."[5] Puritanism and Thomism are equally unacceptable options to Northrop. Unfortunately, he only hints at the way aesthetic immediacy can be meaningfully integrated into United States culture. In this respect he accepts with appreciation the interpretation Alfred Stieglitz puts on Georgia O'Keefe's artistic Abstraction No. 11, The Two Blue Lines: "...the one blue line represents the female aesthetic component; the other, the male scientific component in things. And the common base from which they spring expresses the fact that although each is distinct and irreducible to the other, both are united."[6]

Several philosophers, historians, and sociologists of religion are currently seeking for more adequate explanations for ideological diffusion. This can be
seen in Carl Rashke's paper, "The Asian Invasion of American Religion: Creative Inno-
vation or New Gnosticism?" (Chicago AAR Meeting, 1973). Rashke argues that the phenomenon of an Asian influx should be understood in terms of a contemporary culture
crisis rather than in the innate appeal of the Orient.

## The Aesthetic/Theoretic Polarity

According to Northrop the world is made up of two factors: "the aesthetic
component of things" and "the theoretic component of things". The aesthetic component consists of whatever is directly and immediately apprehended without any conceptual, inferred or postulated addition whatever. This aesthetic component is
unique, and in no way to be understood in terms of anything else. By contrast,
science constitutes the antipode of the intuitive aesthetic component. "It becomes
logically, systematically and deductively formulated, and verified only indirectly
by precisely and theoretically defined experiments. It directs attention away from
the aesthetically immediate, to the inferred component of things."[7] In science
knowledge proceeds through inference (e.g. indirectly verified theory). It is for
this reason that Northrop terms it the theoretic component. Through this use of
terminology the stage is set for an appreciation and integration of intuition and
experimentally verified theoretical science.

Northrop states that the reader must not conclude from his usage that the
theoretic component is a mere idea or subjective construct. It is a part of any
real thing with precisely the characteristics which the verified theory designates.
"It is, however, convenient at times to use the expression 'theoretic component', especially when referring to knowledge, to designate the theory rather than the component in things which the verified theory designates."[8] Following James, Bergson,
and Whitehead, rather than Locke or Hume, Northrop views what is immediately apprehended not as a disjunctive aggregate of atomic sensa or qualities, but as the all
embracing aesthetic continuum in which these are local, determinate differentiations.
He says: "...it is only at its center that it is differentiated and determinate;
(at its periphery) this aesthetic continuum is indeterminate. It seems appropriate,
therefore, to designate and describe the aesthetic component in its totality as "the
differentiated aesthetic continuum".[9] Thus, in a review article, W. T. Stace observed, "It is differentiated because of its variety of qualia. But the aesthetic
continuum need not always be differentiated. It is possible to get rid of all particular differentiations, of all specific determinations, qualia, or feelings. What
is left then is not, as one would expect, nothing, total vacuity, but — surprisingly — the "undifferentiated aesthetic continuum".[10] When so experienced, it is profoundly moving aesthetically and mystically. Stace indicates that Northrop does not
consider the point that what is aesthetically moving has the character of being
aesthetically moving in some particular way, e.g., it produces a feeling of blessed-
ness and not of misery and thus, therefore, not wholly indeterminate.[11]

In contrast to Stace, D. T. Suzuki was quite appreciative of Northrop's
use of the term "undifferentiated continuum". He felt that it was an appropriate
way to indicate what is primarily and immediately given to consciousness. He said:
"To the Western mind, 'continuum' may be better than sunyata, though it is likely to
be misinterpreted as something 'objectively' existing.."[12]

## Determinancy/Indeterminancy

Northrop has been responsible for showing that:

> Orientals are an exceedingly concrete, practical, and realistic
> people; and their religion is best thought of by Westerners as
> something nearer to what the West regards as aesthetics than to
> what the West has regarded as religion...But in saying this, care
> must be taken. For...the aesthetic must be conceived in its
> Oriental sense as the aesthetically immediate for its own sake
> and not in its Western sense as the handmaid of common sense be-
> liefs in external, three-dimensional objects, or of more sophi-
> sticated...scientific, philosophical, or theological objects.[13]

So far so good, but he also states:

> In the case of the major Far Eastern religions, the Divine and
> the 'true self' are identified with the all-embracing, indeter-
> minate, undifferentiated, and hence positively indescribable por-
> tion of the aesthetic component; in the case of theistic religions,
> the Divine and the human soul are identified with certain primary
> factors in the theoretic component of the nature of things.[14]

One senses the tendentious character of such a generalized correlation between "the
divine" and the indescribable in spite of Northrop's insistence that the Eastern traditions (Hindu, Buddhist, Taoist, and Confucian) are neither theistic nor pantheis-
tic "in its uncorrupted form". The generalization which posits a universal perspective underlying four disparate traditions tends to ignore such particular Eastern
expressions as the Anatta doctrine of Buddhism and the impersonal nature of Tao.
Northrop's cultural analysis of "theistic religions" leads him to posit an identification of the Divine (in part, but not completely) with "the invariant element"[15]
in the theoretic component. In his view, "a perfect religion"[16] will conceive of
God as embracing both the aesthetic and the theoretic "divine components".[17]

Evidently part of Northrop's difficulty lies in his tendency to view
reality conceptually and in terms of imputed "essences" rather than experientially.
The phrase "The Orient, for the most part, has investigated things in their aesthetic component"[18] represents a case in point. Here the Western category (investigation) is clearly inapplicable. Northrop is right about the matter of comparative
priority, but incorrect with regard to the mode of expression. A mildly appreciative yet critical assessment of Northrop's viewpoint was offered by E. A. Burtt at
the Second East-West Philosophers Conference in 1949. Burtt says:

> I do not agree with Mr. Northrop in his contention that theoretic
> concepts are generally speaking alien to the East, but it is
> obvious that if he is right there would be no adequate way of
> translating this kind of idea into Eastern languages, nor the idea
> of 'epistemic correlation' through which, in his view, the theoretic
> and aesthetic components are to lie down in peaceful harmony...The
> most important virtues, in my judgment, in Northrop's methodology
> for achieving a 'meeting of East and West' lie in this clear
> realization of the importance of a neutral terminology in which to
> analyze the similarities and differences of Occidental and Oriental
> philosophies, together with his conviction that the analysis can
> and should emphasize the ways in which they complement rather than
> contradict each other. Its most serious defects are his failure to

realize that knowledge in the East, is more than an intellectual affair, his belief that Chinese and Indian philosophies exemplify a single type, and his apparent assumption that a valid reconciliation between East and West can be worked out in advance of active methodological cooperation on the part of thinkers representing these diverse cultures.[19]

Theoretic concepts are by no means alien to the East and several art historians are of the opinion that the Hindu tradition emphasizes the theoretic dimension considerably more than do the Chinese and Japanese traditions.

Generalizations that do not derive from empirical particularities can easily mislead. Such is the case in Northrop's characterization of theism. As he puts it:

> Theism in religion is the thesis that the divine is identified with an immortal, non-transitory factor in the nature of things, which is determinate in character. A theistic God is one whose character can be conveyed positively by a determinate thesis. His nature is describable in terms of specific attributes. All of the Oriental religions...deny this characteristic of the divine. The divine is indeterminate. Theses, specific determinate properties designate what it is not; not what it is.[20]

The following question can be raised: What evidence (in the form of actual teachings) would corroborate and support (or discredit) Northrop's assertion that Western theism is determinate and conversely that the divine is indeterminate in Oriental religious traditions? According to Northrop, Eastern formulations designate what it is not; not what it is. One immediately thinks of corroborative statements in Taoism ("The Tao that can be spoken is not the real Tao.") and in Zen where affirmation and negation are equally transcended in "No-mindedness" which is regarded as going beyond the subject-object schema.

An extensive investigation of the validity of Northrop's determinate/indeterminate characterization would endeavor to ascertain whether his distinction would hold up as a fundamental difference of Eastern and Western sensibilities of the divine or whether upon consideration of extensive instances it would be regarded as an unwarrented generalization. The present paper can only offer a few observations as to the adequacy of the formulation. In support of the indeterminate nature of the divine in the Oriental tradition one thinks of Radhakrishnan who once stated, "By religion I do not mean a creed or code, but an insight into reality...We may climb the mountain by different paths, but the view from the summit is identical for all". Methods may vary, but the goal is the same. Thus understood the life of the inner spirit from the standpoint of Hinduism is freely available to men of variant traditions. In Northrop's view, the realization of Brahman (aesthetic component) is given priority over Hindu ideology (theoretic). The two are not totally separated as theory and practice go hand in hand.[21] As Winston King has put it, "with Hinduism...words and concepts never represent the primary truth. They are purely relative, and reliance upon them may obstruct one's realization of truth. Thruth is to be found in experience and ritual practice. Hence for orthodox Hinduism, one may believe whatever doctrine he will...provided that his practice of ritual and attendant way of life is correct."[22]

Likewise Taoism and Zen emphasize the indescribable portion of the aesthetic component. Zen has stressed the immediacy of truth which must be spontaneously realized. Words are viewed as utterly inadequate to grasp the true nature of reality.

A Zen expression states, "The instant you speak about a thing you miss the mark." For Zen words are snares, "the fog one has to see through".[23] The Four Great Statements of Zen point to "A special transmission outside the Scriptures; No dependence upon words or letters; Direct pointing to the soul of man; Seeing into one's nature and the attainment of Buddahood.[24] Suzuki exposits that Zen has no God to worship. Consonant with the indeterminate experiential emphasis recognized by Heidegger, Barrett and others, Zen seeks realization not conceptualization. "Zen wants to rise above logic, Zen wants to find a higher affirmation where there are no antitheses. Therefore, in Zen, God is neither denied nor insisted upon; only there is in Zen no such thing as has been conceived by Jewish and Christian minds."[25]

Several examples can equally be cited to cast doubt upon the general adequacy of the determinate/indeterminate model to characterize the essential difference between Eastern and Western conceptions of the divine. For instance, Otto's comparison of Eastern and Western mysticism would hardly support such a distinction. No one would dispute that the conception of a theistic God with attributes such as "eternity", immutability", and the like has been enormously influential in Western theology. Northrop echoes Bertrand Russell when he asserts that "All the theistic religions are aggressive...each tends to have a provincial self-righteousness...and all tend to regard religious views other than their own as heathen, erroneous, or inferior."[26] The all-inclusiveness of the assertion makes one wonder if it is correct. Are theistic religions aggressive? Or is it people who are aggressive because of their "true believer" convictions? To the question: "does an exclusivistic or determinative perspective represent what the West wants to share with the East at this point in time?" the answer of Northrop is understandably negative. It can be noted that in our own time some Christian theologians are calling for a 100 year or indefinite moratorium on "missions". But from a rejection of exclusivism does it necessarily follow that the sole contribution of the West to an emerging dialogue is scientific verificationism? Western social, economic, political, and religious thought, although fraught with difficulties, are highly instructive. Should the West with its long philosophical and religious history abandon the attempt to remedy errors and deficiencies?

How appropriate is it to generalize the "Western theistic deity" in terms of specific attributes?[27] What Northrop describes and rejects applies to the Thomistic and Descartian conceptions of the deity. One can, however, disagree with Northrop's definition of theism (the thesis that the divine is identified with an immortal non-transitory factor in the nature of things) on several grounds. His formulation is too definitive. Aristotle and Thomas notwithstanding there is much indeterminancy in Western religious expressions. As Richard Kroner has said:

> Like Aristotle, Thomas distinguished in the visible universe
> the two levels of the celestial, or supralunear, spheres; like
> Aristotle, he believed that the higher one is more divine than
> the lower one, nearer the divine intellect and the divine eternity
> and immutability, so that it can harbor half-divine beings like
> the angels, whereas the lower hemisphere is exposed to the
> vicissitudes of natural and historical change and given over to
> contingency and chance. Man's soul and intellect are regarded as
> the bridge between the two realms...[28]

Much theological and philosophical debate has raged over the issue of divine attributes especially among those who take the arguments for the existence of God seriously. A God with attributes can be "known" with greater certainty and is even more amenable to philosophical disputation as attested by the innumerable attempts to prove and disprove his existence. However, the point here is that an adequate model must take into account not only the viewpoint of a given theological establishment but the dissenting opinions as well. Not all Western religious thinkers would agree that the divine nature is describable in terms of specific attributes. For example, Nicholas of Cusa's Negative Theology which deplores attributes is not just the exception that proves the rule. On the contrary for Nicholas the absolute is beyond all comprehension. We can know it only by contrast to what can be comprehended. Like the early church fathers of the Alexandrian School he insisted that the comprehensibility of the world is but the footstool of an inherent incomprehensibility of the divine and the created order. And so Eckhart, Boehme, and the entire tradition of Western mysticism add fuel to the fire. Likewise, while not a mystic per se, Buber's reference to the "Thou" within an I-Thou relationship is not a "pronoun that stands for some noun, a linguistic symbol of some transcendent reality"[29]

It is precisely the static intransigence of concepts like immutability (a Greek rather than Hebraic conception) that have produced much reformulation and dehellenization in modern theology. Leslie Dewart, a contemporary Catholic progressive, goes so far as to insist that eternity far from being a necessary attribute is a highly unbecoming one. "For an eternal God whose proper abode is a Heaven beyond creation remains essentially the Greek theos even if he is allowed occasional forays into time. In the Christian experience, God does not dip his finger into history; he totally immerses himself in it."[30]

Bernard Groethuysen (a pupil of Wilhelm Dilthey quoted with approval by Buber in Between Man and Man) said that with Aristotle man ceases to be problematic, and with him man speaks of himself always in the third person. He attains to consciousness of the self only as "he", not as "I" ...Man is comprehended only in the world, the world is not comprehended in him".[31] Buber once made a distinction between the dogmatical and the dialogical ways of understanding reality. The dogmatic perspective, he said, always seeks precision, knowledge, explicit formulation and definition; the dialogical perspective is content to allow immediacy to reveal itself in the givenness of an actual situation.

In modern times the notion of a "Deus Revelatus" is out of favor for obvious reasons such as a conflict between science and certain religious forms, the general climate of opinion that has given rise to ever new theologies of hope or despair. Yet in spite of all the acknowledged problems in any form of "god-talk" the tradition of a "Deus Absconditus" continues to hold a strange fascination for theologians be it the "eclipse of God" or "the experience of divine absence".

In view of these considerations it would seem that in actuality the existent world situation is considerably more complex than Northrop indicates. The obvious danger of broad generalizations is oversimplification and Northrop's case is no exception.

## Summary of Northrop's Assumptions

It is always somewhat precarious to set forth another man's premises and basic assumptions because there exists the possibility of misunderstanding. Acknowledging this possibility nonetheless, the attempt should be made because the viewpoint Northrop articulates has been exceedingly influential in both the East and the West. Among the points stressed are the following:

1. In the West philosophies are normative and determinative; religions are derivative and reflect the dominance of given philosophical theory. Progress proceeds through the process of examining, evaluating, and discarding outmoded and fallacious philosophical, political, economic, and religious assumptions. In a discussion of twentieth century culture in the United States[32] Northrop shows how seventeenth century philosophical assumptions such as Lockean individualism, Humeanism,

Quakerism, Congregationalism have and continue to dominate predominant thought patterns while the culture that originally produced these outlooks is long gone. For example, Northrop calls attention to the relative absence of art in traditional Protestantism. Only in modern times has Western art come to have an aesthetics which conveyed the aesthetic component in the nature of things for "its own sake".

2. Confidence in "scientifically informed philosophy". One reviewer has held that it is Northrop's purpose "to show that where Western thought is strong (in its natural science and mathematics) it does not need the East, but is needed by the East; and that where it is weak (in much of its religion and art and philosophy), it needs precisely what the East can give it".[33] Northrop nowhere puts it so explicitly. The deficiencies of traditional philosophy, religion, and aesthetics are exposed but where are the criteria for confidence on Northrop's own grounds (progress through discarding outmoded philosophies)? If the East has much to offer the West and vice versa, then more attention must be given to the matter of the criteria that should be employed for the acceptance and incorporation of Eastern perspectives.

3. The primacy of both the theoretic and the aesthetic components of things. "...the aesthetic factor is as primary...a criterion of trustworthy knowledge and the divine in culture as is the theoretic component."[34] The immediately apprehended "can not be defined away in terms of anything else. (It is)...primary and ultimate."[35] Greek philosophy had assigned a priority to the theoretic function and it is this imbalance that Northrop seeks to rectify. Northrop suggests that an aesthetic/theoretic distinction is developed by Plato. He says:

> Plato, in his famous lecture on the Good, even when designating the female aesthetic component as evil, nevertheless indicated it to be an ultimate, irreducible factor, one of the two 'ground principles of all things' ...it is with this female compassionate, aesthetic component that the good and the divine in the philosophy and religion of the Orient are identified. In fact it is likely that this female ground principle in Plato's philosophy was not original with Plato, but came to him from the East".[36]

He makes the point that in the history of Christianity the differentiated aesthetic continuum was used to convey a theoretically conceived object. Examples of this imitative tendency can be seen in the innumerable madonna with child portrayals the West has known. There is no quarrelling with his contention that such are based on optics, theory of proportion and perspective has predominated in the West. Such art does not use aesthetic materials and the aesthetic continuum for their own sake but "analogically and symbolically to convey the theoretic component of the nature of things of which they are the mere correlate or sign."[37]

4. "The basic task of our time is merging Oriental and Western civilizations". Philosophers were not ready to undertake such a "merging" of viewpoints. Even today a large number (if not the majority) of Western philosophers (and religionists) are as insular and provincial in their view of what constitutes the "truth" as in times past. The analytical establishment no less than the theological one looks upon such efforts as Northrop has outlined with an evil eye. Yet it is this writer's opinion that an emerging world civilization may well be desirable, especially as a long term goal. Nonetheless, an emergent synthesis requires a clearer understanding than has thus far obtained as to precisely what is to be "merged".

The value of Northrop's analysis is that it has raised the question of precisely how and to what extent Eastern and Western formulations of reality are complementary. As I have suggested in what has preceded, I do not believe that he has answered the question raised in a sufficiently satisfactory manner. Northrop's efforts at achieving ideological unity were premature. The Meeting of East and West appeared in print six years after the first East-West Philosophers Conference at which time hope for achieving a world philosophical synthesis was running high. On the flyleaf of Meeting he quotes with approval the statement of Mo-ti — "Where standards differ there will be opposition. But how can the standards in the world be unified?" A common set of language usages is one thing but world philosophical synthesis is another. Differences and the reasons for them are at least as important as similarities. Perhaps he should have reflected more upon the dictum of A. N. Whitehead, his former teacher, that the conflict of doctrines is an opportunity, not a disaster. For Northrop, conflict is ever unacceptable.[38]

The program Northrop outlines is essentially a call for the West to appropriate the complementariness of the undifferentiated aesthetic continuum. In the view of the present writer, this approach offers much as a viable basis for future world culture. It is strange that he does not associate the affinity between O'Keefe's artistic Abstraction No. 11 titled "The Two Blue Lines" with the yin-yang polarity. His appreciation for this work of art is expressed in the words "the one blue line represents the female aesthetic component; the other the male scientific component of things". If the good life for individuals and culture consists of a harmonious relation between the components further attention should be given to achieving equilibrium between the polarities.

Krister Stendahl has spoken of the need for a "...world theology." Such is definitely called for if the day of religious particularity is past (Tillich). Serious thought must be devoted to the coming world civilization. I have tried to show how the philosophy of religion must extend its purview from an exclusively Western agenda if we are to meet this urgent cultural and philosophical challenge. With this in mind one may ask if there is any good reason why the theoretic and aesthetic components cannot be expanded somewhat from the limits Northrop has imposed. If Northrop has suggested the form of East-West interaction, the content needs modification and adaptation. For example, it can be argued that science is but one aspect of a yang modality. Continuing discussions between leading exponents of Eastern and Western thought lends support to the hypothesis that Occidental modes of expression are complemented by Oriental modes of realization and vice versa. Perhaps Northrop should have said: The Occident has stressed formulating things in their theoretic component; the Orient has especially sought to actualize the intuitive component of reality. Neither tradition has been devoid of the yin or yang component, only deficient in some respects. In the spirit of complementariness may increased learning proceed from reflection on the peculiar aspects of internal history and from renewed encounters of East and West.

Footnotes

1.  Meeting, p. 375

2.  Ibid, p. 64

3.  Ibid, p. 162

4.  Ibid, p. 163

5.  Ibid, p. 160

6.  Ibid, p. 163

7.  Ibid, p. 163

8. _Ibid_, p. 303

9. _Loc.Cit._

10. W. T. Stace, "Review of Northrop's Meeting of East and West", _Ethics_, Vol. 57, January 1947, p. 137

11. _Ibid_, p. 138

12. D. T. Suzuki, "Reason and Intuition in Buddhist Philosophy", _The Japanese Mind_, Ed. by Charles A. Moore, East-West Center Press, 1967, p. 94

13. _Meeting_, pp. 403-4

14. _Ibid_, p. 483

15. _Ibid_, p. 484

16. _Ibid_, p. 483

17. _Loc.Cit._

18. _Ibid_, p. 375

19. Charles A. Moore (Ed.) _Essays in East-West Philosophy_, University of Hawaii Press, 1951, p. 119, 123.

20. _Op. Cit._ p. 401

21. S. Radhakrishnan and C. A. Moore, _Sourcebook in Indian Philosophy_ University of Hawaii Press, xxxiii.

22. W. L. King, _An Introduction to Religion_, p. 115

23. J. D. Eusden, Paper on Zen Discipline presented at AAR Meeting, October 1970.

24. D. T. Suzuki, _Zen Buddhism_, p. 9

25. D. T. Suzuki, _An Introduction to Zen Buddhism_, p. 39

26. _Meeting_, p. 411

27. _Ibid_, p. 401

28. Richard Kroner, _Speculation and Revelation in the Age of Christian Philosophy_, p. 187

29. Maurice Friedman, "Dialectical Faith Versus Dialogical Trust", _The Eastern Buddhist_, Vol. IV, No. 1 New Series, May, 1971, p. 162.

30. Leslie Dewart, _The Future of Belief_: Theism in a World Come of Age, p. 194.

31. Martin Buber, _Between Man and Man_, pp. 126-7.

32. <u>Meeting</u>, p. 142

33. Alburey Castell, "Northrop's Meeting of East and West", <u>Journal of the History of Ideas</u> 9:  237-44 Ap. '48

34. <u>Meeting</u>, p. 311

35. <u>Ibid</u>, p. 162

36. <u>Ibid</u>, p. 62

37. <u>Ibid</u>, p. 306

38. At the time of publication, <u>The Meeting of East and West</u> was touted as "the only book by an American philosopher to state the fundamental conflicts in world culture". — Howard Mumford Jones in The <u>New York Times Book Review</u>.

# THE END OF IDEOLOGY AND POLITICAL THEOLOGY

Hiroshi Obayashi

Rutgers University, Douglass College

Since the publication of Daniel Bell's The End of Ideology in 1960, controversies have been carried on as to the plausibility of an end or decline of ideology
in contemporary politics. Both pros and cons with regard to the decline theory of
ideology have argued for their respective positions with empirical evidence. It seems,
however, as though Bell's theory has, with some points to be modified and some empirical evidence to the contrary, an over-all empirical plausibility. It has been gradually clarified that the decline theory does not and cannot imply the disappearance of
ideological elements from the contemporary political scene. But it does imply that
in industrially advanced parts of the world ideology is no longer present in its
original and total sense of the term. Ideological elements are present in any political situation, but politics of today, especially in North America, Western Europe,
the Soviet Union, Japan, Scandinavia and parts of Eastern Europe domestically and
between nations, is no longer a genuine, thoroughgoing politics of ideology.

The alleged end or decline of ideology presupposed certain conceptual limitations in defining the term. Bell's theory clearly stands on the definitional presupposition. He first tried to salvage this concept from the deluge in its usage and
then assigned to it only a limited meaning. Utilizing Karl Mannheim's distinction
between "the particular conception of ideology," and "the total conception of ideology,"
Bell limited his use of this term only to the latter, "total," sense. For the use of
this term in its particular sense only opens the floodgate of its unqualified and im-
precise circulation as a currency in popular rhetoric. In its particular sense, ideology can be used between parties who are opposed on only some issues or policies but
otherwise stand on the common over-all moral basis. It can also easily be used regarding any interest group referring to its shared interest. Any ethnic group or
trade guild or labor union or pressure group or "anti-" group gathered around issues
of various scope and magnitude ranging from the Vietnam war to building a shopping
center. Ideology can conceptually denote just about anything as long as it represents some common interest, as in the case of "consumer ideology," or "anti-abortion-
ist ideology." For this reason, Bell proposed to use the term, ideology, only in
its total sense, clearly defined and limited in its usage.

> A total ideology is an all-inclusive system of comprehensive reality, it
> is a set of beliefs, infused with passion, and seeks to transform the whole
> of a way of life. This commitment to ideology--the yearning for a "cause,"
> or the satisfaction of deep moral feelings--is not necessarily the reflec-
> tion of interests in the shape of ideas. Ideology, in this sense, and in
> the sense that we use it here, is a secular religion.[1]

With this clear limitation in the usage of the term, Bell set out to prove that we
are now living in a post-ideological era.

America provided socialism, which to Bell was one of the prototypical examples of ideology so defined, with a fertile soil and plenty of opportunity to strike
roots and embody its goals. There were in actuality periods of active socialist activity in the recent history of the United States. Socialism, however, did not become a live option and viable alternative for American politics. It was Bell's argument that "the failure of the socialist movement in the United States was rooted in
its inability to resolve a basic dilemma of ethics and politics. The socialist movement, by the way in which it stated its goal, and by the way in which it rejected the

capitalist order as a whole, could not relate itself to the specific problems of social action in the here-and-now, give-and-take political world. In sum: it was trapped by the unhappy problem of living in but not of the world: it could act, and then inadequately, as the moral but not political man in immoral society."[2]

Today, Bell contends, ideologies which had been generated by the nineteenth century intellectuals such as Proudhon and Marx are exhausted. The failure of Socialism in America, continued dehumanization and forfeiture of utopian thrust even in societies where Socialism became reality and the increasing victory of rational expediency over hard-line ideology in the politics of the Soviet Union after Khrushchev, were all made to serve as evidence for Bell's theory of the end of ideology in the industrially advanced sectors of the world. Modern man no longer lives and thinks ideologically. "Ideology, which by its nature is an all-or-none affair, and temperamentally the thing he wants, is intellectually devitalized, and few issues can be formulated any more, intellectually, in ideological terms."[3] Observers who concur with Bell gave support to his theory by adding more convincing pieces of evidence. Seymore Lipset stated that politics became boring in the western world where the passionate exchange of verbal ammunition about such noble ideas as freedom and equality between peoples of left and right who were committed to the ideological goals was now replaced by issues such as milk prices and safety equipment on automobiles for which ideological commitment is utterly unnecessary.[4] Politics has become largely a matter of bargaining and making deals between groups and largely a matter of administration through bureaucratic organizations within a larger community rather than a matter of achieving a social change through a process of class confrontation and struggle. The working class, which had been the torch bearer for an ideology or social change and often a matrix of strong social forces, is now more or less satisfied with its own affluence of the western world. In America politics for them has become the tactics of collective bargaining. Workers and managers confront each other only across the bargaining table where the issues are seldom class oriented or ideologically motivated but rather a matter of greater shares in capitalistic profits.

To add an empirical and statistical support to the general observation of the end of ideology Robert E. Lane contributed the following report which had been extrapolated from the polls taken for this purpose.

> In an age of affluence, (1) social alienation will decline. ... (2) the sense of crisis and of high national, personal and group stakes in national elections declines; political partisanship takes on a new meaning. ... (3) people slowly lose (or relax) their class awareness. ... /diminishing/ the importance of class voting in many electoral districts. ... (4) religious institutions slowly lose their influence over men's thought and behavior. ... (5) the struggle for equality by a deprived racial group will be facilitated by the expanding economy, the availability of governmental resources for special assistance, and the relative security of otherwise challenged and more hostile "opposition" groups. ... (6) there will be a rapprochement between men and their government and a decline in political alienation.[5]

On the basis of such an empirical plausibility one can tentatively accept, though with important qualification to be discussed later, the decline theory of ideology as a working theory that can be applied to the contemporary political scenes.

What should we make of this trend? For one thing, de-ideologization can be considered the secularization process of politics. Gods of ideologies have been dethroned one after another. Ideological deities for whom men had assumed uncompromising

attitudes have relaxed their holds on political decisions. A considerable amount of
political activities are now carried on without references to those ideological deities. What happened to religion in the way of secularization has also happened to
politics. Secularization which was once deplored as the demise of the sacred has
now been discovered to be rather a maturation process for religion. Likewise one
can find de-ideologization, the secularization of politics, rather welcome as a step
in the right direction. Such an interpretation of de-ideologization can be facilitated
especially if one recalls the fact that the degree and extensiveness in human cruelty
that our wars have incurred were proportionate with the intensity of ideological elements involved in it. Outright ideological warfare, not to mention religious warfare,
was the worst kind in which pragmatic limits of destruction were overstepped to the
point of all-out attack and total annihilation. Points to be settled were not considered in terms of any particular problems, but by the total worldview; antagonists
were therefore hated as irreconcilable enemies just as they were the cursed embodiments of devils in religious warfare. Ideological warfare was caused by misunderstanding in locating the sources of human ills and social problems.

Considered in this manner the increasing de-ideologization with its growing
trend of pragmatization can be found encouraging. For it allows a greater latitude
in empirical weighing of alternatives for resolving pressing socio-economic problems
and in achieving some short range political objectives. Bell believes that there is
a growing consensus among contemporary western political intellectuals which includes
acceptance of the Welfare State, recognition of the desirability of centralized power
and acceptance of a system of mixed economy and political pluralism.[6] The wide acceptance of these items which had often been the issues that divided peoples ideologically now dulls the cutting-edges of hard-line ideologies to the point of making them
superfluous in the contemporary political scenes. The pronouncement of the end of
the ideological age is thus made with a note implying that we are growing up.

An observation might be made with regard to the recent trend in theology
from the theology of hope to liberation theologies if we consider them in the light
of this decline theory of ideology. It is interesting to note first that the increasing political turn in theology came during the period marked by the increasing de-
ideologization of politics. From the very outset the trend set by the theology of
hope contained seminal political implications. For hope is hinged on the God who is
"the power of the future and is believed as the creator of the new world."[7] The
power of the future lies not only in the future; it is also at work in the present
as a transforming and creative power. "By future ('advent')," Moltmann said, "we do
not mean a far-away condition, but a power which already qualifies the present through
promise and hope, through liberation and the creation of the new possibilities."[8]
When politics in the industrialized sectors of the world, whether capitalist or communist, has allegedly become less ideological, theology began bearing ideological
overtones, reflecting successively the futurist ideological elements of Ernst Bloch,
the anti-establishment ideology of Herbert Marcuse, the New Left student ideologies
and the liberation ideologies of the revolutionary Third World. One may certainly
try to account for such an ideological turn in theology by saying that it resulted
from questioning the morality of American involvement in Southeast Asia or from
sensitivity to explosive situations in many Latin American countries. It may therefore be interpreted as theology's responsiveness to the changing human situation.
Such explanations are to a large extent correct, but the question still remains.
When politics itself had been de-ideologized in America and Europe, why did theology
belatedly begin hearing ideological overtones in becoming political? Politics is
tending away from ideological questions toward pragmatic and empirical issues. Despite the continued presence of political parties, ideological differences between
parties have become less important in American and European politics. Domestic
politics, and to a great measure international politics as well, in America and
Europe is no longer an area of ideological clashes but has become a format for

collective bargaining. The fact that theology began bearing ideological overtones precisely at the time when politics ceased to do so might appear to provide an empirical proof for a sociological theory that religion (including theology) is always a step behind the times, reflecting trends that have preceded it. It might also be taken as theology's threat to become an ideology surrogate. That is to say, theology which had long been metaphysically abstract, spiritually inward-looking, soteriologically otherworldly oriented, and ethically privatistic and individualistic, hence timid toward any political involvement, might appear suddenly to have become politicized and come to fill the place allegedly vacated by ideologies. Theologians have always warned against reducing their task to the level of mere ideology. The threat, however, has now become real because it seems that the ideological overtones of a number of politically oriented varieties of theology are beyond doubt. One has only to recall that Black Power was theologically sanctioned,[9] Allende's Chilean socialism was welcomed with hosannas once accorded to Jesus' entry into Jerusalem,[10] the nonviolent and sometimes violent revolutions were found in many a theological writings in search of theological justification,[11] and the whole Third World without any qualification was vested with a messianic role in the tomorrow's world against the first and the second world who are the Babylonians and the Romans.[12]

Then the question we must ask has a dual implication. From theology's side, the question is whether the ideological overtones of recent trends in theology might not be damaging to theology qua theology. From politics' side, one can ask if de-ideologizing pragmatic tendencies in contemporary politics signal a step in the right direction of mankind's political maturation. If so, would not theology's ideological overtones constitute a possible reverse in this process, threatening to become ideology surrogates?

## II

In order to answer these questions I would like to go back and examine the end theory of ideology which had been tentatively adopted to set the platform of our discussion and bring the issue into focus.

It goes without saying that socialism, as Bell accurately observed, did not embody itself in America as a social order, and exerted only a limited influence as a moral force. There is an understanding behind Bell's choice of socialism as one of the empirical illustrations for the theory he put forth. Ideology with regard to which Bell pronounced the end is in his own understanding essentially utopian, or at least a social movement which arises as a criticism against the established order and strives to overthrow it and to establish a new social arrangement conceived in a utopian manner. These ideas and movements remain ideological only so long as they are counter forces to the established order of the status quo. This utopian bent of Bell's definition of ideology is clearly exemplified in his discussion of the religious, chiliastic origin of modern socialism. The major impulse of modern socialism was rooted in the "orgiastic chiliasm" of Anabaptist millenarianism. Bell stated, "socialism is an eschatological movement; it is sure of its destiny, because 'history' leads it to its goal. But though sure of its final ends, there is never a standard for testing the immediate means."[13] Socialism, in other words, is a movement "based on a belief in 'history'; but found itself outside of 'time'."[14] The chiliastic nature of socialism can be expanded to the apocalyptic and chiliastic character of ideology in general. The ideologue, according to Bell, "wants to live at some extreme, and criticizes the ordinary man for failing to live at the level of grandeur."[15] Bell continues, "One can try to do so if there is a genuine possibility that the next moment could be actually a 'transforming moment' when salvation or revolution or genuine passion could be achieved. But such chiliastic moments are illusions."[16]

The choice of socialism is far from arbitrary. In Bell's mind ideology is first and foremost the "left" ideology of social change. When he said, "The end of ideology closes the book, intellectually speaking, on an era, the one of easy 'left' formulae for social change,"[17] the definition of ideology was mainly as "left" and as the social force of criticism against the established order but is hopelessly running on a utopian treadmill. One might ask if this is not too limiting a definition of ideology for clearly there is also an ideology of the "right." If there is an ideology of "change," then there should also be an ideology of the status quo. In fact there is a great deal of ideology in the social force that protects the status quo and resists change. The men of affairs who are pragmatically and realistically disposed in dealing with reality may be just as much ideological as utopian socialists are. What is implied in the end theory of ideology is that the old passion for utopian ideals is spent and the mentality of the men of affairs is now prevailing. The mentality of the men of affairs and the predisposition for practical expediency are held to be ideologically neutral by virtue of the instrumental rationality with which they operate. "Left," utopia, the future and change on the one hand, and "right," the established order, the present and the status quo on the other, are opposed to each other as ideological and non-ideological viewpoints. If this is the general formula behind Bell's definition of ideology, and I believe it is, then the presupposition of the whole theory of the end of ideology is very misleading. The "right" is just as ideological as the "left." If the left ideology involves an element of unreality in terms of the mythical fabric woven on the basis of utopian conceptions of the social order, then the status quo ideology also involves "conscious disguises of the real nature of a situation, the true recognition of which would not be in accord with his interests. These distortions range all the way from conscious lies to half-conscious and unwitting disguises."[18] In fact it is mainly to the status quo ideology that Mannheim assigned the term "ideology," rather than to the utopian and eschatological outlook. Whatever the manner in which the term "ideology" was first used during the French Revolution or when it was used by Karl Marx in his polemic against the civil society, it was used to designate its over-all Weltanschauung which provided a framework for and symbolically represented the class values and interests of the Capitalists. It was the ideology of the status quo, resisting changes in its class structure.

The disappearance of utopian impulses from contemporary politics does not signal the end of ideology. The victory of pragmatism and rational expediency must not be interpreted as the departure of ideology. It is true that the utopian type of ideology is quite incompatible with pragmatism and a degree of compromise between them means a proportionate loss of utopian thrust. But that is not the case with the status quo ideology. Pragmatism and rational expediency are exactly the instruments for the preservation of the status quo; they are far from being ideologically neutral. Compromise, avoidance of extreme conditions, gradualism, practicality and confinement within realizable and short range objectives are the seemingly neutral but actually ideologically essential features of the status quo. The status quo ideology of the established order of Capitalism is very much alive. It is true that the utopian visions of our predecessors in the nineteenth century are all burnt out, at least in the political arena. But the consumption of utopian energy does not, to my regret, imply the demise of ideology.

The ideology of the status quo is formidably present as the distortion of human reality. Robert Bellah's sociological concept of Civil Religion in America fits in with this. It is not a utopian ideology of the dispossessed or alienated masses. It is an ideological formulation of the dominant values. "The words and acts of the founding fathers, especially the first few presidents, shaped the form and tone of the civil religion as it has been maintained ever since."[19] Bellah continues, "What we have, then, from earliest years of the republic is a collection of

114

beliefs, symbols and rituals with respect to sacred things and institutionalized in a collectivity."[20] This is the formulation of the religious dimension of the mainstream political life of America, which is legitimated even in the situation of church-state separation. The formulation of the religious in the political realm has often taken the form of an ideology. In fact five of the definitional categories about ideology all point to what constitutes a religion. They are, 1) the cognitive function, which offers a perspective on reality by providing one with things to know and believe, 2) the evaluative function, which provides norms, standards and values for one's behavior and critical evaluation of any situation, 3) the programmatic function, which helps develop plans and programs for attaining goals, 4) the affective function, through which ideology generates emotional power, mobilizes people and converts ideas into social energy, and 5) the broad-based social footing, usually rooted in a class.[21] Ideology thus in its total sense of the term is equipped with everything religion has been known to possess with the possible exception of the doctrines pertaining to death and after-life. Civil Religion in America is a superb specimen of the status quo ideology with democracy, liberty and equality as ideological symbols which have continually distorted American reality.

What Marcuse called "oppressive tolerance" exemplifies the remarkable elasticity of the status quo ideology. Its dexterity in containing critical forces of the opposition, the dispossessed, minorities and youths by giving them vents and longer leashes rather than outright repression is named concession or compromise or liberty in deceptive senses of those terms. "Democracy," has become a term in which the will of the people is ideologically sovereign but in actuality so carefully and intricately institutionalized that it is not the case. "Liberty and equality" were fermented within the bourgeois consciousness against the rigid aristocratic societies of Europe but were never egalitarianly conceived to include non-white population. They were commercial rather than political in their implications, promising free-enterprise and equal opportunity for business ventures protecting mainly the bourgeois interests. With these ideological symbols the ideology of the status quo is as firmly established as ever. It has not softened; it is in full mobilization and utilization of the ideological tools of its own, i.e., pragmatism. The legislation for Civil Rights domestically, and the detente policies and withdrawal from the role of the global police internationally, are just simply new ideological covers for the same old American Civil Religion.

This answers the question raised about the recent politicization of theology. The question was whether the fact that religion and theology began bearing ideological overtones precisely at the time when politics had allegedly become de-ideologized might not appear to provide empirical evidence to the sociological theory of religion as always the follower rather than the initiator of social changes. That is to say, the theory that religion is more priestly (sanctioning agent of the dominant values) than prophetic (initiator of social change) as it might have been considered. We are now able to say that it is not entirely accurate to call our era a post-ideological age. Theology is not picking up the trails of political trends just to stay abreast. If theology is not behind the times, then is it simply echoing concurrent political trends by bearing ideological overtones? Are they meant to replace political ideologies as ideology surrogates?

I must emphasize that politicized theology with its ideological overtones is not trying to become an ideological surrogate. It is striving to unmask the covers of the status quo ideologies which go by the name of pragmatic politics. In this sense political theology calls for the real end of ideology. Daniel Bell's end of ideology was an observer's descriptive statement about the situation of ideology; in reality, however, ideology is not yet dead. Political theology is now calling for the genuine end of ideology. What Bell said as a statement of fact is taken by political theology and now turned into a prophetic pronouncement. Ideologies, both status quo and utopian, are in my judgment distortions of human reality.

Hence, one of the first tasks of political theology is criticism. Both Johannes Metz and Jurgen Moltmann, from their German predilection, honored their own cultural past by tracing the spirit of criticism to the Enlightenment heritage.[22] Regardless of the validity of their chauvinistic claims, the spirit of criticism is the initial task of political theology to unmask the distorted conception of human reality and deceptive assessment of the historical situation prescribed by ideologies. Dorothee Soelle believes, "political theology carries on in the best tradition of liberal theology and preserves precisely the methodological achievements of criticism, analogy and correlation, while enriching them with refinements from sociology and sociology of knowledge."[23] She is further convinced that political theology must push the spirit of criticism, which has heretofore been exercised mainly in historical, literary, and hermeneutical areas, a step further to an ideological criticism. Her critique of Bultmann's existentialist eschatology, "whose interest is served by perceiving the meaning of history always in the present,"[24] is unmistakably an ideological criticism indicting him as guilty of serving bourgeois ideology. Ideological criticism must, however, be executed in the way in which ideological distortion is disclosed. This must be executed by theology without theology's assuming any ideological stance itself. If that happens in theology's ideology criticism, then it would only be another quarrel between two ideologies. In my opinion, this is exactly what happened in the most recent expression of political theology by William Coats where theology is regretfully entrenched in ideological thinking.[25] Coats' penetrating analysis and critique of Capitalism was done not so much from the theological point of view as from an ideological presupposition of some idealistically conceived, perfect, atemporal and imaginary socialism. The point I would like to make here is that the spirit of criticism must be pushed to the point of criticizing ideologies themselves. All ideological viewpoints are to be subjected to politico-theological criticism so that the deception and distortion of reality inherent in the structure of ideology, both utopian and status quo can be exposed.

Theology has been criticial of political ideologies before, always from a Platonic and Augustinian point of view, disdainfully criticizing politics as this-worldly. That is to say, theology's criticism of political ideologies was always made from an apolitical vantage point of asceticism, aestheticism, transcendentalism or apocalypticism. Political theology attempts its criticism not by alienating itself from political reality, but by thoroughly politicizing itself.

Theology has long been apolitical, perhaps because of the fear of lapsing into advocating a pre-modern sacral politics. Even Reinhold Niebuhr who perhaps spoke more actively to and about politics than any other theologian in recent past remained too deeply Augustinian to get theology genuinely involved in politics. He did become a theological spokesman of his time to politcal issues, but he would never have allowed himself to think of politicizing theology. The ground rule meticulously observed by both theologians and politicians of modern times has been a policy of mutual non-interference, i.e., the separation of church and state. This naive assumption which in time became an inviolable law of sanctity was not of theological origin. Its source was in modern European nation-states who invented this device and forced it upon theology for the purpose of silencing any religio-moral indictment. Unsuspecting sectarians helped make this belief into a general principle about the relationship between theology and politics through their millenarian antagonism against civil authorities. The separation of church and state was helpful at first in bringing about the demise of ecclesiastical hegemonies in politics and in establishing the autonomy of modern states. But in the contemporary world, theology is no longer necessarily ecclesiastical, and politics needs theology to avoid its own excesses of normlessness and inhumanity. Politicization of theology is not only not a violation of a theological axiom, but also urgently needed as the fulfillment of theology's

obligation to humanity. Politicization of theology does not imply anything like a
sacral politics or a revival of ecclesiastical hegemony. Political theology should
not be intimidated by ghosts of bygone dualisms.

Thus it is on the one hand the politicization of theology itself, but on
the other hand, more importantly, political theology attempts a thorough politicization of human life in its totality. The politicization of theology must lead to, or
at least in its intent, aim at the politicization of human life. Otherwise, the politicization of theology will only result in idolatry.

In the contemporary West religious life is compartmentalized and divorced
from political life. By the same token political life is relegated to a small com-
partment. Precisely because of this, politics in the modern Western world tends to
be relegated to a small group of professionals who supervise bureaucratic political
machinery. The plight of modern men who are ground under by massive bureaucracies
is the result of their fallacious view that politics is a specialized enterprise
which can be delegated to professional politicians and bureaucrats while most people
indulge in apolitical routines. Politics must concern man's total life. The signals
of transcendence must not be found and sheltered only in a cloistered region of human
experience rendering the rest of human life areligious or secular. By the same token, political commitment must not be rendered as partial, let alone as having little
to do with ultimate concerns. The compartmentalization of political commitment as
only a part of human life entails surrendering to "specialists" through the ballot
box--the worst possible consequence of the division of labor. If the desacraliza-
tion of politics means such a professionalization, then a retrogression toward oli-
garchy would be an easy possibility in which elite political specialists can rule
people through a monstrous bureaucratic machine, taking full advantage of people's
political apathy and ignorance. The divorce between man's impulse toward transcendence and his political commitment thus creates a dangerous future for us.

Political theology "apprehends politics, in the Aristotelian sense of the
word, as the inclusive horizon of the life of mankind," Moltmann stated.[26] To confirm this Gurierrez said, "Nothing lies outside the political sphere understood in
this way. Everything has a political color. It is always in the political fabric--
and never outside--that a person emerges as a free and responsible being, as a person
in relationship with other people."[27] This is not a mere attempt to use the word,
politics, semantically in a wider sense to denote the entire range of life instead
of a limited sphere of it. The aim of political theology is to transform life through
politicization.

Through such politicization, that is, through a reinterpretation of human
life as thoroughgoingly political, theology attempts to disclose the fallacies of
ideology. The easy alliance between politics and ideology, the facile surrender of
the masses to ideological propaganda, and an agitation of the masses into a mob action or a totalitarian docility of the masses under ideological manipulation, are
possible only when people are apolitical. "The point is that ideologists are 'ter-
rible simplifiers.' Ideology makes it unnecessary for people to confront individual
issues on their individual merits. One simply turns to the ideological vending machine, and out comes the prepared formulae. And when these beliefs are suffused by
apocalyptic fervor, ideas become weapons, and with dreadful results."[28]

Only when men are apolitical, i.e., politically apathetic or ignorant or
simplistic, they are vulnerable to ideological mesmerism and manipulation. Ideological simplification of complex human issues, propaganda which fully utilizes those
simplified slogans and prescriptions and mob-like mobilization of mass-energy, not
for people's sake, but for the interests of ideologues, all feed and thrive on men's

apolitical consciousness or political immaturity. It is this that political theology
must address. Political theology aims at thorough politicization of human life,
thereby to isolate ideology as the distortion of political reality. When human life
is fully politicized, men mature and alert in their political consciousness, then
there would be no condition under which ideology could thrive. Political theology
should aim at thorough politicization of human life because the well-being of mankind
hinges upon people's political maturity and freedom from ideological distortion and
manipulation. The thorough politicization of human life means on one hand the inten-
sification of individual man's political awareness; each individual must become mature
in his political awareness and judgement. On the other hand, this leads to the politicization of all members of a community, resulting in the political "priesthood of
all believers," which will now render professional ideological priests (ideologues)
superfluous. The thorough politicization of human life advocated by political theology is the contemporary meaning of the Reformers' principle of universal priesthood.
If there is any meaning to Daniel Bell's catchword, "End of Ideology," it would be
such political maturity which renders ideologues unemployed. The "End of Ideology,"
which for Bell was an empirical theory, is now turned into a prophetic pronouncement
by political theology which calls for that very end of ideology through man's political maturity.

III

Earlier we examined the end/decline theory of ideology. We saw that ideology, when taken to include status quo ideologies, was far from being defunct. If we
go back to the limited application of this theory and take it to refer only to the
utopian type of ideologies, then we can say that Bell's theory has a measure of validity—although I am still persuaded that such limited use of the term is not fully
warranted.

Let us focus now on the utopian type of ideologies and their decline and
try to see what further implication recent politicization of theology and their ideological overtones have. Bell believed that these nineteenth century utopian oriented
ideologies, such as Socialism, Anarchism, Marxism, Communism are all exhausted. Politics of the so-called Socialist and Communist countries of today has become increasingly de-ideologized. "Few serious minds believe any longer that one can set down
'blueprints' and through 'social engineering' bring about a new utopia of social harmony. At the same time, the older 'counter beliefs' have lost their intellectual
force as well."[29] Even those who want to modify Bell's "end" theory into a more
moderate "decline" theory of ideology agreed to the disappearance of ideologies of
the apocalyptic, chiliastic, total and extremist type. The implication of this is
that politics, by becoming ideologically neutral and moderate, has become goal-less.
It is the victory of Realpolitik in its Anglo-American cast. Politics has become
more a discussion of means than ends. In the light of the distortion and inhumanity
which ideologies of the past have perpetrated in their conflicts, the de-ideologization is definitely to be considered a step toward mankind's maturation. But pragmatic
politics has made a virtue of not having any ideals at all. Pragmatization, which is
the other side of the same de-ideologization coin, seems to have promoted a sentiment
which frowns upon ends, goals, ideals and values as soft questions in contrast to the
hard questions of facts, efficiency, practicality and interests.[30] For they are not
questions which are amenable to quantification and technicization through which human
affairs and values are converted into manageable problems and subjected to pragmatic
handling with efficiency as the sole criterion of performance. Pragmatization entails a view of politics as efficient social control, which in turn calls for increasing specialization and professionalization. Professionals in strategy, social
engineering, bureaucracy, management, etc. are looked to for increasingly efficient
dealings in human affairs which are essentially not matters of efficiency-treatment.

"Today when we see bureaucracies perform their work of classifying, herding, expediting, and exterminating when necessary, we know they are machines without devils inside. What is inside is merely a certain conception of knowledge and the self, which has been long growing and which is widely distributed. It is a conception which means by thought only a process of rational and efficient calculation of the most efficient way to handle materials, a conception which trains men how to behave efficiently, but not how to act responsibly."[31] Michael Novak laments that the specialization of professionals is "an escape from responsibility as a human being."[32] Professionals are trained experts who find the most efficient way of combining the available empirical factors within limits set by the known variables to yield the outcome of greatest desirability. They remain strictly within the limits of the given and the so-called "possible." They are extremely impoverished in creativity. They are not the inventors of new human possibilities, but the expert appliers of existing rules. The visions of the end, the ideal or genuinely new possibilities dawn on mankind only when the closed perimeter of such pragmatism is broken through. Pragmatic professionals operate within a closed universe of the given and the practical. It is small wonder, then, that the demise of the end-vision in politics has been closely paralleled by the dissolution of philosophy into logical positivism. The end of ideology in politics coincides with the end of creative power in philosophy, with the beginning of the "one dimensional man," who preoccupies himself with the routine, day-to-day affairs within the cocoon woven of pragmatic sets of alternatives.

Theology welcomes the end of absolutistic ideologies, because ideologies make men idolators by turning ends (human well-being) into means and means (ideological values) into ends. The whole world can testify to the dehumanizing character of ideological entrenchment and clashes. Therefore, in a very real sense, de-ideologization of politics is a step forward in maturation. However, if it means loss of end-vision, theology has to qualify its welcome of de-ideologization of politics. Daniel Bell himself warned, "The end of ideology is not--should not be--the end of utopia as well. If anything, one can begin anew the discussion of utopia only by being aware of the trap of ideology."[33] Politics as man's historical venture can never afford to be without visions or settle for a goal-less expediency. Theology's recent interest in politics and its apparent ideological overtones can be interpreted as an indication that politics should never become a completely pragmatic handling of day-to-day affairs in the absence of any final perspective. As long as politics is man's historical activity, it must bear an orientation toward some goal. Theology's politicization at the time of politics' de-ideologization is a timely reminder to man's political consciousness that it always needs ends. Therefore, it is no accident that political theology has a strong eschatological orientation. Theology thus proves to be quite strongly with the times, even taking initiative in revitalizing the perspectives of an end in the world of increasingly goal-less politics. Theology can be seen to be cultivating an end perspective through its eschatological vision, not just staying abreast of events in order to survive. It is a needed sensitizer of pragmatic politics.

Meaning is the sine-qua-non of human life and activity. And yet pragmatization of politics strips human activity of its meaning. Meaning is created in a contextual relation within a totality or a whole of community. That is to say, if we borrow a linguistic example, words independently are only verbal signs or symbols. Meaning is constituted only when a word is placed in a context of a coherent statement--a community of words. Meaning is not intrinsic to an individual word. It is generated and constituted by an ordered whole in which that word is integrated to play a part. Man as an individual has a spatio-temporal context: history and human community. Man's political conduct has its context of meaning in wider social and historical horizons. Those horizons are symbolically summed up and concentrated in goals and ends. Therefore, the loss of end-vision in the pragmatic settlement of politics into expediency means depriving politics of its horizon of meaning. This in turn implies the reduction of politics from man's historical commitment which is characterized by meaningfulness into a constant repetition of man's atomized actions devoid of meaning and exclusively geared to expediency. Pragmatization of politics with its concomitant loss of end-vision is the dissolution of meaning, the reduction of political conduct into quantified efficiency.

Ideology in the total sense of the term as we have considered it in this essay, is quite incompatible with empirical elements involved in political activities. Ideologies map out unalterably rigid courses of action for achieving their goals. They are idolatrous in that they absolutize finite goals and interests and uncompromisingly rigid about means to go about achieving such idolatrous goals. Politics is man's historical activity which lies in the realm of choice, his weighing of alternatives and consideration of consequences in a pluralistic situation. Theology aspires to revitalize an end-vision for politics without falling into the trap of ideology. Strong as theology's ideological overtones may be, they are not meant to resemble ideology. Theology tries to see itself as providing an end-vision to man's political endeavor.

On the other hand, pragmatic tendencies de-ideologized politics, which binds man only to claims made by the situation and closes the door to any end-vision, result in the loss of a horizon of meaning. The eschatological orientation of present political theology tries to prove itself capable of accommodating dual needs of political existence, viz., empirical openness and ultimate end-perspective.

The eschatological proviso which Moltmann mentioned is an important qualification for political theology.[34] It safeguards the end-vision which political theology is trying to revitalize from lapsing into an ideological one. The eschatological end, as Herbert Richardson stated,[35] must be symbolically definite, but must remain cognitively vague. The end-vision which political theology holds over our political consciousness is symbolically clear and definite because it can be nothing less than the final consummation of the historical process in which the ultimate humanization of man as a whole is to be realized individually and collectively. Salvation in the conventional religious vocabulary points to this ultimate humanization in contrast to a penultimate humanization of which realization can be pursued in the politico-historical realm. The eschatological end-vision is sufficiently vague cognitively so that man's historical striving for penultimate humanization is left open to political endeavor.

The eschatological end stands at the point where history is consummated and in a sense abrogated. The eschatological end therefore cannot immediately become an end which can inspire and inform politics. Consequently, a penultimate humanization is necessary as an intra-historical end, thoroughly political and yet free from ideological ossification, an end which can be pursued in history, never to be exhausted. The penultimate humanization can be formulated as something like "Well-Being of Mankind," which is thoroughly politico-historical and resistant to any ideological misuse.

One can ask then whether what I called penultimate humanization may not be just another name for an ideological end. As I conceive it, penultimate humanization is on the one hand inspired and informed by ultimate humanization and therefore strives to be an end worthy of universal pursuit, transcending all ideological and partisan self-interests. But on the other hand, being a historical end allows for empirical political endeavor, a concrete reckoning with changing historical conditions. It receives the clarity of its directionality from eschatological roots and yet lends itself to constant reformulation through contact with empirical reality. My conception avoids ideological ends which exclude such complementary relationships.

Another possible point of difference is that penultimate humanization pertains to the totality of man, individually and collectively, whereas ideological ends do not. That is to say, the former can never be reduced into an end formulated out of a single-faceted understanding of man. Alienation of man must be understood as happening to the totality of man instead of being flattened into a single-dimensional phenomenon such as an economic or social or psychological alienation. Then humanization (de-alienation) must also be understood in a total sense of the term. Alienation undoubtedly becomes manageable when reduced into a condition in a single-dimensional reality such as when Marx reduced it into economics. Marx did have a more thoroughgoing, and profound understanding of human predicament. But when it comes to formulating it into an ideological propaganda, he had to flatten it into economic interpretation. That is the usual fate and limitation of ideology. Ideological ends are therefore markedly simple, given to easy sloganizing as exemplified by Marxist and Socialist socio-economic views of alienation. Contrary to this, the penultimate humanization which political theology aspires to cultivate in politics is total rather than one-dimensional.

Politics is now called upon to achieve a penultimate humanization, for which empirical openness continues to be important. Penultimate humanization is inspired by the symbolic clarity of ultimate humanization and at the same time enriched by the abundant alternatives made possible by the cognitive vagueness of ultimate humanization. Penultimate humanization which is the goal of man's political strivings is called by the ultimate humanization into history of human possibilities.

## FOOTNOTES

1. Daniel Bell, The End of Ideology (New York: The Free Press, 1960), pp. 399f.

2. Ibid., pp. 278f.

3. Ibid., p. 404.

4. Seymour M. Lipset, "The End of Ideology?" in M. Rejai, ed., Decline of Ideology (New York: Aldine-Atherton, 1971), p. 50.

5. Robert E. Lane, "The United States: Politics of Affluence," in M. Rejai, ed., Decline of Ideology, pp. 168-199.

6. Daniel Bell, The End of Ideology, pp. 402f.

7. Jurgen Moltmann, Religion, Revolution and the Future (New York: Charles Scribner's Sons, 1969), p. 5.

8. Ibid., p. 209.

9. See James H. Cone, Black Theology and Black Power (New York: Seabury Press, 1969).

10. See Renato Poblete, "Socialist and Christian in Chile," Worldview, Vol. 15, No. 4 (April, 1972), pp. 18-23.

11. Gustavo Gutierrez, A Theology of Liberation (New York: Orbis Press, 1973), p. 109.

12. An incisive criticism on this point was presented in Richard Neuhaus, "Liberation Theology and the Captivities of Jesus," Worldview, Vol. 16, No. 6 (June, 1973), pp. 41-48.

13. Daniel Bell, The End of Ideology, p. 288.

14. Ibid., p. 287.

15. Ibid., p. 301.

16. Ibid., pp. 301f.

17. Ibid., p. 405.

18. Karl Mannheim, Ideology and Utopia (New York: Harcourt, Brace and World, 1959), p. 55.

19. Robert Bellah, "Civil Religion in America," in Walter Capps, ed., Ways of Understanding Religion (New York: Macmillan, 1972), p. 245.

20. Ibid., p. 246.

21. M. Rejai, "Introduction," in M. Rejai, ed., Decline of Ideology, p. 3.

22. Jurgen Moltmann, "The Cross and Civil Religion," in Religion and Political Society, edited and translated in The Institute of Christian Thought (New York: Harper & Row, 1974), pp. 37f; Johannes B. Metz, "The Church's Social Foundation in the Light of a 'Political Theology'," in Johannes B. Metz, ed., Faith and the World of Politics (New York: Paulist Press, 1968), pp. 2-18.

23. Dorothee Soelle, Political Theology (Philadelphia: Fortress Press, 1974), p. 18.

24. Ibid., p. 49.

25. William Coats, God in Public (Grand Rapids: William Eerdmann, 1975).

26. Jurgen Moltmann, "Toward a Political Hermeneutics of the Gospel," in Martin E. Marty & Dean G. Peerman, eds., New Theology No. 6 (New York: Macmillan, 1969), p. 81.

27. Gutierrez, A Theology of Liberation, p. 47.

28. Daniel Bell, The End of Ideology, p. 405.

29. Ibid., p. 402.

30. Michael Novak, "The Student Movement and the End of the 'End of Ideology'," in M. Rejai, ed., Decline of Ideology, pp. 303f.

31. John H. Schaar, "Legitimacy in the Modern State," in Philip Green & Sanford Levinson, eds., Power and Community (New York: Random House, 1970), pp. 307f.

32. Michael Novak, "The Student Movement and the End of the 'End of Ideology'," in M. Rejai, ed., Decline of Ideology, p. 305.

33. Daniel Bell, The End of Ideology, p. 405.

34. Jurgen Moltmann, "The Cross and Civil Religion," Religion and Political Society, p. 20.

35. Herbert Richardson, Theology for a New World (London: SCM Press, 1968), p. 24.

THEOLOGY AND ETHICS:
THE PERSPECTIVE OF BLACK PHILOSOPHY

Roy D. Morrison II

Wesley Theological Seminary

        This paper is an essay which is concerned with the relation-
ship between theology and ethics, as this relation is conceived by
black philosophy of culture and religion.  Black philosophy, as philosophy, argues that the cultural liberation of black people presupposes a methodological commitment to philosophical objectivity
and to objective historicity.  The provocative assumption and argument of the paper is as follows:  Theology has an inescapable obligation to consider, as an integral part of its own task, the theoretical
and empirical implications of its ethical content.  G.W.F. Hegel's
romantic subjectivity and his schematized ontological racism constitute
one example which illustrates the imperative character of this argument.  Since, however, the reader cannot be expected to possess an
acquaintance with black philosophy, the essay presents part of its
technical apparatus and then employs that apparatus to make an interpretive analysis of the relation between theology and ethics in a
concrete situation.  The notion of methodological and cultural
enlightenment is the basic model employed in that analysis.


                Black Philosophy of Culture and Religion:
                        Its Genesis and Nature


        Religion is the cultural point of departure for black phi-
losophy because religion is the major repository for the decisive
elements of the black experience in America.  Religion has provided
blacks a cultural guidance system and an instrument for interpreting
reality and suffering.  In the seventh decade of the twentieth
century, black thinkers moved into that arena known as theology.
Much of the academic activity of black thinkers and writers is directly
related to religion.  This is not a unique development in America where
many of the most prestigious academic institutions were inspired and
shaped by religious concerns.  Black theology and black philosophy
have identical motivations.  They both emerge as a consequence of
despair over the utter failure of white philosophy and theology even
to acknowledge the existence of the problem of racism in western
culture.

        Black theology is occasioned by white racism.  The latter is
a cultural and quasi-religious phenomenon which systematically inflicts
various forms of violence upon the blacks of America and of Africa at
all the levels of human transactions.  Responding to this situation,
both black theology and black philosophy of culture and religion are
part of a black enlightenment.  In its narrow sense, this term designates a movement in which a small family of black thinkers has begun
to ask radical questions and to make revolutionary assertions.  One
radical question is why racism seems to be perpetuated by the very
religion and by the very god that are supposed to combat it.  One
revolutionary assertion is that the humanity and personhood of black
people are inviolable, and that we have the right and the obligation
to defend it against all offenses--by man, by theology, and by god.

        In his discussion of black power and black theology, professor
James Cone has explained this consciousness by stating that it
means "complete emancipation of black people from white oppression by

whatever means black people deem necessary."[1] The writing of a black philosophy of culture and religion is one of the available means--though it is not the only one. This consciousness, and its expression, come as a shock to many because blacks were supposed to be satisfied with the promise of some unverifiable eschatological fulfillment. They were supposed to maintain absolute faith that god was in favor of their freedom, despite the paucity of empirical, historical evidence to support that faith. Now, however, the power of critical human reason, the universal sense of justice, and the irreducible authenticity of black cultural particularity have suddenly burst through the artificial boundaries of the parochial religiosity which, because of external pressure, appeared to be adequate in the past.

In its broader sense, the black enlightenment includes black theologians, black philosophers, ethicists, sociologists of religion, historians, poets, and playwrights. Despite the wide spectrum of faiths, cosmologies and world views, certain basic concerns are shared by all of the participants in this movement. We shall mention only four of these. First, it should be noted that black philosophy, black theology and the black enlightenment in general share two foci: indigenization and liberation. Second, they all share a decision to de-emphasize, or to eliminate, the classical role of futurism and eschatological fulfillment in the objective assessment of our cultural situation and the kind of action to be taken. Third, they all--theologians, historians and playwrights-- share a burning intellectual militance at the level of symbol formation. All agree that there must be a restructuring of the decisive secular and religious symbols of our culture. All too often, it is the invisibly reverberating connotations of inherited symbols which perpetuate the cultural dynamics of white racism. The black playwright who shapes indigenous experience and the black theologian who re-interprets the Christian doctrines are equally important in this enterprise of symbol formation.

The thinkers being considered here do not seek an ontological replacement for the supernatural eschatology which placed a snow job over their empirical suffering at the hands of Western culture. Some of the most privileged and some of the most deprived of the black community gather regularly in a black barbershop on Seventy-ninth Street in Chicago. Any listener would immediately realize that there is a single desire, a single expression, that they all hold and understand: "Tell it like it is!" The expression, "Tell it like it is!" is a battle cry of the black enlightenment and is the fourth shared concern that we wish to mention. This expression contains not only an ethical imperative, it also demands an empirically-oriented epistemology. Consequently, by way of including the voice of the black masses, black philosophy of culture and religion posits that expression as a major point of departure for its methodology.

Black philosophy of culture and religion is a natural philosophy in that it presupposes only the equipment and the capacities that men have in common: empirical perception, human reason, the capacity to experience religious awe or the sense of holiness, and the ability to be enriched by participation in secular and/or religious communities.  Its aim is not the construction of a romantic or religious vision of reality however.  It is more concerned to ask whether a particular vision is worth constructing and what are the empirically verifiable consequences of the visions to which men have already made commitments.

Black philosophy, like natural philosophy, is conceived as an inquiry into the first principles or postulates of the various special sciences, including those of philosophy itself.  It has five major divisions:  minimum metaphysics, epistemology, semantics, ethics, and aesthetics.  Division one, minimum metaphysics is non-speculative. It is the study of recurrent, or persisting structures of reality and of the indispensable, inescapable schemata of human thought.  Minimum metaphysics includes all of the postulates and categories which are regarded as "universals" and, apparently, must be employed to achieve an intelligible schematization of empirical data for the sciences of philosophy, nature, theology or of ethics.  Included here are the catagories of space, time, logico-causal relatedness, and substance or process.  Included also are the postulate of the principle of the irreversibility of temporal succession, and the postulate of the existence of an objective, external world.  This constellation of categories and postulates is regarded here as a kind of minimum prerequisite for non-idealistic philosophy, for objectivity, for intelligibility, and simply  for thinking.

Division two is epistemology.  As understood here, it is the critical study of the possibilities, the native perceiving equipment, the procedures, and the limits of human knowledge.  The position held by black philosophy is not empiricistic epistomology.  Rather, it holds that the empirical and the non-empirical components of a scientific system, or of a theological-cultural guidance system, constitute "knowledge"  only in a relationship or a correlation of mutual dependence and coherence.

Black philosophy of culture and religion holds that a chain of theoretical or theological concepts may be ever so long and elaborate; but, that at some point, it must be intelligibly correlated with publicly accessible facts in the sphere of empirical reality.  In this sense, black philosophy is empirically-oriented.  Among other things, this means that it will not indefinitely retain an abstract notion in theology, ethics, theodicy, or in eschatology, if the hypothetically  inferred, deductive consequences of that notion violate empirical experience and objective history.  It will not retain or defend an inherited notion of a god, if that notion, in practice, demands from blacks a passive acceptance of empirical dehumanization.  Empirical orientation also means that the principles of objective validity and publicly empirical historicity must have primacy over all of our theological, mythological, or theoretical projections--not vice versa.

From our perspective, the subject matter of philosophy consists of conceptual theoretical components and of aesthetic-empirical components.  Philosophy, then, is equally concerned with ideas, concepts, objective events and physical entities.  We insist that the two basic kinds of components must be continuously correlated in a manner that results in correspondence, coherence, maximum possible objecti-

vity, and economy of causal explanation. The notions of minimum
metaphysics and of epistemology, so briefly stated here, constitute
the methodological touchstone of the technical apparatus of black
philosophy.

It should be noted that the methodology developed here
is not intended to be racially or ethnically particularistic.
Rather, it is grounded in the universal processes of human reason,
and in the publicly accessible, critical thinking procedures of
methodical philosophy. Also, it is positively related to the methods
of modern science because of its immediate kinship to the notion of
the "two-termed epistemic correlation" as developed in the works of
F.S.C. Northrop and of Albert Einstein.[2]

Division three of black philosophy is semantics. It involves meaning, linguistics and the objective referents of systems
of communication symbols. Black philosophy holds that a thinker,
even a theologian, should practice semantic integrity, semantic precision, and that he should be willing to make an unambiguous specification of the categories and the objective referents for his
language. Black philosophy insists upon the metaphysical postulate
of the law of non-contradiction as a presupposition for intelligible
semantics. Aside from any residual persuasive power in the arguments
of Aristotle's Metaphysics,[3] or in Kant's Critique of Pure Reason,[4]
blacks have a practical reason for this position.

Black persons have to deal with white interpreters of the
American Constitution, white theologians and ethicists, and with the
importers of speculative phenomenology. When they speak of man, or
of human beings, from the operative categories and connotations of
white philosophy, we want to know if they mean to include us, or if
there is a silent dialectical disclaimer which excludes us from history, from culture and from the status of human beings. For a black
person, it is crucially important that the spokesmen of a culture say
what they mean and mean what they say. A person who practices
semantic deception with himself and with others while attempting to
approach ultimate reality, will not hesitate to do likewise when dealing with individuals and with races that have been historically and
philosophically designated as less than human.

Division five, aesthetics, will be omitted. Therefore,
division four, ethics, is the last one to be defined here. Within
certain etymological and psychological limits, a culture or a thinker
has a right to modify the definitions of terms and categories. Such
a defining process is now under way in the black enlightenment in
regard to the notion of ethics. The black thinkers ask what is
ethics for. If it is merely an intellectual pursuit, maintaining
the status quo, and disassociated from the real world of violence
and injustice, it is irrelevant to black people.

Likewise, in black philosophy, ethics is the sophisticated
study of oughtness, and it is simultaneously an activist enterprise
of theology and of philosophy. The abstract ethical thinking, and the
religious contemplation are done for the sake of the comprehension
of truth--and for the sake of effecting empirical change, from the
perspective of black philosophy of culture and religion, only part of
the ethical task has been executed when the academic methods, cate-

gories and value judgments have been delineated on an abstract, intellectual plane. The crowning function or role of ethics in human experience is to make radical, sustained changes in the normal condition of man and thereby to improve the general quality of human relationships.

The preceding discussion has presented a part of the technical apparatus of black philosophy of culture and religion. Using this apparatus, our enterprise appropriates that which is intelligible and viable in the critical tradition of occidental natural philosophy and then employs it to trace the relation between the categories, methods, theologies, theoretical ethics and the empirical behavior of white western culture. At the same time, it seeks to schematize the wide-ranging elements of black experience into a communicable structure, and to present to the white world a philosophically intelligible picture of the way that it appears from the perspective of black people.

### The Notion of Enlightenment:
### Black Philosophy at Work

Certain sustained behavior patterns of Western thought and religion demand attention from the enterprise of black philosophy --both from its American and from its African contributors. These patterns include the antipathy for empirical reality, the long-term alliance of Christianity with Greek and with German idealism, and Christendom's internal collaboration with white philosophy. Any analysis of the reasons for these behavior patterns is difficult. However, three pre-enlightenment procedural tendencies can be designated and possibly evaluated.

First, there is the fallacy of misplaced solutions. In practice, this involves centuries of formulating non-empirical solutions for empirical problems. Second, there is the tendency to give subjectivity primacy over objectivity. This leads to the deliberate relinquishing of philosophical objectivity and of objective historicity as criteria or as goals in one's interpretive enterprises and in relating oneself to reality. Third, there is the tendency to give a revealed, or a gnostic, or a mystical content primacy over critical method.

It is the contention of black philosophy that the religion which embodies these three procedural tendencies must be studied-- as one would study a foreign religion. The need for such study arises from the strong suspicion that these three tendencies systematically prevent major segments of western culture from deciding that the empirical, practical implications of ethics are a part of the proper concern of theology and of religious philosophy. All of the available evidence indicates that this cluster of procedural tendencies continuously leads men to become fascinated by, and satisfied with, intellectual solutions while the empirical situation continues to fester.

The notion of "study," as employed here, means (a) the use of the technical apparatus of black philosophy and (b) a methodological approach which utilizes the accumulated typologies and the scientific attitude shared by the established enterprises known as the psychology of religion, the history of religion, and the philosophy of religion. Such study involves nothing less than a philosophical "distancing," a philosophical "differentiation" which will call attention to the situational and culturally relative character of all the religions that are a part of our concern. This proposal applies equally to the religion of Plato; the religion of the Jewish psalmists and prophets; the religion of Jesus, Paul and the Synoptic writers; the religion of the American slaves; and the religion of the counter-enlightenment German romanticists (Hegel, Schelling, Tillich, and Heidegger).

It is instructive to recall some of the events which illustrate the fallacy of misplaced solutions. Standing at an early stage of Western culture, Plato has no empirical way to authenticate his idea of a social order. So--he casually violates the notion of objective historicity by orally bringing into existence a 9,000 year old city which he knew was not real.[5] According to Schweitzer's analysis, Jesus of Nazarath mentally converted John the Baptist into Elias in order to complete the Jewish eschatological calendar of events which had to precede the coming of the messiah.[6] St. Paul, faced with the fact the crucified Christ had not made an empirical return, invented and projected the mystical body of Christ as an invisible but objective reality. He thereby initiated an 1,800 year investment of effort to defend the reality of the non-empirical entity and to solve the empirical problem. The crux of Paul's solution was the expectation of dramatic, externally initiated change. This is the eschatological variant of the non-empirical solution and blacks appropriated it when they were the beneficiaries of a slavery-time Christianity. History has been educating black people however, and they are now moving on to the intellectual militance of James Cone and to the "reverent agnosticism" of the enlightened black preacher.

The history of non-empirical solutions is a decisive part of the story of Western idealistic philosophy and its alliance with Christianity. When in historical trouble Western man has often formulated an intellectual, non-empirical solution for himself. When powerless, systematically dehumanized races or cultures have sought redress, he has attempted to seduce them with non-empirical solutions. This procedural tendency still characterizes the cumulative guidance systems which function in the west. What black people seek is liberation from the non-empirical solution.

At the end of the German Enlightenment, a movement began which eventually saw the emergence of four towering figures: Hegel (1770-1831), Schelling (1775-1854), Tillich (1886-1965) and Heidegger (1889--), All were deeply and ambiguously affected by the impact of Kantian epistemology and its alleged limits of human knowledge. All four conducted a desperate attempt to overcome those designated limits,

while simultaneously acknowledging that they had some irreducible
validity. These men became the architects of the religion of
counter-enlightenment German romanticism. We shall consider two
of these figures, Hegel and Tillich, with emphases on the notion
of enlightenment and on the thesis that there is an obligatory
relationship between theology and the empirical implications of
its ethical content.

       The presentation of a black philosophy implies that there
is a white philosophy. This is in fact true. A white philosophy is
a system of thought which so organizes methodology, epistemology,
mythology, symbols and the notion of ultimate reality that the
resultant cultural guidance system consistently and effectively
dehumanizes non-white persons. America has a white philosophy and
it is stated by Chief Justice of the United States Supreme Court,
C. J. Taney. Speaking of the Negro slaves, he states that

> They had for more than a century before been regarded as beings
> of an inferior order, and altogether unfit to associate with
> the white race, either in social or political relations; and
> so far inferior that they had no rights which the white man was
> bound to respect; and that the negro might justly and lawfully
> be reduced to slavery for his own benefit. . . This opinion
> was at that time fixed and universal in the civilized portion
> of the white race. It was regarded as an axiom in morals as
> well as in politics, which no one thought of disputing. . .[7]

The Supreme Court no longer speaks in this fashion. However, the white
guidance system that supported Chief Justice Taney's statement still
functions in America and is continuously experienced by black people.

       The spokesman for the Supreme Court was a jurist, not a
Christian theologian. Consequently his development of racism is some-
what limited. It is within the religion of counter-enlightenment
German romanticism that we find the apotheosis of white philosophy.
In order to support this statement, we now turn to G.W.F. Hegel.

       Hegel brings the sophistication of German academic philo-
sophy to the task of making a cosmic apologetic for white racism.
In the "introduction" to the Philosophy of History, he spends approximately twenty pages[8] on that which he calls the geographical basis
of history. In this remarkable passage, he repeats the notion that
the idea of the Spirit unfolds or reveals itself in the emergence of
the empirical world. He continues the basically Platonic method of
hypostatizing ideas to explain what he believes to be an ontological
structure of reality. Hence such notions as "Family," "Law," and
"Universality" are capitalized. In order to provide permanent
support for white racism, he weaves it into his ontological cosmogony.

Hegel has a dynamic, evolutionary notion of history and of physical reality. Here, we simply mean that, for him, "realization," "movement," and "development" occur on the way to the status of substantial objective existence--or, on the way to the status of fully developed humanity with moral sensitivity, theological perception, and the possibility of developing a culture. In Hegel's romantic vision of history, the idea has not yet revealed itself to the Negroes of America and of Africa sufficiently for them to "realize" the status of human beings. He explains that incomplete status:

The peculiarly African character is difficult to comprehend, for the very reason that in reference to it, we must quite give up the principle which naturally accompanies all our ideas--the category of Universality. In Negro life the characteristic point is the fact that consciousness has not yet attained to the realization of any substantial objective existence--as for example, God, or Law. . . The Negro, as already observed, exhibits the natural man in his completely wild and untamed state. We must lay aside all thought of reverence and morality--all that we call feeling--if we would rightly comprehend him.[9]

Hegel agrees with Chief Justice Taney that Negroes are better off in slavery than outside of it.[10] At the conclusion of these pages, he decides never to mention Africa again because "it is no historical part of the World; it has no movement or development to exhibit. Historical movements in it--that is in its northern part--belong to the Asiatic or European World."[11] At this point, Hegel has schematized his ontological racism into the voluntaristic unfolding of the world-spirit. He has solved the problem of the existence of the black people of the earth by excluding them from history--in his head. He then gives this romantic, subjective dream world primacy over the objective facts of black historicity. He presents the world-spirit and the inferiority of black people as knowledge--a content which cannot withstand the scrutiny of any critical method--and for which he offers no intelligible epistemology. Hegel thus embodies the three anti-enlightenment procedural tendencies that we have cited above. What we have here is the classic case of a racist tail wagging the theological dog. Moreover, in response to the troubling question of Wm. R. Jones, "Is god a white racist?", Hegel has provided an answer for the religion of counter-enlightenment romanticism: "Yes, our unconscious god is indeed a white racist". . .

We now have before us a view of the problem that the black thinker faces relative to the current practice of importing entire world views and entire systems of categories from other cultures. Not only are those importations often intrinsically incompatible with black experience, but the imported racism serves to reinforce the domestic racism which already operates in America. Aside from the question of whether the architects of romanticism are talking about anything that is real, there is the question of whether such material is morally fit to be imported for the use of anyone, black, white, red or green. This is an ethical problem.

A first reading of Hegel's philosophy of history makes a black person wonder how he could have been stupid enough to put his

racism in print. Reflection indicates, however, that he was not
stupid, he was safe. From his experience in Germany, and from his
encounter with American visitors, he knew that there was nothing in
Christianity that would condemn or disqualify him simply on account
of his white racism. This is an ethical problem, and it leads back
to one of the main arguments of this paper: The theologian, in
his methodology, must consider ethics and its empirical implications
an integral part of his task.

We now turn to another major architect of the religion of
counter-enlightenment German romanticism, Paul Tillich. He informs
us that a problem arose in the 19th century German situation as a
result of the

> breakdown of the religious tradition under the impact of
> enlightenment, social revolution, and bourgeois liberalism.
> ...
> The Existential philosophers were trying to discover an
> ultimate meaning of life beyond the reach of reinterpre-
> tation. ...
> Historically speaking, Existential philosophy attempts to
> return to a pre-Cartesian attitude, to an attitude in which
> the sharp gulf between the subjective and the objective
> "realms" had not yet been created, and the essence of
> objectivity could be found in the depth of subjectivity.[12]

Certain observations must be made here. First, the religion
of counter-enlightenment German romanticiam is situational and hence
culturally relative--on Tillich's own account. Second, there is no
such thing as an ultimate meaning of life beyond reinterpretation.
Third, we do not believe that the split between subjectivity and
objectivity was created by men or by the German Enlightenment.
Rather, we contend that men possibly became more conscious of its
significance during the Enlightenment. Fourth, Tillich and his
companions did not react to the Enlightenment, but to a romanticist
interpretation of that movement and its possible consequences. There
are viable, non-romanticist interpretations of the German Enlightenment and its significance for man. Such non-romanticist interpretations have their own validity and are attractive to many oppressed
and deprived people of the earth who appreciate and need critical
thought, technical reason and the benefits of the technology which
can flow from this approach to reality. Fifth, the notion of
returning to a pre-Cartesian attitude strikes us as counter-enlightenment regression toward undifferentiated mystical darkness. It is a
decision to go backward rather than forward. Tillich himself speaks
of

> a philosophy which was distinctly anti-enlightened and
> deeply influenced by romanticism, namely German clas-
> sical philosophy and, in particular, the system of Hegel.[13]

The real key to Tillich's methodology is in his relationship to pre-enlightenment German mysticism. He declares that if we
wish to understand the Christian faith, we must abandon the kind of
methodology that is characteristic of Aristotle and turn to the

symbolic procedures of Jacob Boehme, a sixteenth century German mystic who vainly pursued metaphysical alchemy.[14] Tillich also classifies himself as a romanticist.

> One side of this so-called romanticism is my relationship to nature. It is expressed in a predominantly aesthetic-meditative attitude toward nature as distinguished from a scientific analytical or technical-controlling relation. It is the reason for the tremendous emotional impact that Schelling's philosophy of nature made upon me--although I was well aware that this philosophy was scientifically impossible.[15]

Another fascinating statement suggests that Tillich was programmed early in life for his work as an architect of counter-enlightenment romanticism:

> The difficulties I experienced in coming to terms with reality led me into a life of fantasy at an early age. Between fourteen and seventeen, I withdrew as often as possible into imaginary worlds which seemed to be truer than the world outside. In time, that romantic imagination was transformed into philosophical imagination. For good and for ill, the latter has stayed with me ever since.[16]

From the beginning to end, this kind of thinking informs and guides the religion of counter-enlightenment German romanticism and Tillich casually provides fragments of explanation because he honestly does not see anything wrong with living in a world which allegedly "transcends" objectivity and empirical reality. The work of Paul Tillich is the ultimate embodiment of the three pre-enlightenment procedural tendencies cited above.

Having cited two architects of the religion of counter-enlightenment romanticism, we now turn to a major figure in the cultural movement which we call the black enlightenment. William R. Jones, the internal critic of black theology, has written a book titled Is God a White Racist? In that work, he conducts a relentless, empirically-oriented critique of the classical approaches to theodicy, injustice and racism in Jewish[17] and Christian theology. Both white and black theology can find their philosophical indictments here. Professor Wm. R. Jones advances the principle that god is the sum of his acts. The consequence , he maintains, is that "we cannot appeal to an alleged self or character that is independent of or in disharmony with the veritable acts of the person."[18] Hence, Jones "makes conclusions about who God is on the basis of what he has done for black people..."[19] His argument also insists that we should

not come to our analysis of the divine nature with the
presupposition of His intrinsic goodness for all of mankind but let this conclusion emerge, if at all, on the
basis of His actual benevolent acts in behalf of all. . .[20]

The principle affirmed here is that the black theologian
should not desire or expect to fit black theology into the
customary Christian or biblical mold. Rather, he should
determine whether the biblical faith and the Christian
tradition fit the needs of black liberation.[21]

A primary reason for raising the question, Is God a white
racist? is to force the black theologian to consider every
theological category in his arsenal, and in the whole
biblical and Christian tradition, in terms of its support
for oppression. This is the import of the de novo approach
described here.[22]

We do not know what methodology Professor Wm. R. Jones
will employ in other works. In this book, however, we find that
the basic principles of an enlightenment methodology are explicit
and decisive. These principles are compatible with those of the
German enlightenment; therefore they are in diametric opposition
to those of counter-enlightenment German romanticism. The principles include (1) The primacy of objectivity over subjectivity.
(2) The primacy of method over content. (3) The inviolability
of objective historicity. And (4) the use of an empirically-
oriented epistemology. The theologian's idea of God, for example,
must be determined by, and must correspond with, the objective,
empirical facts of the human condition.

It is frequently asserted that Immanuel Kant effected a
copernican revolution in Western philosophy and that Schleiermacher
effected a similar revolution in Protestant theology. In our
judgement, the critical methodology of Wm. R. Jones constitutes
another copernican revolution--one in the history of Judeo-
Christian approaches to theodicy and to the verification of the
attributes of ultimate reality. In the language of black philosophy, it is the principle of empirical orientation which makes
his approach so radical for black and for white theology--and
also makes it a symbol of the black enlightenment.

We hear the insistent knocking of humanism on the door
of Western culture. And, the question is whether the working
theologians have been trying to protect the integrity and personhood of man--or whether they have invested their energies, and
their sophistries, in the preservation of a particular idea of
god--an idea which does not correspond to our objective, empirical
knowledge of the racism over which that god presides in history.
Given the theological and cultural problems which we all face, it
is no surprise when Professor Jones states that his theological
position is "secular humanism."[23]

We shall now propose four questions which can be contem-
plated at the reader's leisure.

1. Are the architects of the religion of German romanticism talking about anything that is objectively real?

2. Is there any factor or power in that religion which would enable it to exorcise the ontological racism that Hegel has schematized into it?

3. Can the _Idea_, the Prius, the Unconditioned, or Dasein do anything, perceive anything, provide any information, or make a clear choice between ethical alternatives?

4. Objectively, and in empirical practice, how is the religion of counter-enlightenment German romanticism different from, or superior to, an acknowledged ethical humanism?

We now offer an assessment, in the light of the material and the arguments that have been presented above. A cultural enlightenment is a ragged, fragmentary, halting kind of thing. However, certain clear indicators can be recognized. One is the now operative decision that black people have the cosmic and cultural _autonomy_ (an Enlightenment notion) to judge the inherited Christian _idea_ of god on the basis of its empirical moral behavior in relation to black people. We have already cited this decision in the methodology of Wm. R. Jones. One other example must suffice at this point. Professor James Cone[24] has proclaimed that if god is a creator and ruler of a world in which "black people _must_ suffer. . . then he is a murderer."[25] Cone also sees that traditional eschatology must be discarded because it "implies that absurdity has won." He argues that non-empirical solutions for empirical problems involve "a Platonic grasp for another reality because one cannot live meaningfully amid the suffering of this world."[26] He insists upon the inviolability of the personhood of black people and his entire theology of black power is empirically-oriented.[27] He is quite clear in his insistence that black people should not and will not be placated with solutions that are located in the dreamworlds of Western idealism, or in the futurisms of the Judeo-Christian tradition.

It is our contention that the religion of the counter-enlightenment German romanticists is a deliberate attempt to reinstate primitive, non-critical methods and attitudes in philosophy and in theology by sanctifying the three escapist tendencies cited above. From our perspective, this means that counter-enlightenment romanticism does not represent progress or admirable sophistication. It does not move forward; it moves backward. It is an attempt to erect a piece of romantic architecture that will primarily perform only the functions of the most primitive religions: to ward off the terrors of history and to thwart and to diffuse the intellectual suspicion that the cosmos is ultimately silent. If this situation is acknowledged, then Western man can realize that his allegedly "modern" religions are not, in principle, superior to the religions of earlier times--and that his ethical problems are largely of his own making.

In Professor William R. Jones' approach to theodicy, we find the relentless insistence that black theology must examine all

of the categories and methods of the Christian tradition which
might support oppression.  Likewise, black philosophy of culture
and religion demands a critical identification of the methodological factors in the Western philosophical and religious tradition
that lead to dehumanization.  We have identified three of these
factors and have designated them as "procedural tendencies;" the
tendency to accept the fallacy of misplaced solutions, the tendency
to give subjectivity primacy over objectivity, and the tendency to
claim possession of a verified content which cannot and must not be
examined by a critical method.  These tendencies lead to a continuum
of escapism from reality and, in practice, they have had the
consequence of dissassociating theology from the empirical implications of its ethical content.  The uncritical acceptance of Hegelianism
is a case in point.

Enlightenment and its attendant liberation do not come by
request or by appeals to the piety and nobility of men.  The
possession of power leads to the illusion of innate superiority, and
men do not surrender such illusions voluntarily.  Moreover, those
who possess power almost always have contempt for those who are
powerless.  The experience of the American Indian is a case in point.
People have to possess some minimum amount of power to avoid being
the objects of contempt and the objects of violence which is not
even perceived by their oppressors.  Consequently, the black
enlightenment is a thrust toward cultural collegiality in terms of
participation, and in terms of the external acknowledgement of the
authenticity of black culture and its intellectual perspectives.
This involves nothing less than a redistribution of the cultural
power that is operative in the West.

In conclusion, we wish to make one statement of clarification.
Despite its title, black philosophy gives primacy to ethical, humanistic universality, rather than to ethnic or racial particularity.
Therefore, it ever remains an invitational enterprise; it proceeds
in the hope that white persons as well as black persons, and red persons,
and yellow persons will elect to participate in a genuine
cultural and ethical enlightenment--and thereby to enhance the quality
of life in the human community.

Notes

1. James H. Gone, <u>Black Theology and Black Power</u> (New York: Seabury, 1969), p. 6.

2. F.S.C. Northrop, <u>The Meeting of East and West</u> (New York: Macmillan, 1946), pp. 442-454; Cf. p. 294f.  See also Albert
   Einstein, "Reply," <u>Albert Einstein:  Philosopher-Scientist</u>
   (Evanston:  The Library of Living Philosophers, 1949), Vol. 7,
   p. 683f.

3. Aristotle, <u>Metaphysics, The Basic Works of Aristotle</u> (New
   York: Random House, 1941), p. 10061 & 1006b.

4. Immanuel Kant, <u>The Critique of Pure Reason</u>, trans. by Norman
   K. Smith (New York: St. Martin's, 1965), p. B 189-193, B 625.

5. Plato, <u>The Timaeus</u>, trans. by Cornford (Indianapolis: Bobbs-
   Merrill, 1970), Section 26c-e.

6. Albert Schweitzer, <u>The Quest of the Historical Jesus</u> (New York;
   Macmillan, 1948), p. 375f.

7. Henry Steele Commager, ed., <u>Documents of American History</u> "Dred
   Scott vs Sanford, 1857," (New York: Appleton-Century, fifth
   edition, 1949), p. 342.

8. G.W.F. Hegel, <u>The Philosophy of History</u> (New York: Dover, 1956),
   p. 79-99.

9. <u>Ibid.</u>, p. 93.

10. <u>Ibid.</u>, p. 96.

11. <u>Ibid.</u>, p. 99.

12. Paul Tillich, <u>Theology of Culture</u> (London: Oxford University
    Press, 1959), p. 106f.

13. Paul Tillich, <u>Systematic Theology</u> (Chicago: The University of
    Chicago Press, 1957), Vol. II, p. 23

14. Paul Tillich, "Preface," John J. Stoudt's <u>Sunrise to Eternity
    - A Study in the Life and Thought of Jacob Boehme</u> (Philadelphia:
    University of Pennsylvania Press, 1957), p. 7f.

15. Paul Tillich, "Autobiographical Reflections," in <u>The Theology
    of Paul Tillich</u>, ed. by Kegley and Bretall (New York: Macmillan,
    1964), p. 4.

138

16. Paul Tillich, On the Boundary (New York: Scribner's, 1960) p. 24f.

17. William R. Jones, Is God a White Racist? (Garden City: Anchor Doubleday, 1973), p. 175-184.

18. Ibid., p. 10.

19. Ibid., p. 14.

20. Ibid., p. 14.

21. Ibid., p. 142.

22. Ibid., p. 143f.

23. Ibid., p. 172.

24. For a white thinker's understanding of the universal elements in James Cone's theology, see Glen R. Bucher, "Liberation in the Church: Black and White," Union Seminary Quarterly Review, XXIX, No. 2, (Winter, 1974), 91-105.

25. James Cone, Op. Cit., p. 125.

26. Ibid., p. 123.

27. Ibid., p. 11f. See Chapters I & V.

# BEYOND GALILEI AND BULTMANN : THE PROBLEM OF CHRISTIAN ETHICS

William VanderMarck

DePaul University, Chicago

It is the purpose of this paper to address itself to the problem of Christian ethics (briefly formulated in # 8) by trying to come to terms with the problem of Christology (or revelation).

1. Numerous studies have recently been published, and reviewed, concerning the question, whether there is a Christian ethic, or not.[1] Although the answers tend to be affirmative, they are not always very precise. Many suggest a Christian "intentionality", "life style", "inspiration", and the like. Some, while very precise (e.g., Delhaye, to be described in # 9), may appear unrealistic, and unacceptable to many. None of the recent publications addresses itself to the question of Christology. Gustafson, in his admirable and comprehensive study, acknowledges it as "worthy of exploration in philosophical theology" but excludes it from his own investigation.[2]

2. Rudolf Bultmann has profoundly challenged the understanding of Jesus, and provoked a deluge of studies, often critical. One remarkable and significant feature of the Bultmann debate is an apparent misunderstanding by some of the critics to the effect that demythologizing would imply the end of analogical and metaphorical speaking about God.[3] Bultmann, in rejecting this charge,[4] has been supported, and criticized, by Ogden.[5] While there undoubtedly was a misunderstanding, Farrer's assertion has been left standing, that Bultmann "has no taste for this line of inquiry".[6]

Bultmann rejects the significance of "das Historische" while emphasizing that of "das Geschichtliche", thus seemingly reviving the distinction between the historical Jesus and the Christ of faith (Martin Kähler). He appears to declare the historical (i.e., "das Historische") irrelevant with regard to faith. However, even while emphasizing the existential encounter with Christ (i.e., "das Geschichtliche"), he remains convinced that without the historical ("historische") fact there would be no redemption, salvation, etc.

The post-Bultmannians (Ernst Fuchs, Bornkamm, Käsemann, etc.), shying away from Bultmann's approach, re-emphasize the historical.

The unresolved issue of the Bultmann debate is the apparent, and seemingly insignificant, misunderstanding about analogy. It provides the key for an advance beyond Bultmann to where the historical (both as "historisch" and as "geschichtlich", which makes the distinction superfluous) is at once essential and irrelevant (see # 6).

3. Bultmann uses the word "analogy" a few times.[7] He reinterprets it within the context of his own existential approach. He ignores the classical meaning of the term, thus encouraging the criticism by Farrer [8] and Ogden.[9]

If analogy is an unavoidable condition of our speaking about God,[10] then historical statements about God are true only if, and to the extent that, they are analogical, metaphorical, symbolical.

At this point one would wish to avoid any and every misunderstanding. Qualifying a statement as analogical is preserving the truth about God from univocity, i.e., from misunderstanding and false interpretation. One can deny historical facts only after someone else has first asserted them. Therefore, if a historical statement about God does not (per definition) assert historical facts, then there are no historical facts that one could possibly desire to deny.

Paul Tillich has warned for the phrase, "only a symbol". He has stated that "nonanalogous or nonsymbolic knowledge of God has less truth than analogous or symbolic knowledge" (his emphasis), and also: "The use of finite materials in their ordinary sense for the knowledge of revelation destroys the meaning of revelation and deprives God of his divinity".[11]

The question before us is a theological one. We cannot ask the biblical scholars for their assessment of the facts before we start our inquiries, for their fundamental criterium is the same as ours. They study the Bible, not Homer or Virgil. They distinguish between the Bible and pseudepigrapha and apocrypha, between the Bible and the documents of Qumran, between the Bible and the gnostic writings. They do so not on the basis of historical or literary criteria but because of the Christian tradition.

If that tradition asserts, (1) that the Bible speaks about God, and further, (2) that every human statement about God is unavoidably analogical, metaphorical, or symbolical, then we seem ill advised to assert, or to assume, (1) that the Bible teaches us historical facts, or (2) that its historical statements are univocal.

To assert, or to assume, that this is nonetheless the case, may temporarily have the appearance of common sense, evidence, orthodoxy, and other desirable qualifications. However, we know from experience that it was very temporary indeed in the case of Galilei, not to mention the confrontations with paleontology, the history of the Near East, form criticism, etc.

The question is not, to deny anything, least of all historical facts, but to investigate what the meaning is of historical statements about God, since they are by their very nature analogical. This leads us now to a confronation with the question of "timeless and eternal truth".

4. Among the participants in the New Quest of the historical Jesus circulates an argument so common that one feels almost constrained to accept it at its face value. It states that the irrelevancy, let alone the elimination, of the historical Jesus will make us fall back into that "timeless and eternal truth" which is so characteristic of Lessing, Kant, Hegel, Strauss, etc.[12] It is almost ironic that the main target of this argument, Rudolf Bultmann, had already formulated that same objection, in his programmatic article, with regard to von Harnack.[13]

The argument does not spell out what is objectionable about "timeless and eternal truth". This is somewhat amazing, mainly for two reasons. (1) Given our inexperience with timelessness and eternity, it would not be too surprising if one were simply trying to express that something is true at all times. E.g., the objections against Bultmann must certainly be based on premises that are true at all times. Otherwise their authors would never have formulated them. (2) There is another reason which seems rather significant. The theological

141

tradition, following the Bible and St. Augustine, has always referred to God as "eternal truth". Since no one, to my knowledge, has ever accused this tradition of belief in a "deus otiosus", one wonders what is suddenly so objectionable in "eternal truth", and why it would lead to, or imply, a denial of the Incarnation,[14] docetism,[15] gnosticism,[16] myth,[17] mere ideas,[18] etc.

Of course, if the objection against "timeless and eternal truth" is not really an objection against "timeless and eternal truth", then it becomes somewhat less clear exactly in which respect modern authors disagree with Lessing, Kant, Hegel, Strauss, von Harnack, etc.

5. Docetism is usually defined as the conviction that Jesus only seemingly, and not really, appeared in the flesh. Although it is obvious that Karl Barth and others disagree with Bultmann, it is difficult to see how one can level the accusation of docetism against anyone who does not deny the historicity of Jesus.

This is even more true in the case of the analogical understanding of God's incarnation. It not merely asserts this reality. It also refuses to downgrade this reality in a univocal understanding. It not merely asserts God's historicity. It also refuses to cut this historicity down to the size of our limited human experience and conceptuality.

6. Sometimes the term gnosticism indicates what is usually called docetism. Generally, though, gnosticism is defined as the conviction that salvation is only for those who share a secret knowledge. This raises a question that exceeds the radius of the Bultmann debate.

Because of the way faith is often described within the confines of Christianity, one might find himself forced to conclude that only those who share the knowledge of faith qualify for salvation. (Whether faith is described as confidence, trust, personal relation, etc., is irrelevant to the extent that one who does not share the knowledge does not actually accede to this trust, etc.)

If this is gnosticism, then the alternatives are:
(1) All Christianity is in effect gnosticism.
(2) This description of faith is not quite adequate.
If we must affirm the second alternative, we will be free to disregard the first one.

The description of faith leaves indeed something to be desired. Thomas Aquinas, in a very profound statement, calls the "veritas prima" (timeless and eternal truth, if one so desires) the object of faith. This means, in a medieval context in which the ordinary emphasis is on the "articles of faith", that God as he actually confronts man is the "object of faith", i.e., that which "specifies" faith (in the strict sense of determining what faith is). Since this confrontation with the ubiquitous God incarnate is, if one may use that expression, an unavoidable fact of life, Christian faith, or unbelief, has to be a facet (or rather the innermost reality itself) of everyone's life. God incarnate, the (perhaps) unknown but actual term of all man's activity, "specifies", in the strongest sense of that word. Faith is the unachieved, gratuitously given dimension and innermost reality of man's existence, whether man has any awareness of that or not.[19]

Since "specification" creates, and indicates, reality but not a material addition, there can be no trace of gnosticism (nor of docetism).

Further, it should be obvious that the created reality, the historical, plays an indispensable role in the revelation of the timeless and eternal truth. For this reason it was earlier (in # 2) called "at once essential and irrelevant".

Finally, one may wonder whether this supports Karl Rahner's view about "anonymous Christians". The answer is affirmative, to the extent that Rahner's "supernatural existential" tends toward asserting what Aquinas formulates as the actual divine term of man's activity, really "specifying" and "transforming" this activity.

Another question altogether is, whether the term "anonymous Christians" may carry the suggestion, despicable to some, that "they really belong to us". If God incarnate is the real specifying term of all human activity, then the term "anonymous Christians" (if one were to use it) would recognize Christ, not honor a particular group of men. Of course, if the term in actual use would convey a different meaning, one might be rather reluctant to apply it.

7. There exists presently a trend to consider Christ as an example, be it the prime example, of God's redeeming action in all of history.[20] To some extent similar to this is the trend to consider other ways of salvation than that through the historical Jesus.[21]

This is an ambiguous phenomenon. On the one hand it contradicts the Christian conviction, that "there is only one Mediator between God and man, the man Christ Jesus" (1 Tim. 2: 5). On the other hand it confirms the fact that there is something amiss with the emphasis on the historical Jesus. If, however, historicity is understood analogously with regard to God, one can agree with Ogden, Curran, and Gustafson, while using a terminology which is less offensive to the reader of 1 Tim. (Col. 1, Phil. 2, etc.)

8. If the preceding observations are correct, then the term "Christian ethics" can have two distinct meanings.
(1) From a theological point of view, i.e., because God incarnate reaches every locale and every moment of history,[22] any ethic can be called Christian because of its positive human elements. Thus one expresses that God incarnate as term or object "specifies" any and all human activity.
(2) From a sociological (or empirical) point of view, i.e., from the point of view of any religious group calling itself Christian, "Christian ethics" will signify this group's ethics because of its references to Christ's teaching, Christ's example, Christian tradition, etc.

9. Given the analogical understanding of God's incarnation and historicity, and the distinction between a theological and a sociological meaning of the term "Christian ethics", one can discern the position of those involved in the recent discussion.

Gustafson's description of the empirical reality of Christian ethics is the most complete and consistent example of a sociological interpretation that I am aware of. By being pragmatic he avoids the ambiguity that other authors find themselves in. There is one caveat: he states that it is a mistake to suggest, "as the churches seem often to do", that Christian morality is "higher" or "better".[23] His cautious wording about what the churches seem to do, is right on target. The documents of the second Vatican council, to mention one obvious example, suggest often that faith "ennobles" ("elevat") human morality.[24] If one understands that as a strictly theological statement, as I think one should, it is in perfect

harmony with Gustafson's warning not to consider the sociological reality of
Christian ethics as higher or better.

Josef Fuchs appears to have this in mind when he places the Christian
nature of ethics primarily in its "transcendental" rather than in its "categorial"
aspects, i.e., in faith rather than in justice, courage, chastity, etc. His
emphasis on transcendental specification suggests a strictly theological position.
However, two elements produce a certain ambiguity in it:
(1) His identification of "specificity" and "content" [25] may, and partly does,
suggest material difference rather than strict "specification", in which case we
are in fact in the area of empirical description.
(2) The categorial exceptions of virginity, &c. (also noted by Delhaye), point to
sociological observations.

Charles Curran denies the "existence of a distinctively Christian ethic"
because of the sociological observation that non-Christians do act similarly, have
similar goals, and so on. Finally, however, he argues that his essay "does not
signal the end of Christian ethics", in terms almost literally borrowed from
Vatican II.[26] A cost-conscious homemaker might advise him that, if he will look
carefully at his own work, he may not even need "better hermeneutic tools".[27]

Space does not permit to review other authors entitled to consideration
in this context, with one exception. Delhaye [28] appears to represent the position
that Gustafson thinks it would be a mistake to defend, i.e., that Christian ethics
is superior in every respect. Delhaye is critical, not merely of Fuchs, but also of
a natural law morality as exemplified in those pillars of orthodox instruction,
Genicot - Salsmans and Noldin (315), and reflected in Vernon J. Bourke's History of
Ethics (317). He is critical of Hegel, Feuerbach, Marx, and Sartre (317-8), of Karl
Barth, Rudolf Bultmann, bishop John A. T. Robinson, Dietrich Bonhoeffer, Paul
Tillich, Ernst Bloch, and Jürgen Moltmann (319-22), of Johann B. Metz, M. Valsecchi,
J. Blank, and Alfons Auer (322-5). He does, however, declare his agreement with
Augustine, Thomas, Vatican II, and pope Paul VI (329-32).

Delhaye reminds his readers that a learned man will realize that a
"species" is part of a "genus", and that Christian ethics has as much right to be
called a "species" as has Aristotle's, the Stoa's, Kant's, etc. (326) The specifying difference, for Delhaye, is in God's revelation, and it affects even the
area of "categorial" morality (328-37). Therefore, the prudence of the Christians
is superior to that of the pagans, and so are their intersubjectivity, their
justice, their religion, their magnanimity, their patience, their humility, their
sexuality, their celibacy, and their marriage (337-9).

The purpose of this extensive description, contrary to what it perhaps
suggests, is not negative but positive. Everyone will recognize it as a classic
example (of the Roman Catholic variety) of what many a theologian's position with
regard to Christian ethics used to be in the not so distant past.

In the light of the preceding observations it is not difficult to see
that Delhaye has the distinct merit of taking "specification" very seriously: it
really affects the entire area of "categorial" morality. The flaw of his position
lies, somewhat ironically, in his understanding of "specification". He insists on
pointing out empirical differences, whereas he ought to realize that human
morality is really, though invisibly, transformed because of its real, though invisible, specifying term which is God incarnate. In scholastic language: there is
a real transubstantiation without accidental change, not a merely accidental
difference without real transubstantiation.

Although Delhaye's position appears to be extreme, it mainly suffers from
the same inaccuracy concerning "specification" that may be observed in other
positions. "Right" and "left", as so often, have much more in common than appear-
ances might make one believe.
Of course, they also share the univocal understanding of God incarnate which unavoidably, it seems, leads one away from specification to material differences,
from substance to accident, from theology to sociology. One would almost logically
add: and from God to man. To suggest that final step, however, would be most unfair
to the authors involved, although not necessarily to the publications that they
have authored.

10. Thus we return full circle to the real problem of Christian ethics,
namely, Christology. The dilemma of today's theology is: either Christ existed
historically or he did not. Since the latter appears unacceptable, we seem forced
to accept the former, and with it "Christian ethics", and so on.

I suggest that we recognize the dilemma for what it is: part of the always
present threat of anthropomorphism and univocity, i.e., a lack of truth. God's incarnation exceeds the boundaries of seemingly self-evident and obvious human categories and concepts. It is a more-than-historical fact indeed.

Bultmann's program of demythologizing and existential interpretation has
played a major role in the theology of the last three decades, partly as an object
of scorn and criticism. If there is a main weakness in his theories, he shares it,
I submit, with an entire period in the history of theology that has never come to
terms with the real implications of the case Galilei.

-----

Footnotes

1. See: Richard A. McCormick, "Notes on Moral Theology", Theol. Studies
30 (1969) 641-4, 654-68; 32 (1971) 71-8; 34 (1973) 53-5, 58-61; 36 (1975) 77-85;
Josef Fuchs, Existe-t-il une "morale chrétienne"? Gembloux: Duculot, 1973;
Philippe Delhaye, "La mise en cause de la spécificité de la morale chrétienne.
Étude de quelques prises de position récentes et réflexions critiques", Rev. Théol.
de Louvain 4 (1973) 308-39; bibliography in Ephem. Theol. Lovan. 49 (1973) 523*-27*;
50 (1974) 271*-5*; Klaus Demmer, Die Lebensentscheidung. Ihre moraltheologische
Grundlagen. Munich, etc.: Schöningh, 1974; Stanley Hauerwas, Character and the
Christian Life: A Study in Theological Ethics. San Antonio: Trinity Univ. Press,
1975; James M. Gustafson, Can Ethics Be Christian? Chicago - London: Univ. of
Chicago Press, 1975.

2. Op. cit. 85.

3. Austin Farrer, "An English Appreciation", in: Hans-Werner Bartsch (ed.),
Kerygma and Myth. Vol. I. London: S. P. C. K., 21964, 212-23; Julius Schniewind,
"A Reply to Bultmann. Theses on the Emancipation of the Kerygma from Mythology",
ib. 45-101; Friedrich K. Schumann, "Can the Event of Jesus Christ Be Demytholog-
ized?" ib. 175-90; Gustav Brøndsted, "Two World Concepts - Two Languages", ib.
Vol. II. 1964, 216-305; Walter Künneth, "Bultmann's Philosophy and the Reality of
Salvation", in: Carl E. Braaten & Roy E. Harrisville (edd.), Kerygma and History.
A Symposium on the Theology of Rudolf Bultmann. New York - Nashville, Abingdon
Press, 1962, 86-119; Regin Prenter, "Myth and Gospel", ib. 120-37; Charles C.
Anderson, The Historical Jesus. A Continuing Quest. Grand Rapids: Eerdmans, 1972,

185; Donald M. Baillie, God Was In Christ. London: Faber & Faber, [8]1960, 108; Heinrich Ott, "What is Systematic Theology?" in: James M. Robinson & John B. Cobb, Jr. (edd.), The Later Heidegger and Theology. New York: Harper & Row, 1963, 77-111; Léopold Malevez, "Rudolf Bultmann et la critique du langage théologique", in: Georges M. M. Cottier (ed.), Comprendre Bultmann. Un dossier. Paris: Éd. du Seuil, 1970, 59-89; Georges M. M. Cottier, "Jésus-Christ et la mythologie. Analyse des présupposés épistémologiques", ib. 90-129.

4. "Bultmann Replies to His Critics", Kerygma and Myth (footn. 3). Vol. I, 191-211; Jesus Christ and Mythology. New York: Ch. Scribner's Sons, 1958, 68-9; "Reply", in: Charles W. Kegley (ed.), The Theology of Rudolf Bultmann. New York: Harper & Row, 1966, 257-87.

5. Schubert M. Ogden (ed.), Existence and Faith. Shorter Writings of Rudolf Bultmann. Cleveland - New York: World Publishing Co., [4]1965, 15; Schubert M. Ogden, Christ Without Myth. New York: Harper & Bros., 1961, 91-3; "The Understanding of Theology in Ott and Bultmann", in: Robinson - Cobb (edd.), The Later Heidegger and Theology (footn. 3), 157-73; "Bultmann's Demythologizing and Hartshorne's Dipolar Theism", in: William L. Reese & Eugene Freeman (edd.), Process and Divinity. The Hartshorne Festschrift. LaSalle, Ill.: Open Court Publ. Co., 1964, 493-513; "What Sense Does It Make to Say, 'God Acts in History'?" The Reality of God, and Other Essays. New York: Harper & Row, 1966, 164-87; "The Significance of Rudolf Bultmann for Contemporary Theology", in: Kegley (ed.), The Theology of Rudolf Bultmann (footn. 4), 104-26.

6. Op. cit. (footn. 3) 217.

7. See footn. 4.

8. Op. cit.(footn. 3) 217.

9. See footn. 5.

10. See: Farrer, Schniewind, Schumann, Brøndsted, Künneth, Prenter, Anderson, Baillie, Ott, Malevez, Cottier (footn. 3); Ogden (footn. 5); Paul Tillich, Systematic Theology. Vol. I. Chicago: Univ. of Chicago Press, [8]1963, 131; Wolfhart Pannenberg, "Möglichkeiten und Grenzen der Anwendung des Analogieprinzips in der evangelischen Theologie", Theol. Lit. Ztg. 85 (1960) 225-8; "Analogy and Doxology", Basic Questions in Theology. Vol. I. Philadelphia: Fortress Press, 1970, 211-38. Of the many recent studies about analogy the following may be mentioned here: David Burrell, Analogy and Philosophical Language. New Haven - London: Yale Univ. Press, 1973; Bernhard Gertz, Glaubenswelt als Analogie. Die theologische Analogie-Lehre Erich Przywaras und ihr Ort in der Auseinandersetzung um die analogia fidei. Düsseldorf: Patmos, 1969; Julio Terán - Dutari, "Die Geschichte des Terminus 'Analogia entis' und das Werk Erich Przywaras", Philos. Jahrb. 77 (1970) 163-79; George P. Klubertanz, St. Thomas Aquinas on Analogy. Chicago: Loyola Univ. Press, 1960; Hampus Lyttkens, The Analogy between God and the World. Uppsala: Almqvist & Wiksells Boktryckeri, 1952; Ralph M. McInerny, The Logic of Analogy. The Hague: Nijhoff, 1961; Studies in Analogy. Ib., 1968; Michel Gervais, "L'analogie selon saint Thomas d'Aquin et Karl Barth", Laval Théol. Philos. 29 (1973) 187-92; Battista Mondin, The Principle of Analogy in Protestant and Catholic Theology. The Hague: Nijhoff, 1963.

11. Systematic Theology. Vol. I, 131.

12. Baillie, Op. cit. (footn. 3) 28; Helmut Thielicke, "The Restatement of New Testament Mythology", Kerygma and Myth (footn. 3). Vol. I, 138-74 (144-5); Walter Künneth, Op. cit. (footn. 3) 106; Clark Pinnock, "Theology and Myth: An Evangelical Response to Demythologizing", Bibl. Sacra 128 (1971) 215-26 (220, 224); Jacques Colette, Histoire et absolu. Essai sur Kierkegaard. Paris: Desclée & Cie: 1972, 160-81; Carl E. Braaten, History and Hermeneutics. Philadelphia: Westminster Press, 1966, 64; Günther Bornkamm, Jesus of Nazareth. New York: Harper & Row, 1960, 23; Gerhard Ebeling, Theology and Proclamation. Dialogue with Bultmann. Philadelphia: Fortress Press, 1966, 64; Ernst Fuchs, Studies of the Historical Jesus. Naperville, Ill.: Alec R. Allenson, Inc., 1964, 7; Wolfhart Pannenberg, Jesus - God and Man. Philadelphia: Westminster Press, 1968, 186; Charles Anderson, op. cit. (footn. 3) 58; Klaus Hollmann, Existenz und Glaube. Entwicklung und Ergebnisse der Bultmann-Diskussion in der katholischen Theologie. Paderborn: Bonifacius-Druckerei, 1972, 91-2; Schubert M. Ogden, Christ Without Myth (footn. 5) 41-2, 163. Ogden now takes a critical position with regard to this argument: "On Revelation", in: John Deschner, Leroy T. Howe, and Klaus Penzel (edd.), Our Common History as Christians. Essays in Honor of Albert C. Outler. New York: Oxford Univ. Press, 1975, 261-92. See also my article, "Bijbelonderzoek, analogie en theologie", Bijdragen 35 (1974) 372-92.

13. "New Testament and Mythology", Kerygma and Myth. Vol. I, 13; see also: Jesus Christ and Mythology (footn. 4) 78, 79, 82; "The Case for Demythologizing. A Reply", in: Karl Jaspers and Rudolf Bultmann, Myth and Christianity. An Inquiry into the Possibility of Religion without Myth. New York: Noonday Press, 1958, 70.

14. Baillie, op. cit. (footn. 3) 28; Joachim Jeremias, "Der gegenwärtige Stand der Debatte um das Problem des historischen Jesus", in: Helmut Ristow & Karl Matthiae (edd.), Der historische Jesus und der kerygmatische Christus. Berlin: Evangelische Verlagsanstalt, 1960, 12-25; Bultmann, opp. cit. (footn. 13).

15. Karl Barth, "Rudolf Bultmann - An Attempt to Understand Him", Kerygma and Myth. Vol. II, 83-132; Ch. Anderson, op. cit. (footn. 3) 56, 120.

16. Künneth, op. cit. (footn. 3) 107.

17. Bornkamm, op. cit. (footn. 12) 23; Pannenberg, op. cit. (footn. 12) 186; Braaten, op. cit.(footn. 12) 64.

18. Ernst Fuchs, op. cit. (footn. 12) 7; Ch. Anderson, op. cit. (footn. 3) 58.

19. Thomas Aq., Summa Theologiae III, q. 1, a. 1; see also my article, "Faith: What It Is Depends on What It Relates to. A Study on the Object of Faith in the Theology of Thomas Aquinas", to be published in Rech. de Théol. Anc. et Méd.

20. Schubert M. Ogden, "What Sense .." (footn. 5); Christ Without Myth 144. There may be some new nuances in his recent article, "On Revelation" (footn.12).

21. Charles E. Curran, "Is There a Distinctively Christian Social Ethic?" in: Philip D. Morris (ed.), Metropolis: Christian Presence and Responsibility. Notre Dame: Fides, 1970, 92-120 (110-11, 120); James M. Gustafson, Can Ethics Be Christian? (footn. 1) 164.

22. I borrow the expression from Thomas Aquinas who explains the causality of Christ's resurrection. and similarly that of the sacraments, through

the "virtus divina", "quae praesentialiter attingit omnia loca et tempora" (<u>Summa Theologiae</u> III, q. 56, a. 1, ad 3; and <u>passim</u>). The same terms are used to describe God's ubiquity (<u>op. cit</u>. I, q. 8) which "specifies" man's activity (<u>loc. cit</u>. art. 3). See also Ogden's emphasis on God's ubiquity in "On Revelation" (footn. 12).

23. <u>Op. cit</u>. (footn. 1) 177, 80 (emphasis added).

24. <u>Dogm. Const. on the Church</u>, 13; <u>Past. Const. on the Church Today</u>, 76; see also 23, 40, 48, 49, 52, 72, 90.

25. <u>Op. cit</u>. (footn. 1) 10.

26. <u>Op. cit</u>. (footn. 21) 114-5, 120.

27. <u>Op. cit</u>. 117.

28. <u>Op. cit</u>. (footn. 1).

LINGUISTIC STRUCTURE AND THEOLOGY


William L. Power
The University of Georgia


Today there are some theologians who believe that it is
their task to construct theories about God which are, meaningful and
true.  These theologians further believe that the traditional
questions of theology are still the fundamental questions to be
answered.  Briefly stated, these questions are:  (1) who or what is
God?  (2) does God exist? and (3) what particular or unique relations
hold between or among God and his creatures?  Also, there is some
consensus that the best way of handling questions (1) and (2) is to
do so in the context of a natural theology, while question (3) is to
be dealt with in some sort of revealed theology.

All of these assumptions, of course, are open to debate;
yet, if anyone believes these assumptions correct or takes them as
working hypotheses, then certain methodological issues at once
become crucial.  Some of these issues pertain to the structure of
informative or descriptive discourse, for answers to the above questions will be formulated in declarative sentences or statements of
some natural language.  Thus, anyone who sets out to construct
theories along the lines I have suggested would do well to become
thoroughly familiar with the design and use of the tool of his or her
theological trade.

At present, there are four basic ways of approaching the
problem of linguistic structure in theology.  There is the way of
existentialism and phenomenology, the way of structuralism, the way
of ordinary language philosophy, and the way of contemporary formal
logic.  There may be others, to be sure, but of the four, the latter
is perhaps the least understood and the least employed by present
day theologians.  This, I believe, is very unfortunate for two reasons.  First, symbolic logic and semiotics are very powerful tools
of analysis and construction.  Secondly, this logic and metalogic are
continuous with and an extension of the formal logic and the grammatical, semantical, and rhetorical theories of the Patristic and
Scholastic periods of Western theology.  As such, this logic and
semiotic may indeed provide the linguistic and logical underpinning
of a systematic theology which is similar to and as powerful as the
theologies of these two past ages.

In the first section of this paper, I will discuss some of
the recent developments in logical and metalogical theory, mainly
that form of logic which Richard M. Martin calls "philosophic logic".[1]
In the second section of the paper, I will discuss the application of
philosophic logic in the discipline of systematic theology.  In this
paper, however, I will only be concerned with the structure of natural
theology.

I

It is generally maintained by historians of formal logic
that there are three creative periods in Western logic. The first
of these occurred in the third and fourth centuries B.C., the
second from the twelfth to the fourteenth centuries, and the third
began around the middle of the nineteenth century and is still in
progress.[2] The Ancient period was dominated by the term or class-
logic of Aristotle and the propositional logic of the Megarian-Stoic
school. The Scholastics, while interested in the theories of valid
deductive inference inherited from the ancients, were mainly concerned
with the grammatical, semantic, and rhetorical structure of the Latin
language. To be sure, the ancients were also interested in semiotic
issues, but the Scholastics made them their prime concern. The
present period is usually divided into two stages which, in many ways,
recapitulates the two preceding periods. In the first stage of the
present period, the two ancient logics are brought together into one
theory; and in the second stage major attention is directed to
semiotic or metalogic issues.

From its very beginnings contemporary formal logic has been
closely associated with mathematics and issues pertaining to the
foundations of mathematics; however, most of those who were developing
the new logic envisioned a quite general theory which could be applied
in all disciplines of human inquiry. This aim lies back of Leibniz's
desire for a universal language developed in the form of a calculus
which would be the basis for all sciences. While Leibniz is generally
recognized as the early forerunner of the third creative period in
Western logic, the first stage of the present period opened in 1848
with George Boole's work on a calculus which he saw could incorporate
Aristotle's logic and Stoic logic into one theory and with Augustus
De Morgan's work on a logic of relations. This early investigation
culminated in the publication in 1879 of Gottlob Frege's Begriffs-
schrift. This monumental study contains the first complete system of
first-order logic which embodies a viable logic of relations based on
a theory of multiple quantification. Frege's other major contribution
lies in the area of higher-order logic and in his attempt to reduce
parts of mathematics to logic. Frege's brilliant contributions,
Giuseppe Peano's work on the axiomitization of arithmetic along with
his simplified symbolism over that of Frege, as well as the contributions of others were all brought together in Whitehead and Russell's
classic Principia Mathematica (1910-13). Whitehead and Russell's
systematization of the propositional calculus, quantification theory,
and set theory signals both the ending of the first stage of the
present period as well as the beginning of the second stage.

Since 1914 major developments in formal logic have taken
place in the area of metalogic or semiotic. The term 'metalogic'
first occurs in a paper by Lukasiewicz and Tarski in 1930, and some
historians of logic cite Tarski as the founder of metalogic and
designate 1930 as the starting point of the second stage of the present
period. Frege, however, already had distinguished between the language
used and the language mentioned, and the well known division of
metalogic into syntax, semantics, and pragmatics go back to the
writings of Peirce as early as 1879 in which he speaks of semiotic as

consisting of pure grammar, logic proper, and pure rhetoric (2.229).*
Charles Morris accepted Peirce's view of semiotic as a science and
designated the three divisions as syntactics, semantics, and pragmatics.[3] Carnap then followed Morris' convention, but changed
'syntactics' to 'syntax'.[4] From that time on semiotic has been
referred to in terms of the three sub-divisions: syntax, semantics,
and pragmatics. For a period of time, under the influence of Carnap,
many formal logicians did not view pragmatics as a "pure" or
systematic discipline of logic but regarded it as a problem for the
empirical investigation of language. By 1962, and perhaps as early
as 1955, Carnap acknowledged the importance of "pure" or systematic
pragmatics and, in so doing, brought himself in line with Peirce and
Morris.[5]

In spite of the fact that most of the founders of symbolic
logic and semiotic viewed their work as providing a framework for
discourse about all domains of inquiry, contemporary logic's close
ties to mathematics has led many people to equate symbolic logic with
mathematical logic. According to Richard Martin, this equation is
quite unfortunate. Because of the wide range of application of the
former and the very restricted range of application of the latter,
symbolic logic and mathematical logic should be viewed as two separate
fields of study. In short, unless formal logic is viewed as "the
most fundamental of the sciences and a leading humanity" it is in
danger of losing its proper identity. Martin goes on to note that just
as "Peirce and Frege had to struggle valiantly to free logic from the
algebraic model of Boole and earlier workers . . . now in the late
twentieth century . . . there is again a struggle to free logic from
the grip of those who have only mathematical interest."[6]

No one, to my knowledge, has done more to preserve the
proper identity of logic as the most fundamental of the sciences and
a leading humanity than has Martin. This he has done by developing
what he calls "philosophic logic" in distinction to mathematical logic
which is concerned with such topics and problems as the theory of
mathematical systems, proof theory, set theory, model theory, the
theory of recursive functions, computer technology, and various other
issues in metamathematics. For Martin, the most important logic for
the various sciences and humanities is not higher-order logic and
higher-order metalogic or semiotic but rather elementary first-order
logic and elementary first-order semiotic. It is this logic which
provides the core of rationality, and it is this logic which "meddles
with all subjects" (Peirce's expression as cited by Martin) in the
sense that it seeks to provide logical and linguistic forms in which
any subject matter can be discussed intelligibly.[7]

Every beginning student of symbolic logic knows of elementary first-order logic as consisting of the truth-functional calculus
and quantification theory with identity. Into this logical notation

---

*All references to Peirce's writings are to Collected Papers of Charles
Sanders Peirce, edited by Charles Hartshorne, Paul Weiss and Arthur W.
Burks (Cambridge: Harvard University Press, 1931-1958), 8 Volumes.
As is the standard practice, references to Collected Papers are given
by volume number and paragraph number.

almost any declarative sentence or statement of a natural language
can be translated, and valid deductive arguments can be constructed.
As I mentioned above, first-order logic had been well formulated by
the close of the first stage of the present period, and little has
been added to this logic since about 1913. What beginning students
of symbolic logic are most unfamiliar with is the growing body of
semiotic theory, especially of the first-order semiotic that Martin
views as essential to philosophic logic. It is this theory, as
formulated by Martin, that I now want to discuss.[8]

        While semiotic can be understood rather broadly as consis-
ting of the theory of any sort of sign which can be taken by some
organism for some object, first-order semiotic is usually restricted
to the symbols and expressions of a natural or artificial language
which can be used by some person to discourse about some subject
matter. As such it is of a narrower scope than that of the general
theory of signs or that of empirical or structural linguistics. For
the discourse of common sense and science, however, first-order
semiotic appears to have no equal. Like the higher-order metalogics,
first-order semiotic is divided into syntax, semantics, and pragmatics -- but of a first-order nature.

        In a first-order syntax, one is exclusively concerned with
the symbols and expressions of a language and the ways they can be
combined or related to form complete sentences and valid deductive
arguments. In first-order syntax, one is also interested in classifying the various symbols and expressions of a language. For example,
one refers to a linguistic sign or series of signs as a name, a
predicate, a primitive term, a defined term, a definite description,
an indefinite description, a declarative sentence, a primitive
sentence, and a derived sentence. One can also refer to the logical
symbols or expressions as a variable, a place-holder for a predicate
or a declarative sentence, a sentence matrix, a connective, an existential or universal quantifier, a sign for identity, and a valid
rule of inference or a valid argument form. Other syntactical notions
could be mentioned, but these are the most important.

        Syntax, which is the theory of the relations between or
among the symbols and expressions of a language, is not of much
interest to common sense, science, and the humanities until one
begins to give an interpretation to the various symbols in terms of
the way these symbols or expressions relate to concrete objects or
events. For example, a name is said to designate a particular object
or event in some domain of discourse and a predicate is said to
denote severally the individuals of a domain of discourse. In the
statement, "Lucky is our pet dog.", 'Lucky' designates a particular
dog whereas the predicates 'pet' and 'dog' multiply denotes all pets
and all dogs. In philosophic logic, a statement is considered as
either true or false; thus, the statement, "Lucky is our pet dog.",
is true if and only if Lucky is our pet dog and false if he is not.
In the statement, "Kevin is the brother of Keith.", 'Kevin' designates one of my sons and 'Keith' designates another one of my sons.
The predicate 'brother' denotes all pairs ordered by the relation of
being a brother. My statement "Kevin is the brother of Keith." is
also true if and only if Kevin is the brother of Keith, otherwise it
is not. I may go on to discourse about all individuals of a domain

or some individuals of a domain, and even assert that there are no
members of a domain.  I can also truth functionally combine all sorts
of simple statements into compound statements using the truth-
functional connectives.  Some of these statements will be empirically
true or false and some will be analytically true or false.  In the
latter category, take as an example the statement, "Lucky is our pet
dog or Lucky is not our pet dog.".  If I have assigned a designata
to 'Lucky' and denotata to 'pet' and 'dog' (assuming that 'our'
designates my family), then by virtue of that assignment as well as
the interpretation of the connectives 'or' and 'not' by means of
truth tables the above statement will turn out to be true and it
could not be false.  In a similar vein, if I assign an interpretation
or denotata to the predicate 'unmarried' and 'male' and define
'bachelor' as 'an unmarried male', then the statement, "All bachelors
are unmarried males.", will turn out to be true, and it could not be
false.  If I want to utilize the logical grammar of quantification
theory, then the most important semantical task that I have to do is
to specify that the bound variables of quantification will range over
the individual or individuals of a particular domain.

So far, I have not discussed the problem as to what predicates designate as in the case of intensional logics and intensional
semantics.  In a manner of speaking, one can assert in first-order
logic and first-order semantics that predicates designate properties
or classes and relations without these "objects" being taken as values
for variables.  But when one begins to analyze these "objects" in a
first-order semantic theory as designata or intensions of predicates,
they all turn out to be virtual entities.[9]

Whereas syntax is exclusively concerned with the symbols
and expressions of a language and the way they relate to each other,
and semantics is concerned with the relations of these signs to the
objects for which they stand, pragmatics is concerned with the relations that hold between those engaged in communication and the
symbols and expressions of the language they are employing.  Paraphrasing an apt characterization of Frederick Ferré, pragmatics has
to do with what people do with language as well as with what language
does to people.[10]  Pragmatics can also take into account the relations between the user-interpreter of a language and the objects or
events which a language stands for in some way.  In short, pragmatics
deals with human beings or persons, language, and the objects or
events and the various sorts of relations that hold between all three
domains.

In much traditional theorizing about human beings, thoughts,
actions, and feelings are construed as entities in and of themselves.
In systematic pragmatics, however, they are treated as relations
that hold between persons, objects or events, and language (other
non-linguistic signs are also of crucial importance).  For example
I know that Lucky is our pet dog, and I know that Keith and Kevin
are brothers of each other.  I also accept the sentences, 'Lucky is
our pet dog.', and 'Keith is the brother of Kevin', as true.  In
Martin's work on pragmatics, Lucky, Keith, and Kevin would be considered the objects of my belief, and the above sentence the conditions

of my belief.[11] This suggests that belief and acceptance are
tri-adic relations that hold between a person, some sign or signs,
and some objects or events. All sorts of actions can be dealt
with in pragmatics and so can various sorts of attitudes, emotions,
and sensibilities. For example, I feed Lucky, enjoy Lucky, put
Lucky on his leash, and take him to the vets. I adopted Keith, I
fathered Kevin, love them both, enjoy some of their behaviour and
dislike some of their behaviour, take them fishing, drive them to
school, feel sympathy for them when they are sick, and take joy in
their accomplishments and feel sorrow in their failures. Inasmuch
as all these cognitive, conative, and affective relations hold
between persons, things, events and language, some time reference is
necessary for clarity. Some pragmatic forms are:

'Person X believes of Y at t (where 't' is some time
reference) on the condition of a (where 'a' is some sign or
symbol) that such and such'

'Person X accepts a (where 'a' is some statement) at t on
the condition that C (where 'C' indicates criteria for the
confirmation of statements)'

'Person X acts upon Y at t to bring about E (where 'E' indicates some goal or consequence)'

'Person X trusts Y at t because X accepts a as true of Y'

It can be noted that judgments of moral value and moral obligation as
well as judgments of aesthetic value can best be handled in pragmatics.

First-order logic and first-order semiotic constitute the
heart of philosophic logic according to Martin; however, this logic
needs to be expanded to include a logic of events as well as a
calculus of individuals to adequately deal with events and the part-
whole relation.[12]

In most first-order systems of logic, it is assumed that
names or individual constants designate concrete or enduring individuals and that the bound variables of quantification range over the
individuals of a well-specified domain of discourse. The Polish
logician Kotarbinski maintained that every meaningful statement asserts
something about intersubjectively observable, spatio-temporally local-
ized things. This position, which he called "reism", has had many
adherents, and it tends to agree with common sense. Lucky, Keith, and
Kevin are normally treated as objects of this sort. There may,
however, be other sorts of concrete or enduring objects which are not
observable either with the natural senses or with an artificial instrument to extend the power of the natural senses. Certain sub-atomic
entities are not observable; yet, they are treated as "real" hypothetical entities within current physical theory. The same appears to
be the case in regard to the universe as a whole. It is not
observable, but it has a locus and endures for a finite span of time
or an infinite span of time.

If Kotarbinski's reism is modified to take into account non-observable hypothetical entities as well as observable ones, one is still confronted with a major issue in terms of logical and linguistic form. If one wants to construe enduring or concrete objects as a sum or fusion of a class or virtual class of events, or if one wants to discourse about events as different sorts of entities than concrete or enduring objects, then a logic of events seems a necessary complement to first-order logic and first-order semiotic. For example, I may treat Lucky, Keith, and Kevin as a fusion of the processes going on within them and the events that happen to them. Or if I want to distinguish them from such processes or events, I still may want to talk about events which are parts of their life histories. While I can assert that Keith hit Lucky in the symbolism of first-order logic as 'Hkl' or 'kHl', I cannot express the event of Keith hitting Lucky. Perhaps I need some form like '(kHl)e' to express the goings on between Keith and Lucky. At present, a logic of events is in its early stages of development, but when it is developed in relation to the calculus of individuals, it promises to be a valuable tool in analysing the part-whole relation as well as the problem of time and space.

## II

In _Religion in the Making_, Whitehead writes: "To-day there is but one religious dogma in debate: What do you mean by "God"? And in this respect, today is like all its yesterdays."[13] Whitehead's question is interesting, for he is focusing on the word 'God' and its meaning. But what is the meaning of 'meaning'? In philosophic logic, the question of meaning is un-packed in terms of syntax, semantics, and pragmatics.

In terms of logical syntax, the word 'God' must be classified either as a primitive proper name or an abbreviation for a definite description (an expression beginning with the definite article having the form 'the one individual such that so and so'). If the former, the term is treated as undefined; if the latter, the term is introduced into discourse definitionally. Syntactically viewed, 'God' must be one or the other for any user of the term. If one, however, dropped the capital 'G' and replaced it with the lower case 'g', then 'god' would be either a primitive predicate or a defined general term.[14]

C. S. Peirce, the father of modern semiotic, once asserted that the singular term 'God' is "the definable proper name signifying Ens necessarium; in my belief Really creator of all three Universes of Experience" (6:452). Setting aside for the moment the semantic and pragmatic elements of Peirce's claim, as well as what he understands to be the three universes of experience, it is interesting to see how Peirce apparently treats 'God' as an abbreviation for 'the necessary being' and 'the creator of all three Universes of Experience'. As such, the name is not taken as primitive. While Peirce believes that 'God' has a unique referent, it is important to note that in term of mere syntax, producing a definition for a name in the form of a definite description does not provide a unique designatum for the name. As Richard Martin points out, "the existence and uniqueness of the entity described must be established before such a definition is useful."[15] In short, as long as we are only concerned with the symbols and expressions of a language and the relations that hold between these symbols and expressions we refer to nothing extralinguistic.

While syntax is a very respectable discipline and is basic to a complete semiotic theory, as suggested in section I above, it is not of much interest until one begins to assign designata to the names of a language and denotata to the predicates. Also, syntax is not of much interest until one begins to inquire as to why a particular name, predicate, or definition is used rather than another. To flesh out the syntactical skeleton, we must be interested in the semantic and pragmatic meat. For example, it is obvious from the quote of Peirce that he believed that 'God' designated the necessary being or the creator of all three universes of experience. But is there such a unique designatum? And did Peirce demonstrate the existence and uniqueness of the entity described? If he did, should I accept the statement 'God exists.' as true? One might also ponder why Peirce associated the name 'God' with the identifying descriptions 'the necessary being' and 'the creator of all three universes of experience'. Did he draw upon established usage or is he introducing any new definition? Moreover, should I accept these identifying descriptions as abbreviations for the singular term 'God'?

In semantics, one is concerned not only with the relations that hold between the symbols and expressions of a language but also with the relations that hold between these signs and the objects to which they refer or for which they stand in some way. A name is said to designate one and only one object when a designatum is assigned to that name, and a predicate is said to denote multiply the objects of a domain when denotata are assigned to that predicate. In turn names and predicates, along with the appropriate marks of punctuation, are combined into complete singular, general, or relational statements. These statements can then be combined to produce compound statements of various sorts by means of the truth-functional connectives. Also, any statement is treated as either primitive or derived and as either analytically true or false or as empirically true or false. These are the basic semantic notions as we have seen, and they should find exemplification in our discourse about God if that discourse is meaningful and true.

Let us assume, at least for the time being, that Peirce is correct in associating the descriptions 'the necessary being' and 'the creator of all three universes of experience' with the term 'God'. That is, he is correct from the point of view of monotheistic religion. Let us also assume that the name 'God' is not primitive but that it is introduced into discourse definitionally. If one can establish that there is one and only one necessary being and creator of all three universes of experience, then a referent or designatum for the name 'God' will be provided and the statement 'God exists.' will be true. But how can one do that? There are several moves which would be un-appropriate from the point of view of philosophic logic. One might just assert that there is one and only one necessary being and creator of the three universes of experience and simply will to

believe that there is. On the other hand, one might take some
authority's word that there is such an entity. One might even assert
that there is one and only one such a being because he or she is
inclined to believe that there is or that he has a strong hunch to
that effect. None of these moves, however, would be acceptable to
the philosophical logician, for in them there is no appeal to
empirical evidence or to logical evidence.

If by empirical evidence one means roughly some sort of
public observational procedure whereby a statement which asserts a
state of affairs or event which could be otherwise is confirmed or
disconfirmed, then one might surmise that the very notion of a
necessary being and a creator of all three universes of experience
excludes as relevant that sort of evidence. One might even want to
argue that the very definition of 'God' as 'the necessary being' and
'the creator of all three universes of experience' entails the statement 'God exists.', as in the case of certain forms of the ontological
argument. Yet, to paraphrase Martin, producing a definition does not
guarantee either existence or uniqueness; and without that guarantee
one has no semantical right to claim that 'God' has a designatum or
that the statement 'God exists.' is true.

Now if empirical evidence is not relevant to the establishment of the existence and uniqueness of the entity described by
the definite descriptions 'the necessary being' and 'the creator of
all three universes of experience', then there is only one other
option from the point of view of philosophic logic. This option is
to demonstrate within the context of some metaphysical theory that
there is one and only one necessary being and creator of all three
universes of experience. The form of this demonstration would be to
show that from the syntactical and semantical rules and primitive
statements governing the symbols and expressions of that theory the
conclusion could be derived that there is one and only one necessary
being and creator of all three universes of experience. And since
within that theory 'God' would be considered as the abbreviation for
'the necessary being' and 'the creator of all three universes of
experience', then 'God' would have a referent or designatum and the
statement 'God exists.' could be treated as an analytic truth within
that theory. In short, specifying who or what God is, and that he is,
is a task for natural theology.[16]

It is important to understand how the philosophic logician
views the metaphysical task. First and foremost, metaphysics is
treated as a science. It is a science, however, which aims at describing the most general characteristics of the common world disclosed
in experience as well as explaining those features. That is, the
metaphysician aims at constructing a theory about the invariant structure of reality at any time or at any place. The basic "bricks" of
his theory are the universal predicates which apply to the various
sorts of entities that make up whatever there is or might be. Like
the regional predicates of the special sciences, the universal predicates of metaphysics must be assigned denotata; yet, unlike the
regional predicates of the special sciences, the universal predicates
have a universal range of application. In Whitehead's terminology,
these universal predicates should be "adequate" along with being
"consistent", "coherent", and "applicable."[17] Of the four criteria

by means of which a metaphysical system is evaluated, adequacy guarantees the semantic linkage of the universal predicates to the world disclosed in experience. And if there is one and only one hypothetical entity that is the explanatory principle of all that is or might be, then no doubt some name will be introduced definitionally to designate that entity.

In my example drawn from Peirce, the three universes of experience are the three sorts of entities that are always discernable in experience. These "modes of being" are (1) the being of positive qualitative possibility or simple quality of feeling; (2) the being of action-reaction or dynamic fact of relatedness; and (3) the being of law or thought (6:455, 4.545ff.). Peirce oddly refers to these sorts of things as Firstness, Secondness, and Thirdness.

In terms of syntax, the words 'Firstness', 'Secondness', and 'Thirdness', would be universal predicates which would apply to every concrete thing. Peirce believed that God was the source of Firstness, Secondness, and Thirdness, and attempted to arrive at God as the hypothetical entity that explained these universal features of experience by means of what he called an abductive argument. This is his famous Neglected Argument for the existence of God (6:457). While abduction may indeed be a legitimate form of inference, in addition to deduction and induction, from the point of view of philosophic logic, an argument for the existence of God must exhibit the deductive form. To make Peirce's claim work, one would have to show that from the syntactical and semantical rules and axioms that govern his universal predicates one could demonstrate deductively that there is one and only one necessary being and creator of all three universes of experience. Whether this could be done is, to my knowledge, still to be shown.

While I have a great admiration for Peirce both as the founder of modern semiotic and an ardent supporter of scientific metaphysics, and while I think he was on the right track in associating the definite descriptions that he did with 'God', I have focused upon Peirce mainly for the purpose of semiotic analysis. In short, I have not been trying to bake any bread of natural theology, to utilize an apt expression of Martin.[18] I am only interested in how it might be done from the point of view of philosophic logic.

Which metaphysical system can best articulate the monotheistic vision of God for our time is a judgment that each systematic theologian must decide. If one does not believe that metaphysics is important for theological purposes, or if one does not believe that scientific metaphysics is possible, then the sorts of things I have suggested in the second section of this paper will not make much sense. And if one further believes that theology is beyond logic and more akin to poetry or story, then what I have said about the application of philosophic logic to theology will even make less sense. My own belief is that metaphysics is here to stay along with logic and that the theologian can hardly do without them if he is to speak and write meaningfully and truly of God. For those systematic theologians who are interested in natural theology, it is my belief that one should choose one's metaphysical system not mainly because of its utility in articulating the monotheistic vision of God but because it is true and because there are good reasons for believing that it is.

# FOOTNOTES

[1]Richard M. Martin, Logic, Language and Metaphysics (New York: New York University Press, 1971) p. 6.

[2]I. M. Bochenski, A History of Formal Logic, trans. and ed. Ivo Thomas (1960; rpt. New York: Chelsea Publishing Company, 1970), p. 11. This work, along with that of W. & M. Kneale, The Development of Logic (Oxford: Oxford University Press, 1962), are the two standard histories of formal logic.

[3]Charles W. Morris, Foundation of the Theory of Signs in International Encyclopedia of Unified Science, Vol. 1, No. 2. (Chicago: University of Chicago Press, 1938), pp. 6-7.

[4]Rudolf Carnap, Foundations of Logic and Mathematics in International Encyclopedia of Unified Science, Vol. 1, No. 3. (Chicago: University of Chicago Press, 1939), p. 3.

[5]Paul Arthur Schilpp, ed., The Philosophy of Rudolf Carnap (LaSalle, Ill.: Open Court, 1963), pp. 861-862.

[6]Richard M. Martin, Belief, Existence, and Meaning (New York: New York University Press, 1969), p. 5.

[7]Martin, Logic, Language and Metaphysics, p. 4.

[8]Ibid., see especially Chapters I and VI.

[9]Martin, Belief, Existence, and Meaning, see especially Chapters VI, VII, VIII, and IX.

[10]Frederick Ferré, "A Renewal of God-Language?" The Journal of Religion, 52, No. 3, (1972), 288.

[11]Martin, Belief, Existence, and Meaning, p. 101.

[12]Martin, Logic, Language and Metaphysics, pp. 14-16.

[13]Alfred North Whitehead, Religion in the Making (New York: The Macmillan Company, 1926), pp. 67-68.

[14]Richard M. Martin, "On Bochenski's Logic of Religious Discourse," International Philosophical Quarterly, 6, No. 4. (1966), 658.

[15]Richard M. Martin, "On the Logical Structure of the Ontological Argument," The Monist, 57, No. 3. (1973), 298.

[16]See the work of Bowman L. Clarke, Language and Natural Theology (The Hague: Mouton and Company, 1966). Also, among others "Theology and Philosophy," Journal of the American Academy of Religion, 38, No. 3, (1970), 276-288.

[17]Alfred North Whitehead, _Process and Reality_ (New York: The Macmillan Company, 1929), pp. 4-6.

[18]Martin, "On Bochenski's Logic of Religious Discourse," 664.

# LONERGAN'S TRINITARIAN INSIGHT

John Carmody

The Pennsylvania State University


With the recent publication of Method in Theology,[1] Canadian Jesuit Bernard Lonergan (b. 1904) has moved out of a whispered, esoteric reputation toward the deanship of Engligh-speaking Roman Catholic theologians. Because of Method of Theology's scope, which is nothing less than the redesign of theology into a collaboration of eight functional specializations (research, interpretation, history, dialectic, foundations, doctrines, systematics, communications), Lonergan now commands serious study from anyone professionally seeking Christian faith's understanding. However, Method in Theology is hard going, for at least two reasons. First, it proceeds in terms of a philosophy of mind entailing "transcendental method" and "intentionality analysis."[2] If one knows this philosophy's forebears, Verbum and Insight,[3] some of its difficulty is eased, but it remains knotty epistemology. Second, Method in Theology is prescriptional, meta-theological. It seldom indicates what such specializations import concretely, as performances with the stuff of Christian tradition.

Now, there seems no easy solution to the first cause of Method in Theology's difficulty. Though secondary analyses can help,[4] the task of appropriating one's consciousness, internalizing Lonergan's theory of mind, remains a lonely business of introspective psychology. Regarding the second cause, however, prospects are better, for Lonergan himself has written four sizeable treatises that are good indices of what his method concretely implies. They are little known--largely because they are in Latin--and, interestingly, Method in Theology does not mention them.[5] Nonetheless, they show the work that prepared Lonergan's prescribing.

In this article, then, I shall 1) make available an important and representative portion of Lonergan's theological performance, as a basis for 2) offering some critical comments on his views' practical import and utility. The performance is the second chapter of De Deo Trino, II: Pars Systematica, where Lonergan elaborates the divine processions as the foundation of an ordered understanding of the Christian God. It is a good specimen of the work preceding Method in Theology, since it applies Lonergan's basic achievement in Verbum and Insight, his understanding of human understanding. As we observe him applying this understanding to the Trinity, we shall witness his "analogical" conception of systematic theology, as well as his updated version of the doctrine that human kind is imago Dei. After this observation, we should be positioned to start the calculation of Method in Theology's utility.

## The Analogical Conception of the Divine Processions

### 1. Preparation

As performer, Bernard Lonergan has specialized in dogmatic theology and systematics. Dogmatically, he views theology in terms from Pius XII's Humani Generis: "That is the most noble task of theology which shows how the doctrine defined by the Church is contained in the sources . . . in that sense in which it is defined.[6] Systematically, his mentor is Vatican I: "Reason indeed, enlightened by faith, when it seeks earnestly, piously, and calmly, attains by a gift from God some understanding, and that most fruitful, of mysteries, partly from the analogy of those things which it naturally knows, partly from the relations, the mysteries bear to one another and to the last end of man . . .[7] So, taken comparatively, Lonergan's dogmatics aims at presenting what the Church believes, while his systematics aims at the ordered, synthetic understanding of this belief.[8]

De Deo Trino, II then depends on the positive exposition of Trinitarian faith laid out in De Deo Trino, I.[9] Its concern is to order these dogmata--to present them in terms of their inner logic, their conceptual relations as primordial or derived. Such presentation Lonergan refers to as the via doctrinae, the way or order of teaching.[10] In the chapter of our interest, dealing with the divine processions, his concern is with the first step in teaching Trinitarian doctrine systematically. Since he is a good scholastic, Lonergan takes this step measuredly, through three "assertions" and four "questions." Assertions are positive teaching or theses. Questions are subordinate, usually disputed issues whose clarification removes impediments to grasping the assertions. They are the chapter's core. Preceding them, however, are introductory materials that set the problem of understanding the divine processions in context.

"The fundamental Trinitarian problem is that 1) the Son is both from himself and not from himself, and 2) the Holy Spirit is both from himself and not from himself, and 3) the Son and Spirit are not from themselves differently." (DDT, 66) As God, these persons are from themselves: independent, non-derived. As Son and Spirit, however, they originate--by respectively being born from the Father ("Light from Light, true God from true God"), and "proceeding from the Father" (and the Son).[11] Finally, then, they originate differently, since the Son is generated and the Spirit proceeds by spiration.[12] What teaching the divine processions entails is making these distinctions coherent, intelligible. Later chapters, on the divine relations, persons, and missions display the rest of Trinitarian theology that the doctrine of the processions undergirds.

To deal with the processions, Lonergan invokes Aquinas, because "concerning how the divine processions may be understood, some opinions are erroneous, others are insufficient, still others are less well proposed--and finally there are Saint Thomas' opinions." (DDT, 68) The erroneous opinions err by excess or defect. By excess, the semi-rationalists would demonstrate the divine mysteries, and so have been condemned by Vatican I.[13] By defect, some would deny even an imperfect understanding of the mysteries. They also conflict with Vatican I.[14] "Insufficient" opinions remain external, verbal--like

those that affirm two processions but fail to show why there are only
these two. Finally, opinions "less well proposed" use the psychological
analogy (based on the human processions of understanding and love),
but handle it clumsily--for instance, by concentrating on the sensitive rather than the intellectual dimensions of human understanding.
Here Lonergan has Scotus in mind. Aquinas is surehandedly intellectualist: "The human soul understands itself through its act of understanding, which is its proper act perfectly demonstrating its power
and nature.[15] Following Aquinas, then, Lonergan takes out after the
notion of intelligible emanation, in which Aquinas found the key to
Trinitarian understanding.

Intelligible emanation may be treated philosophically,
historically, or theologically. Historically, Verbum testifies to
Lonergan's long textual studies in Aquinas' sources and innovations.
Philosophically, Insight elaborates the cognitional theory, epistemology, and metaphysics implied in a modern appropriation and development
of Aquinas. So in De Deo Trino, II the only task is speculatively
theological: to acquire that awareness of our minds requisite for
some understanding of the divine processions. Towards this acquisi-
tion Lonergan asks the reader to consider his or her own mental
experience.

We all know by experience what intercedes between a rash
judgment and a true one. The former is proffered without sufficient
evidence, while the latter is so founded in the perception of evidence
that it has a certain intellectual necessity, that it cannot be avoided.
What is lacking in the rash judgment, but present in the true, is
intelligible emanation.

Similarly, we all know from experience what intercedes
between a definition repeated by memory and a definition proffered
because we have perceived something by understanding it. The former
is simply a matter of emitting sounds, from sensitive habit, while
the latter is an expression of intellectual success. When we understand we can vary our examples, express ourselves diversely, under
the direction and necessity of our insight itself. Intellectual or
intelligible emanation is what is lacking in the memory-person, what
is present in the insight-person--"which emanation is nothing other
than the reality that whoever understands, by this very fact that he
understands, proffers definitions, explanations, illustrations through
a certain intellectually conscious necessity." (DDT, 71)

Finally, all of us know from experience what intercedes
between an inordinate act of the will, repugnant to reason, and an
honest, obligatory, holy, ordered volitional act. Goodness that is
perceived, approved by reason, and imposed on the will so obligates
us that we either cede rationally to its dictate or are rendered
irrational for choosing against it. What is present in the honest,
rational choice, but lacking in the morally evil, irrational choice,
is again intelligible emanation. Here it consists in the fact that
on account of a good intellectually perceived an appetite potentially
rational (the will) is made rational actually, effectively.

On the basis of these experiences, Lonergan proceeds to his
definition of intellgible emanation: "the conscious origin of a real,

natural, and conscious act from a real, natural, and conscious act, both within intellectual consciousness and by the force of this same intellectual consciousness as it has been determined by the prior act." (DDT, 73)  To clarify some of the definition's terms he notes that "conscious" means "present to the subject."[16]  "Within intellectual consciousness" connotes a psychological, not a metaphysical consideration.  Such consciousness is constituted by acts of the intellect and will.  The "force" of intellectual consciousness implies the intellect's transcendental exigencies--those that regard the totality of intelligibility, truth, being, goodness.  The "determination" of one intellectual act by another indicates a causal nexus--e.g., defining because one has understood, and in terms of this understanding.

## 2.  Assertions

Having cleared the foreground, Lonergan can next move to the heartland.  This is staked out in three "assertions" about the divine missions.  The first reads, "The divine processions, which are per modum operati, are somewhat understood according to the similitude of intelligible emanation.  And, there seems to be no other analogy that will serve to form a systematic conception of divine procession." (DDT, 75)  The key technical notion, "per modum operati," is defined as "an internal procession [origin of one thing from another] in which the act that arises is really distinct from the act that originates it.  It is not distinct according to absolute being, however, but rather according to relative being.  Its mode of determination is metaphysical and external [its source act and originated act are specified according to general ontological notions like act and potency], and it has been thought out [precisely] to clarify the divine mystery." (DDT, 76)

The goal of this assertion is technically to formulate the problem involved in understanding creedal affirmations like that of Quicumque:  "The Father is neither made, nor created, nor generated by anything or anyone.  The Son is only from the Father--not made nor created but generated.  The Spirit is from the Father and the Son-- not made nor created nor generated but proceeding."[17]  By transposing this doctrine into equivalent technical terms ("per modum operati") and analyzing it analogically with the conceptual tool of intelligible emanation, Lonergan hopes to express some understanding of the mystery.  After indicating other opinions less nuanced than his own view of theological understanding, he moves to the assertion's argument.

That divine procession is per modum operati is a strict deduction from the truths of faith through metaphysical notions and principles known to all.  Divine procession is not creation or making; it is not external; it is internal, but neither as a processio operationis (from potency to act) nor as a processio operati (from act to act with absolute real distinction, as in creatures).  What satisfies dogmatic conception of the Trinity is, then, only the technical notion per modum operati, which saves the divine unity by insisting on only relative real distinction and internal procession.

Now, if one supposes there is intelligible emanation in God, it follows that there is processio per modum operati.  In other words, the analogical employment of "the psychological analogy" (in Lonergan's intellectualist version of its Thomist form) so deals with divine

procession as to produce, logically, the technical equivalent of its
dogmatic conception. But, what is entailed in supposing divine intelligible emanation? First, that in God there is intellectual consciousness, determined by an act that must be infinite, in such dynamic wise
that this consciousness demands procession. Next, because of the
divine simplicity and sufficiency, the originating and derived acts
must both be infinite. This makes it possible, third, that the procession be an origin of God from God, where principle and principled
are really distinguished only as regards relative being.

What supposing divine intelligible emanation entails, then,
is such a coherent, "deductive" arrangement of the dogmatic elements
that some understanding (not increased knowledge) of faith results.
In other words, good systematic theology results: the precise moment
of this deductio ex suppositione is that mediated, imperfect, analogous
understanding of the divine mysteries praised by Vatican I. Supposing
divine intelligible emanation, one can sufficiently reconcile God's
infinity of act and dynamism of consciousness, the consubstantiality
of the proceedent and the reality of the procession, to understand
dimly the Trinitarian mystery. Reconciliation, of course, does not
mean full comprehension, coruscant understanding. Full comprehension
would involve grasping the root unity to which the elements organized
by the hypothesis of divine intelligible emanation are reduced. Since
this is an infinite rational and moral consciousness, and we humans
understand infinity only negatively, we have no positive, full comprehension of God's Trinitarian consciousness. Our knowledge remains
"covered by a veil of faith and as though wrapped in a cloud."[18] What
we do have, however, Vatican I called "very fruitful."

Lonerganian theological understanding, then, is modest,
delicately balanced. It is ever confessing that the mystery of God
is greater--Deus semper major.[19] However, this does not render it
sloppy or compliant. In tough terms, Lonergan finishes his first
assertion by declaring that no analogy but intelligible emanation is
adequate for Trinitarian speculation. To buttress this declaration,
he hammers home a tight "dialectic"[20] of the conceptions that serve
of fail speculative Trinitarian theology's exigencies. The signal
blows in this dialectic include demonstrations that 1) the needed
analogy is from a created procession in which a strictly spiritual
act arises from a strictly spiritual act according to a strictly
spiritual mode of proceeding, and 2) the optimal form of this activity
in human experience is our generation of inner words in understanding
or judgment, and our consequent acts of love, as these constitute
our existential autonomy. Poised on this analogy, one can 3) consider
God as he constitutes his own Trinitarian existential autonomy from
eternity. Only intelligible emanation, then, offers the spirituality,
actuality, and constitutive or determinative consciousness that may
mediate something of divine procession into human terms.

In his second assertion, Lonergan moves to specify his
analogy's application: "Through the similitude of intelligible emanation two, and only two, divine processions can be conceived, namely
that of the Word from the Speaker and that of Love from both [Word
and Speaker]." (DDT, 92) Here the new terms requiring explanations
include "speaker" ("a principle of intelligible emanation insofar as

it is determined through an act of understanding"), "word" ("the immanent term of intelligible emanation from a speaker"), and "love" ("the fundamental act of the will"). (DDT, 92-3) In addition, the declaration of terms defines "spirans" as "a principle of intelligible emanation insofar as it is determined both through an act of understanding and also through a consequent word that is a judgment of value."[21] A "breather" or "spirator," then, is a notional or intellectual lover.

The content of this assertion has varying degrees of certitude. That there are two divine processions is of divine and catholic faith.[22] It is a common theological opinion that they can be conceived according to a certain intellectual and voluntary emanation. It seems to be Saint Thomas' opinion that they should be conceived according to the intelligible emanation of word from speaker and love from both.[23] The intent of the assertion, then, is to continue a Thomist tour of the via synthetica--the organizing, teaching path of systematic theology. Having determined that intelligible emanation is the key, one tries to unlock the first door to the Trinitarian mystery: how many intelligible emanations can be conceived in God? Since only two may be found, the psychological analogy is congruent with what is known by faith.

Lonergan advances this synthetic step with the following arguments. First, two divine processions can be conceived on the analogy of intelligible emanation, because God is the highest being, in whom there must be perfect understanding, formal truth, and the goodness of love itself. But every affirmation that humans know is true insofar as it emanates from an understander, while every spiritual love that humans know is right and holy insofar as it proceeds from a true affirmation of good. Therefore, if any intelligible emanations can be conceived in God, surely the emanation of Word from Speaker and Love from both can be conceived. And these two processions, if they are postulated in God, cannot be reduced to only one, because "to emanate from a word" and "not to emanate from a word" are contradictory. The emanation of love is from a word; the emanation of word is not from itself but from an understander, a speaker. Since God cannot be contradictory, two divine processions can be conceived.

Lonergan argues that God has only two processions analogously conceivable through intelligible emanation by insisting that only one understanding, one word, one love can be conceived in God. This is so because in God there is only one simply infinite act, through which all being, truth, and goodness are attained. By implication, then, there are only two processions, since one love has only one emanation, one word has only one emanation, and the divine understanding cannot intelligibly emanate from any principle other than itself.

Assertion three reads, "The logic of generation properly so called is followed in the divine emanation of the Word, but not in the emanation of Love." (DDT, 96) The assertion's point, then, is to specify how the only two divine processions differ. Since Lonergan finds the difference between understanding and love analogous to the difference faith places between generation and spiration, he considers that this assertion also confirms the aptness of the "psychological analogy."

Concerning the certitude of the assertion, it is noted that the Son's being generated and the Spirit's not being generated are matters of divine and catholic faith.[24] Similarly, that the Son is the same as the Word is of divine and catholic faith.[25] Finally, it is the opinion of Aquinas and other theologians who follow Augustine that "word" has the same import as "son"--which opinion was approved by Pius VI.[26]

The assertion's argument unfolds in three steps. These deal, respectively, with generation strictly so called, the mode of conceiving divine nature, and the difference between the emanation of the word and the emanation of love. Generation strictly so called is defined as "the origin of a living thing from a conjoined living principle in similitude of nature." (DDT, 97) Generation is therefore different from creation, because creation's principle is not conjoined to the living thing that it originates. Similarly, generation is not the name for Eve's origin from Adam's rib, because it is not natural for a woman to be made from a rib. Finally, one should note that the natural similitude in question should arise by the force of the generative emanation itself.

Next, one must consider how the divine nature is to be conceived, since this is the nature whose similitude the generation of the Word involves. Such consideration has difficulties. First, it is difficult to verify the Aristotelian notion of nature ("the principle of motion and rest in that in which it is first and through itself and not accidental"), because God's simplicity allows no distinction between the principle of his operation and that operation itself. Second, if nature be considered not as principle of operation but as essence, then it may be acknowledged in God--but not as something that we understand. In this life we do not know what God is. Consequently, the most proper name for God seems to be "the one that is," because this name is taken from God's act of existence. It omits all formal determinization, in order to signify a certain infinite sea of substance.[27]

Despite the difficulties, however, Aquinas made God's act of understanding his substance and nature. To reconcile this denotation with the equally Thomist nescience indicated above, one must agree that we do not know God through a species proportioned to the divine essence but only analogously. A species is a form in the knower allowing for intentional union. What we know analogously, however, we may order, in such wise that something about God may be placed first, in the mode of a nature or essence. This something is God's understanding, on which his infinity, aseity, simplicity, and whatever else we don't know may be seen as following. They follow in a manner like to creatures' attributes following on creatures' essences. Again, if God's nature be considered under the formality of the intrinsic principle of operation, it falls out that this nature is intellectual. Through faith we know of divine persons distinguished and constituted by relations of origin. Since these origins are the emanations of Word from Speaker and Love from both in the divine intellectual consciousness, it follows that the principle of this divine "motion" is intellectual.

The third step in setting up the assertion's argument is to compare the emanations of Word and Love. To this end, Lonergan suggests a four-fold distinction of 1) a thing itself, 2) the understanding of something, 3) the word for something, and 4) the love of something. Intellectual consciousness is so related to reality that first it understands something; then from its understanding it speaks the thing's true name or word; third, from understanding and word it breathes love of the thing; and fourth, by the force of this love it is borne to the beloved thing.

Now, there is a true word for something insofar as a perfect similitude of the thing is formed within consciousness. Therefore, the emanation by which the word arises is concerned with forming the similitude of something. On the contrary, one has love of something insofar as the lover is inclined, borne, impelled to the thing loved-- insofar as he is united with it, clings to it. Therefore, the emanation by which love arises is concerned with inclination, impulse, clinging.

This difference between verbal and amorous emanation may be illustrated by the frigid, "light" bearing of scientists, who are concerned only with forming intellectual similitudes of things and so remain detached, uncompelled to embrace them. Quite differently, the lover is so occupied with the external goodness of the beloved that he may be called blind. But if one could avoid blindness, by understanding, and levity, by will, a certain perfect circle of consciousness would be completed. One would so begin from reality that it would be perceived by intellect, then represented by a word, then so loved that one would return to the reality itself.[28] At any rate, whether this circle is completed or not, it is clear that the emanation of the word is internal and concerned with truth, while the emanation of love is external and concerned with goodness. The intrinsic logic of the word's emanation, then, is to form a true interior similitude of reality, while the intrinsic logic of love's emanation is to actuate an inclination toward reality itself.

So, the emanation of the Word satisfies the notional requirements of "generation," but the emanation of Love does not. The Word's emanation is an origin, because all emanation is original. It is the origin of a living thing, because God is living and the divine Word is God. God is a conjoined living principle, because the principle and term of an emanation within consciousness are conjoined. The Word's emanation establishes a similitude of nature because God's intentional being is the same as his natural being. Therefore, his Word, similar by intentional being, is similar by nature. The divine emanation of Love, however, not being for the formation of a similitude but for impulsion or adherence, fails in one of "generation's" characteristics. Accordingly, faith develops a different designation for the Spirit's procession: "spiration."

### 3. Questions

Chapter two of De Deo Trino, II concludes with four
"questions." They aim at clarifying subsidiary issues attendant on
the three main assertions, and we may deal with them rather summarily.

The first question inquires whether human understanding is
distinct from human inner words of definition or judgment. The answer
is yes, because in both definition and judgment our acts of understanding have different objects than have our acts of verbal emanation. In
judgment, understanding perceives a sufficiency of evidence, while
verbal emanation affirms something true or denies something false. In
definition, a quiddity existing in bodily matter moves our intellectus
possibilis to perceive intelligibility, while this perception then
prompts the inner dictation of the object's whatness.[29]

Second, can it be demonstrated by the light of natural reason
that there is a Word in God? By conciliar decree (Vatican I), the
factual answer is no.[30] To understand this answer, however, one must
consider the "necessity" of verbal emanation. In human knowledge,
inner words of definition or judgment are necessary because the object
moving our knowledge (the quiddity of a material thing) differs from
the terminal object our understanding intends (all being). To ascend
from this beginning to that end, we require inner words as media of
progressive transcendence. Since God's understanding has no moving
or terminal object but himself, he has no naturally perceptible necessity for an inner Word.

Third, does God's Word proceed from an understanding of
creatures? On the one hand, it seems not, since God's Word is necessary and eternal, while creatures are contingent and temporal. On
the other hand, Saint Thomas taught that God understands himself and
creatures in one act, speaks himself and creatures by one Word.[31]
This apparent conflict dissolves if one has a sure hold on intellectual consciousness as the analogy for God's knowledge. Then it appears
that the necessity in intelligible emanation comes from the conscious
intellectuality of the subject. Applied to divine understanding, this
enables one to subsume God's understanding of creatures (secondary
objects) under his understanding of his own divine essence (primary
object). Whether one considers possible creatures under the aspect
or being or possibility, or considers actual creatures past, present,
or future, all these exist, are possible, or are actual by reference
to the divine essence they participate or the divine power that actuates them. But God knows them in his essence or actuates them through
his power by understanding, speaking a Word, and breathing Love. The
more accurate relation of God's knowledge of creatures to his divine
procession, then, is that creatures are known, spoken, and loved in
dependence on the Word and Spirit, not vice versa.

The fourth and last question is whether "the beloved in the
lover" is constituted or produced through love.[32] In other words,
is the union to which love is impelled the same as the loving itself
("constituted") or is union something additional ("produced")? The
theological moment of the question is how to conceive the procession
of the Spirit. Those holding for a productive love[33] parallel

generation and spiration. As generation develops a word, so love
develops union. Those agreeing with Lonergan that love is constitutive conceive the second procession as flowing from the first.  In
this case, spiration develops from generation's word.  Lonergan
assembles texts from Aquinas that justify his constitutive interpretation,[34] but the edge of his conviction is internal experience.
There he finds that we love because of value judgments, and that our
love itself constitutes the dwelling in us of what we love.


## Critical Comments

We have now examined a basic portion of Bernard Lonergan's
theological performance on the Trinity.  I find it has merits, difficulties, and important implications for the assessment of Method in
Theology.  We can conclude by considering these findings.

The merits of Lonergan's systematic treatment of the divine
processions are at least two.  It is clear and it is deep.  In terms
of general orientation or method, Divinarum Personarum Conceptio
Analogica is unusually lucid.  Lonergan paces each step in the full
light of day, against a map unfurled from the beginning.  Moreover,
his methodological clarity is not simply logical.  It has historical,
dogmatic, and transcendental roots.  Historically, it derives from
Aquinas' capping of the medieval scholastics' development of the distinction between the way of discovery ("via inventionis") and the
way of teaching ("via doctrine").  Dogmatically, it is directed by
Pius XII's description of theology's submission to tradition and
Vatican I's calibration of theology's rational instrumentality.
Transcendentally, its powerhouse is Lonergan's own cognitional theory,
epistemology, and metaphysics.

This latter, transcendental rootage is the most important,
and it gives Lonergan's theology great depth.  Externally, Insight
and Method in Theology spotlight transcendental method--the recurrence
to consciousness' constitutive operations--in its forms antecedent
and consequent to De Deo Trino.  Internally, a little familiarity
with Lonergan's regular homing to consciousness, and creative theore-
ticians' normal ways, generates the growing conviction that Aquinas,
Pius XII, and Vatican I are "authoritative" because they conveniently
confirm what an original mind has found for itself.  This is not to
deny that they have guided Lonergan's way, tipped his truth's hand.
It is to say, however, that the cogency of De Deo Trino, II is internally derived.  The light by which Lonergan flies is the transparency
of his own mind.

More specifically, Lonergan's treatment of the divine processions is lucid and deep because the mind he has made transparent
is, both traditionally and analytically, the counter-player, homologue,
analogue of the Trinitarian mystery.  Traditionally, the human person
is eikon and morphe of the biblical God.  In the Christianity subsequent to Augustine's De Trinitate, the theological person has been
invited to probe his or her memory, understanding, and love, to verify
the godly image, instance the impressions of divine mentality.

Analytically, Lonergan's chapter attacks the primordial divine structure with the primordial human structuring. The dynamic what and how of human interiority are made the probe of its own and all exteriority's ground.

It is clear, then, that "the psychological analogy" places one at a double, concentric "go." It places one at the starting block round which circle theology's director, resource, verifier (the human mind) and its intended object (the fontal, basal, terminal Mystery). Lonergan's technical achievement is to chart this concentric position carefully, precisely. In his hands the psychological analogy pivots between a human mind appropriated with great discipline and a divine "mind" extrapolated most scrupulously. The genius in his second chapter's deployment of the analogy is the translation of confessional faith from the common-sense horizon of conciliar dogma to the theoretic horizon of technical terms like processio per modum operati, technical hypotheses like divine intelligible emanation. This involves carefully sifting the dogmatic elements, to show that processio per modum operati is a precise, intelligible expression for the reality left when one has eliminated "creation," "making," "processio ad extra," etc., and then trying to understand how processio per modum operati might occur--what analogy it might bear to occurrences we humans experience.

Both moves exploit the cognitional theory elaborated in Insight. Further, both utilize the traditional conviction that the human person is God's image. Insight develops the notions of common-sense and theory, which come to specify Lonergan's understanding of doctrinal development and systematization.[35] The traditional conviction of imago Dei collects the basic assumption and hints: "God is somewhat like us, and the point of resemblance is our minds." When a theology specifies its mind's moves, and argues persuasively (if implicitly) that this mind is the divine Mystery's most intimate presence and reflection, it is clear and deep in rare measure.

Nonetheless, Lonergan's theology of the processions harbors some problems. Perhaps paradoxically, they seem to be the reverse side of the methodological and scholastic coin in which he pays handsome dividends. Methodologically, there is an arbitrariness about Lonergan's conception of dogmatic and systematic theology that is likely to trouble today's reader. I find its focus to be the directive quotations from Pius XII and Vatican I that we have mentioned several times. Insofar as these directives are matters of convenience --ways in which Lonergan might convince, seduce, calm his Roman audience and censors--they are no major problem. As noted above, I find them less intrinsically directive than his own cognitional theory. However, one would have to suspect Lonergan's express words not to credit him with believing in magisterial direction, papal infallibility, the understanding of theology enounced by Pius XII and Vatican I. Since I find such suspicion precarious, if not insulting, I take Lonergan's submissions seriously. Thereby, I wonder about the critical freedom and adequacy of his outlook.[36] And it does not help that no Protestant or Orthodox views even brush De Deo Trino's fair parchment, except as occasional adversaries.

        Regarding dogmatic theology, Pius XII's directive is easily
liable to promote eisegesis. No little sophistication would be needed
to go to one's sources with an authoritative interpretation of their
meaning in hand and not simply read that interpretation into them.
Lonergan is nothing but sophisticated, and he expended considerable
energy on the problems of hermeneutics and doctrinal development.[37]
Nonetheless, I have not found his Christological interpretation of
scripture impeccable,[38] and the impact of dogma on his Trinitarian
speculation must be carefully measured. What place should be given,
for instance, to a critique (on transcendental grounds) of the creedal
affirmations that furnish his speculation its content? Method in
Theology may conceive dialectic and foundations as providing for this
task.[39] De Deo Trino, II gives it no place or play. It just assumes,
for instance, that "generation" is the faith-truth about the Son's
relation to the Father. Moreover, it parses the consequents of "generation" in Aristotelian terms, accomodating divine procession to a rather
crude natural biology.

        This Aristotelianism indicates a second problem with De Deo
Trino. As its systematization uncritically accepts ancient dogma's
setting of its questions, so it does its own conceptualizing work in
alien, if not extrinsic, terms. For Thomist terminology is alien to
the twentieth century. By Lonergan's own reckoning, it is unaware of
the historical, scholarly, and intentionality horizons developed by
modernity.[40] Despite Insight's moves into modern horizons, De Deo
Trino is fettered by a scholasticism still strongly medieval. Recently,
Lonergan has made oblique reference to the "impossible" conditions
under which he was forced to work in Rome.[41] A major pressure point
where these conditions impinge on his performed theology is in their
scholastic categories. This is almost cruel: a cognitional theore-
tician is forced to use the outmoded language of faculty psychology;
a scholar convinced that "metaphysical" categories are wooden is
forced to speculate in them. Insight (1957) shows that Lonergan was in possession of the tools to write very different theology texts than he
chose to write (in 1964). An interesting question about his own
psychology is why he chose to capitulate to the Roman system. Lonergan
maneuvers, fights for working space, but from the beginning his vic-
tories are condemned to be flawed. Act and potency, intellection and
volition, nature as essence and nature as principle of operation--these
are not viable terms for a contemporary understanding of God.

        Which means, finally, that Method in Theology lacks concrete
illustrations, specific performative fruits, that would render its
prescriptions compelling. To move from the transcendental precepts
that legislate "authenticity" ("be attentive, intelligent, rational,
responsible") to Christian or Roman Catholic Trinitarian speculation
one has to pass more fiery brooks than Lonergan's cartology allows.
His own performances beg the question how dialectics and foundations
come to the apologetic and fundamental theology of Vatican I, Pius XII,
Edward Dhanis.[42] It simply is not patent that being in love unrestrict-
edly ("religion")[43] imperates the choice of Jesus, let alone what Nicea,
Chalcedon, or Ephesus make of Jesus' God. Equally, the horizons un-
veiled by "authenticity" specify no contemporary bowing to the concep-
taulizations of the Roman Magisterium. The history of religions reveals
myriad ways of being authentic; the contemporary mental sciences bring

eams of research to bear on the rise of "God" in human consciousness.[44]
uture doctrinal and systematic theology would seem more difficult than
ethod in Theology, let alone De Deo Trino, implies.

Winningly, Method in Theology, and even more recent publica-
ions, provide a Lonerganian basis for peace in the midst of such
ifficulty.[45] They forthrightly assert the primacy of love over
nowledge, Mystery over kataphatic theology. Without despising knowl-
dge, expression, or the intersubjective nearness of the precisely
hristian God, they view God's salvific will as regularly achieving
ts goals outside the Christian traditions and their categories. As
n elderly, wise observer, Lonergan now seems to view theology sub
pecie aeternitatis. He does not give it all over as straw he re-
ains confident that intellectual work can diagnose contemporary
ultures' aberrant, amnesiac mental stress; but he seems relatively
nconcerned about reducing his methods to perfect concreteness, rela-
ively unconcerned about the perduring value of his own performances.

The implications I draw from Lonergan's Trinitarian insight
or Method in Theology, then, are quite liberating. First, the future
heology it sponsors is to be respectful of the past, but not inden-
ured to it. For all that Method in Theology repeats Vatican I's
onceptions of theological speculation,[46] De Deo Trino offers performa-
ive grains of salt. Second, "authenticity" so stresses the appropria-
ion of one's spirit, and so finally roots in religious love, that
nconverted, rather heteronomous pronouncements of ecclesiastical
uthority may be peacefully bypassed. The business of theologians in
he future is to probe confessional experience, symbolization, convic-
ion with contemporary analyses of consciousness, reaching what systema
hese analyses, not past fathers, find most adequate. This they should
ive their churches, letting them make of it what they will.

Third, the faith-certainties anchoring such theoretic inde-
endence or boldness are not going to issue from Rome, Geneva, or any
external magisterium. They are rather to be expected from the inner,
fruitful Spirit, who shadows and prompts our time on the way down that
is the way up.[47] If we go down, to the gravity of judgmental self-
criticism, to religious endurance of the Holy Mystery, we may hope to
grow clarified, purged, convicted of the sin that mars God's eikon,
ersuaded that a source, word, and breath we thought we were seeking
as already found us.[48] We may hope to be persuaded, finally, that
this living God's perichoresis in us creates our tradition, gathers
our church, specifies theology's authorities, tasks, and method anew.

174

## Notes

[1]New York:  Herder and Herder, 1972.

[2]Transcendental method deals with the basic, structural, never absent operations of consciousness.  Intentionality analysis is similar, focusing on consciousness' dynamics and finality.

[3]See Bernard Lonergan, Verbum:  Word and Idea in Aquinas (Notre Dame: University of Notre Dame Press, 1967), and Insight:  A Study of Human Understanding (New York:  Philosophical Library, 1957).

[4]See e.g., David Tracy, The Achievement of Bernard Lonergan (New York: Herder and Herder, 1970).

[5]The works are:  De Constitutione Christi Ontologica et Psychologica,[4] De Verbo Incarnato,[3] De Deo Trino I:  Pars Dogmatica,[2] and De Deo Trino II:  Pars Systematica.[3]  All were published by the Gregorian University Press, Rome, 1964.  See Method in Theology, p. 390.

[6]See Denzinger-Schönmetzer, Enchiridion Symbolorum,[32] (Freiburg: Herder, 1963), no. 3886.  Hereafter this will be referred to as DS.

[7]See DS 3016.

[8]See De Deo Trino, II, pp. 36-42.  In Method in Theology dogmatics is replaced by the more general "doctrines."  Hereafter, reference to De Deo Trino, II will be placed in the text as, e.g., DDT 36-42.

[9]De Deo Trino, I has five dogmatic theses affirming 1) the consubstantiality of the Son with the Father; 2) the divinity of the Holy Spirit; 3) the unity of God and distinction of persons; 4) the procession of the Holy Spirit from Father and Son; 5) the permanent mystery in the Trinity.  All of these rest on full documentation.

[10]See De Constitutione Christi, pp. 42-56.

[11]See DS 125, 126, 150.

[12]See H. Denzinger, Enchiridion Symbolorum [31] (Freiburg:  Herder, 1957), no. 460, 691, 704.

[13]See DS 3041.

[14]See DS 3016.

[15]Summa Theologiae, I, q. 88, a. 2 ad 3m.

[16]See DDT 73. Lonergan's regular accent is on the subjective, experiential side of consciousness. It is for him not perception of oneself as an object, but the oblique self-awareness of oneself as subject. See De Constitutione Christi, pp. 83-99.

[17]See DS 75.

[18]See DS 3016.

[19]See De Deo Trino, I, pp. 249-298; Method in Theology, pp. 340 ff.

[20]See Method in Theology, pp. 235-266.

[21]DDT 92-3. Lonergran draws many of these terms from stated texts of Aquinas.

[22]On the question of theological "notes"--degrees of certitude--see E. J. Fortman, "Notes, theological," The New Catholic Encyclopedia, Vol. 10, p. 523.

[23]See, e.g., Sum. Theol., I, q. 93, a. 6.

[24]See DS 75.

[25]Lonergan gives no citation for this.

[26]See Sum. Theol., I, q. 34, a. 2, ad 3m; Augustine, De Trinitate, VII, ii; H. Denzinger, Enchiridion Symbolorum, no. 1597.

[27]DDT 98, with reference to Aquinas, Sum. Theol., I, q. 13, a. 8.

[28]Here one hears overtones of the Trinity's perichoresis (circuminsession).

[29]See Verbum, especially pp. 97-140.

[30]See DS 3041.

[31]See Sum. Theol., I, q. 34, a. 3.

[32]This is misnumbered V in the text.

[33]John of Saint Thomas, and most Thomists.

[34]E.g., Contra Gentiles, IV, 19, 4; IV, 19, 7; IV, 19, 8; IV, 24, 12; Sum. Theol., I, q. 37, aa. 1, 2; q. 38, a. 1; q. 36, a. 2.

[35]See Insight, pp. 33 ff., 173 ff.

[36]See Charles Davis, "Lonergan and the Teaching Church," in Foundations of Theology: Papers from the International Lonergan Congress 1970, ed. Philip McShane, S.J., pp. 60-75; David Tracy, "Lonergan's Foundational Theology: an Interpretation and a Critique," Ibid., pp. 197-222.

[37]See De Deo Trino, I, pp. 3-28; II, pp. 7-64; Insight, pp. 562-594.

[38]See John Carmody, "The Biblical Foundation and Conclusion of Lonergan's De Verbo Incarnato," Andover Newton Quarterly, 15 (1964), 124-136.

[39]See pp. 235-293.

[40]See Method in Theology, pp. 314 ff.

[41]See Bernard Lonergan, Philosophy of God, and Theology (Philadelphia: The Westminster Press, 1973), p. 15.

[42]Dhanis was a colleague of Lonergan's in Rome, and apologetic mentor for Lonergan's De Verbo Incarnato. See his Testimonium Jesu de Seipiso⁵ (Rome: Gregorian University Press, 1964).

[43]See Method in Theology, pp. 101-124.

[44]See, e.g., John Bowker, The Sense of God: Sociological, Antropological, and Psychological Approaches to the Origin of the Sense of God (Oxford: Clarendon Press, 1973).

[45]See Lonergan's replies to various questions in Philosophy of God, and Theology.

[46]See p. 336 and passim.

[47]See Eric Voegelin, Order and History, III: Plato and Aristotle (Baton Rouge: Louisiana State University Press, 1957), p. 52 ff.

[48]Lonergan frequently refers to this notion from Pascal (Pensees, vii, 553). He does not give his edition.

# THE SOCIAL SELF AND HISTORICAL RELATIVISM
### Jerry A. Irish
### Wichita State University

Social selfhood (I) and historical relativism (II) are prominent subjects in H. Richard Niebuhr's religious thought. Their treatment gives us a perspective on Niebuhr's definition of revelation as organizing principle and transforming power (III) and his understanding of Jesus Christ as symbolic form (IV).

## I. Social Selfhood

The self is fundamentally social in the sense that "it is a being which not only knows itself in relation to other selves but exists as self only in that relation."[1] The significance of Niebuhr's claim is first seen in self-consciousness or reflexive selfhood, the capacity of the human subject to experience itself as object. Something as routine as navigating a car through rush hour traffic or describing an event to a friend would be impossible if we could not transcend our immediate involvement, if we could not witness our own activity. Niebuhr contends that self-reflexiveness is rooted in the individual's relations to other selves. The duality of self as subject and self as object is only real in the remembered, contemporary, or anticipated presence of at least one other. Though the same self is both knower and known, its self-knowledge is mediated by another self or group of selves. An individual becomes an object to itself by taking the position of the other, by seeing itself as others see it.

Game playing illustrates many of the social conditions for reflexive selfhood. The rules of the game establish a cooperative environment, and the players put themselves in the positions of their teammates or opponents in order to play their own positions effectively. As a baseball shortstop I become proficient by learning my own moves in relation to those of the other infielders. I can only execute the double play if I have "taken the position" of the second baseman fielding a ground ball between first and second. Only if I "see myself" as the pitcher sees me can I take the pickoff throw with a man leading off second.

An obvious example of reflexive selfhood and its basis in social relations is the phenomenon of conscience. Niebuhr describes the conscience as a "moral dialogue, the phenomenon of a duality in the self in which one is judged, counseled, commanded, approved or condemned by an <u>alter</u> in the <u>ego</u>."[2] In conscience I represent myself to myself, not directly, but through the mediation of an other. Niebuhr contends that the "alter" in the "ego" is not primarily an idea or a law. It is another self or a group of selves. "Conscience is a function of my existence as a social being, always aware of the approvals and disapprovals of my action by my fellow men."[3]

Niebuhr uses the term <u>social companion</u> for the other person that mediates self-reflexiveness. The social companion is similar to the Thou in Martin Buber's sense of the word.[4] The other in whose presence the self is reflexive is also a knower and an evaluator. We can only take the position of the other if the other has a position to be taken. It is the reciprocal character of I-Thou relation that facilitates self-reflexiveness or reflective selfhood.

177

For Niebuhr, the individual who avoids I-Thou relation fails to exercise real selfhood. We need not imagine a desert island or a withdrawn recluse in order to illustrate the avoidance of reflective selfhood. Anti-personnel bombs are effective because the pilot does not see his victims as persons torn apart and maimed by metal fragments. He does not take the position of the other, and thus he escapes seeing himself as a mutilator whose devastation far exceeds that of the slayer who wields his knife in some dark alley. The failure to take the position of the other and the consequent loss of self characterizes those loveless marriages in which the parties agree, perhaps unconsciously, to fulfill certain habitual roles such as breadwinner, babysitter, or bed partner.

The encounters that constitute the self - social companion relation are "particular demonstrations of an enduring movement or particular parts of a continuous discourse."[5] Were they merely unrelated atomic events they would provide no basis for self-reflexiveness. Individual actions become personal in the context of acts that precede and follow them. Only as the social companion acts upon and reacts to the self with some consistency can the self take the position of the social companion in self-knowledge and judgment.

The I-Thou encounter itself takes place in a context of relations. The Thou displays some constancy in its interaction with other Thous as well as in its interaction with the self. We come to know a friend not simply as an isolated individual, but as a participant in a context that extends beyond our friendship. Patterns of behavior are established among the members of the community in which the I and the Thou participate. "The social self is never a mere I-Thou self but an I-You self, responding to a Thou that is a member of an interacting community."[6] Niebuhr's concept of social companion includes this plurality of Thous. Reflective life in relation to social companions is I-Thou, I-You existence.

Through the mediation of social companions the reflective relation that exists between I and Thou can also exist between the self and the self's community. In addition to its unique identity as a self, the Thou may represent a community of selves. The impact of communal judgment mediated by social companions is concrete rather than abstract. Self-evaluation of one's own professional competence, for example, comes from taking the position of particular professional colleagues.

The social self is always a member of an I-Thou-You complex, which is to say, the self is always in the presence of social companions. So it is that social selfhood exhibits a triadic form. "When the Thou is present to me as a knower, it is present as the one that knows not only me but at least one other; and it knows me as knowing not only the Thou but something besides it. This encounter of I and Thou takes place, as it were, always in the presence of a third, from which I and Thou are distinguished and to which they also respond."[7] In the case of the social companion, the third in relation to both I and Thou is at least one other Thou. The I-Thou-You or self - social companion complex is the elementary triadic form of social selfhood. It is a constituent in all the self's more complex relations.

Niebuhr distinguishes between two basic triadic forms in which the self and its social companions participate. The nature triad represents the self's simultaneous relation to social companions and natural entities. By "nature" Niebuhr has in mind those actualities that we know, but that apparently do not know us or themselves, that "large world of events and agencies that we regard as impersonal, as purely objective or thing-like in character."[8]

We are natural beings. However, our participation in the world of things and Its is not simply "natural" because we are also social beings. As a social self one cannot divorce one's responses to natural phenomena from ever-present social companions. It makes a difference whether we enter the forest as representatives of Boise Cascade or the Sierra Club. It is equally difficult to isolate social activity from nature. Technological society's attempt to ignore this truism in its definition of progress has resulted in the pollution of our water and air.

A significant feature that comes to light in our discussion of the nature triad is the self's partial but ever-present dependence on its social companions, the Thou and the You. In a description of the conscience, Niebuhr puts this matter as follows: "Both those who maintain that the self is its own sole legislator and those who regard all such legislation as pure echo of social injunctions seem to be mistaken. The authorship is a joint authorship."[9]

The phrase joint authorship draws our attention to a paradox: not only is the self in society, society is in the self. We simply cannot escape the influence of social reason. No matter how thorough our denial of the structures and beliefs of our particular society, that denial itself must be couched in social language and bear sufficient continuity with social attitudes so as to be understood. There is a fate-like character about the society "in" the self. We are born into certain relations and others force themselves upon us. Our freedom of choice in social companions is limited. Yet alongside these "givens" there is our own experience, our own appropriation, modification, or rejection of our social social companions' understanding. The limitations of social selfhood do not preclude the individual's own contribution to the joint authorship of self-knowledge and self-judgment. "The viewpoint which is imposed upon him by his birth at this point of history and under these particular conditions is not only a limitation but also an opportunity for discovery, not only a confinement to a relative insight but also an obligation to make the best of his insight."[10]

The social self's dependence upon its companions is a factor in all human relations. Returning to our representation of triadic form, there is always a self, social companion side. This is an avenue of reflexiveness among I, Thou, and You. In the case of the nature triad, the other two sides are formed in relation to a third entity that is not reflexive. When the third is a mediator of self-knowledge, either literally or symbolically, the relation in question is no longer "natural" in Niebuhr's sense, and we have an instance of the second basic triadic form.

The cause triad is a form of social relation characterized by commitment or loyalty.[11] In this case the third is an object or an objective to which the self is devoted. It may be another person, an institution, a program or an ideal. Devotion to this cause relates the self to other devotees of the same cause. A triad is formed in which self and social companions are loyal to one another by virtue of their loyalty to a common cause.

The cause triad is exemplified in family relations. Sibling rivalry that flourishes within the family often disappears when brothers and sisters perceive a threat from outside the family. Parents often remain social companions beyond the time of any deep love for one another simply "for the sake of the children." In these cases the family is a focus of commitment, a third that relates self and other as brother and sister, or mother and father.

The mutual loyalty characteristic of the cause triad may be seen in a black person's growing solidarity with fellow blacks. Black allegiance is a late development in compaison with the cohesiveness of immigrant groups in the United States. This delay is one consequence of a slavery system in which natural units of commitment such as family and tribe were systematically disintegrated by slave traders and owners. The process was extended beyond the days of legal slavery by a system of economic and political competition that often pitted the black person's desire to better his or her personal lot against loyalty to race. This phenomenon suggests still another example of a cause triad, the situation in which black and white cooperate out of a common commitment to economic development. This often results in the prosperity and the plight of black bourgeosie in the midst of militant black power.

In these examples, the third in the triadic situation displays characteristics that distinguish it from its counterpart in the nature triad. First, a cause is personal in the reflective sense. It is a source of self-knowledge and self-evaluation. The reciprocity of self and cause is mediated by persons with whom the self identifies. The personal element here is the same feature Niebuhr points to when he asserts that the demands of conscience are made by representative Thous, not by abstract others or an isolated Thou. The committed self is known and evaluated by the cause to which it is committed, but this self-knowledge and evaluation is mediated by social companions, remembered, present and anticipated.

Another feature of the cause that distinguishes it from the third in a nature triad is its reference to something beyond itself. Individuals who represent family commitment or racial loyalty point beyond their particular community to its cause. "They represent not the community only but what the community stands for."[12] Honesty between parent and child represents what is to be sought in all one's relations. The black solidarity called for by advocates of black power is in the name of all oppressed peoples of color.

A third feature of cause triads is that they are often overlapping and at cross-purposes. It would be quite enough to weigh the political claims of my nation upon myself and upon other nations. But this cannot be done in isolation from familial, vocational, and religious claims. I must be a father, teacher, churchman, and citizen all at once. Each of these roles is the personal focus of a network of relations among Thous. My social companions in one enterprise may appear as Its in light of some other cause to which I am committed. The causes themselves are unstable, their relevance and ranking varying from situation to situation.

There is a process of movement in the realm of personal commitment. If the third in the self - social companion - cause triad points beyond itself to another cause, then a new triad is formed with a different constituency of social companions. If the patriot's representative figures appeal to liberty in calling for national allegiance, then the patriot may finally join forces with liberty seeking persons from other nations. This may separate the patriot from some fellow citizens while uniting him with others. There will also be different faces among the group of representative Thous who now mediate the patriot's self-knowledge. This movement among causes involves the self in a progression of assessments that gives it some independence from its immediate social relations. When the third in a cause triad no longer points beyond itself, the adherents to that cause constitute the final court of appeal in self-judgment. If, for example, the ultimate cause is the nation, then some of the self's relations with foreign nationalists may be called into question by fellow patriots who interpret such relations as treasonous.

The triadic form of the self's relational interaction is grounded in the social nature of selfhood. Because the self is social, it cannot engage in isolated, one-to-one relationships. The entity to which the self is related in any given situation may dictate the number and variety of social companions, but it cannot eliminate them altogether. Because this third can be a natural object or a cause, an impersonal It or a reflective Thou, there are the two kinds of triadic relation we have discussed. Whether a triadic relation is of the nature or the cause variety is not determined solely by the third in question. The interest or disposition of the related selves may be the determining factor. Likewise, the same selves and social companions may be mutually related to natural objects and to causes simultaneously. Niebuhr's distinction between the two kinds of triadic relation is best stated in terms of the total relationship, and neither kind of triad can be ignored. The self always stands in the natural world and in a society of selves with all its claims and allegiances.

Social selves are also **time-full** selves. We exist not only in relation to one another, but in relation to the past and the future. Niebuhr grounds his analysis of the temporal self in the intimate relation of selfhood and present. The self's temporal situation is one of relations between the self and **compresent** others and events, others and events that are present **with** the self. In order for the other, the not-myself, to influence my relations it must be present still, now, or already. Self-awareness, however weak or strong, involves this compresence of the not-myself. Could I withdraw completely from such compresence, I would lose all sense of self and time. In Niebuhr's notion of compresence the temporal dimension of selfhood is understood in conjunction with the social dimension, for the compresence of an other, be it personal or impersonal, also involves the presence of social companions. Self-existence is social-temporal existence.

Time is a fundamental dimension of selfhood because the relational interaction of the social self is continuous. Memory and anticipation are acknowledgments that the relations in which the self is currently participating grew out of previous relations and will themselves develop into new relations. Were it not for the continuous interaction that the temporal dimension seeks to articulate, none of the systems or patterns of constancy that facilitate self-reflexiveness would ever emerge. Self-identity would be a meaningless notion.

The nature-cause distinction as it applies to the temporal dimension of selfhood is apparent in the two ways a self can relate to particular historical figures. To some citizens of the United

States Abraham Lincoln is simply the sixteenth president, following James Buchanan and preceding Andrew Johnson. Such citizens speak of Lincoln in terms of speeches and documents that were once instrumental in effecting certain significant changes in the course of events. Other Americans relate to Abraham Lincoln as a fellow citizen and a representative figure for the present causes of federal union and civil rights. They appeal to Lincoln in their criticism of present institutions and practices. He is a personal symbol of the nation and its professed allegiance to the cause of human dignity for all men and women.

The number and character of the self's social companions and the quality of these relations in time will be influenced by the way in which the self is related to particular historical figures and events. "Events may be regarded from the outside by a non-participating observer; then they belong to the history of things. They may be apprehended from within, as items in the destiny of persons and communities; then they belong to a life-time and must be interpreted in a context of persons with their resolutions and devotions."[13] In terms of the nature triad, persons are fated to their particular histories. We all take our place in a series of events that can be located along a time line. Seen in this way, relations in time are given. In terms of the cause triad, selves have some freedom in the interpretation and appropriation of their particular histories. We are related according to commitments and loyalties to causes that endure. All citizens of the United States relate to Lincoln as the sixteenth president. Some of them relate to him as a companion in the cause of racial justice. Because they do, Lincoln is still present, a representative Thou to whom they refer in self-judgment.

The social self's relations in the present extend into the past and the future. In this sense time is a condition of self-identity and self-understanding. The self is in time. But the relevance and impact of past and future compresences is also influenced by the self's present relations to its own particular compresent others. In this sense time is conditioned by self-identity and self-understanding. Time is in the self. Past and future are extensions of the present, and the present is always rooted in the self. In one case time is a framework for the impersonal, non-reflective relationships of the nature triad. In the other case it is an ingredient in the personal self-reflexive relationships of the cause triad.

A third dimension of human existence is the relation of social-temporal selves to what Niebuhr describes as the "radical action" whereby we have our being and have it in a particular society and time. "The radical action by which I am and by which I am present with this body, this mind, this emotional equipment, this religion, is not identifiable with any of the finite actions that constitute the particular elements in physical, mental, personal existence."[14] The self, confronted with the mystery of its very being and its being in a particular social-temporal context of relations with other beings, is made aware of its most primitive relation. This relation is with something beyond space and time, the last reality, "the creative and destructive power, whence all things come and to which they all must return."[15] This whence and whither of our being here and now seems an impenetrable mystery. Is it an alien power or a positive force? Is it simply fate, or nothing? For the moment we can identify it only as the one beyond the many, the final reality, the abyss we confront when we ask how it is that we have life and have it here and now.

When the self stands in relation to this last reality, it stands in relation to all beings. All existents are members of this triad; the extent of the self's social companions in this relationship is universal. It may be that in relation to this final third the self has its unity and its uniqueness, its integrity in the midst of pluralism. But Niebuhr points out how readily we ignore this other and the central self it reveals. The childhood question, "What am I?" becomes "What is man?" or, even more abstract, "What is a rational creature?"[16] Genuine selfhood is diminished in this progression.

To ignore the question of our identity in the ultimate context of being and time is to stand in relation to the last reality as the third in a nature triad. We understand this other as non-reflective, impersonal in its regard for the beings that pass before it. To ask the ultimate question, to seek the final boundary of our social-temporal existence, apparently adds nothing to our self-knowledge.

It might also be possible to stand in relation to the last reality as the third in a cause triad. Reaching the end of the movement through causes that point beyond themselves, the self might be related to the ultimate other as a personal force that is not indifferent to the state of the universe. Whether the final reality were demonic or gracious, whether its concern were best characterized as death-dealing or life-giving, would be another matter. But in either case, as a reflective cause it would influence the self's relations with its social companions. As personal, the object of the self's absolute dependence would affect all the self's relations in being and time.

## II. Historical Relativism

Relativism is a necessary consequence of the self's relational being. Our experience of other entities is always in terms of the relation in which we stand to those entities; ". . . all knowledge is conditioned by the standpoint of the knower."[17] Niebuhr analyzes this relational standpoint of the knower in terms of psychological, historical and religious relativism.[18]

Psychological relativism. Niebuhr distinguishes three factors that result in psychological relativism. First, all persons are restricted to a certain range of sensitivity, and particular persons have limitations within that range. None of us is able to hear certain audio frequencies that are heard by other animals, and some of us are unable to hear sounds that are easily heard by most humans. Limited sensitivity, either through the absence of the necessary faculty or through neglect, is also true with respect to the more complicated and subtle combinations of the senses.

A second factor in psychological relativism is the restriction imposed by each individual's perspective. Where and when we stand in space and time makes a difference as to what we are able to experience. I cannot witness a robbery on the other side of town while I am reading in my study. As a customer standing in the bank I do not see the robbery as I would if I were passing in the street as the robbers make their escape. The relational self has its uniqueness, in part, by virtue of the particular standpoint it occupies in space and time. No one else can fully share my point of view. But this particular standpoint also sets limits on what I am able to experience and know.

Along with the limitations imposed by sensitivity and perspective, there is the limitation imposed by reason. The mental tools
we bring to any event restrict what we are able to know of that event.
It takes more than acute sense organs and a seat on the fifty yard line
to experience the game of football as football. Without at least some
prior knowledge of the rules of the game, the scene is simply one of
semicontrolled violence. The organization and understood meaning of
the data observed depends upon the rational categories employed by the
observer.

Niebuhr's recognition of psychological relativism is not a
denial of the reality of what is seen and understood under the particular limits of sensitivity, perspective and reason. "It is not evident
that the man who is forced to confess that his view of things is conditioned by the standpoint he occupies must doubt the reality of what
he sees."[19] The symphony is real even though I only sense some of its
movement in harmony and range. A robbery has actually taken place even
though I only saw the thieves leap into the getaway car. The football
team has been penalized fifteen yards even though I do not understand
the offensive holding rules. To acknowledge psychological relativism
is simply to acknowledge that objects are known under the conditions
of the knower's relation to those objects.

Historical relativism. Historical relativism is a further
specification of psychological relativism. It is entailed by the historical nature of reason itself. If it is the case that objects are
known under the conditions of the knower's relation to those objects,
and if it is also the case that no self-other relation can be completely
abstracted from the self - social companion relation, then social reason
is an ingredient in all knowledge. Social reason, like the social self,
changes through time. The mental tools employed by the medieval scholastic were not those of the first century Palestinian Jew, nor are our
rational forms just like those of our grandparents. A person's particular place in space-time is also a point in social-cultural history.
That particularity affects not only one's vision, but the rational
equipment one brings to that vision. Historical relativism, as the
phrase is used by Niebuhr, means that the categories of reason themselves, not just their employment, are relative to the standpoint of
the observer: ". . . our reason is not only in space-time but . . .
time-space is in our reason."[20]

It is important to grasp more precisely what Niebuhr means by
reason in order to understand the significance of historical relativism.
He discusses reason in terms of the categories, concepts, patterns,
images, and symbols that we employ in our interpretation of the entities
with which we stand in relation. These rational tools have a wide range
of applicability, and Niebuhr gives them no precise definition. Basically, however, they function in the apprehension and expression of our
actual situation. "We human beings grasp and represent all reality
that presents itself to us or comes within our reach with the aid of
analogies, metaphors, ideas and images."[21]

Sometimes the image comprehends and articulates a single,
fairly unified, entity, feeling or event. The outline of the Empire
State Building represents New York City. A flower often stands for
the precious beauty of love. Sometimes a symbol in its particularity
serves as the interpretive clue for a pattern of meaning that encompasses numerous entities, feelings, and events over an extended period

of time. Such images lend form and intelligibility to experience by relating particulars to one another in larger wholes that are themselves meaningful. The tools of reason are patterns of interpretation, images that structure our relational interaction in meaningful contexts.

Symbolic form is a term Niebuhr employs in describing the function of reason. A symbolic form is an interpretive image that simultaneously represents and shapes experience. In Niebuhr's usage, somewhat different than that of Ernst Cassirer, the concept of symbolic form stresses the reciprocity between subject and object, the active role played by both observer and observed in the formation of knowledge.[22] In citing art as evidence of man's symbolic, image using character, Niebuhr states that pictorial representation "not only mirrors but guides men's changing apprehensions of actuality."[23] The dual function of symbolic form is evident in Niebuhr's description of responsibility. Responsibility theory with its four elements (response, interpretation, accountability, social solidarity) is a conceptual scheme abstracted from the symbolic form of man-the-answerer. It serves as a report of experience and an instrument of analysis.

Symbolic forms are not chosen arbitrarily. They are products of interaction between subject and object, between the experiencing self and the reality experienced. "Actuality always extends beyond the patterns of ideas into which we want to force it."[24] Some symbolic forms are more adequate than others because they comprehend a greater part of our experience. So it is that Niebuhr prefers responsibility symbolism to that of man-the-maker and man-the-citizen. The imagery taken from the common experience of persons in responsive dialogue brings into focus aspects of the relational self that other images ignore or obscure. New situations are forever modifying our images as reports of experience. These same images, as instruments of analysis, are continually shaping the understanding of things that informs our response and thereby modifies the situation.

Interpretive images emerge and function in all manner of human activity. Sometimes they are profound and disclose hitherto unrecognized dimensions of reality. Sometimes they are superficial and their use easily exceeds their scope, distorting our comprehension of the real. In John Updike's novel Rabbit Run we watch Rabbit Angstrom try to understand his present, demonstrating the MagiPeel Method of economizing vitamins and living with an alcoholic wife, in terms of an image from his past, basketball stardom in the local high school.[25] We know the frustration that comes with a self-image that does not quite fit. At another level of reasoning, we may have debated the pros and cons of American foreign policy in Southeast Asia in terms of the "domino theory," an image taken from our experience on another continent at another time. Or we may have noted the difference it makes whether we see our environment as a living organism or a complex machine, and whether we conduct ourselves as though on a battlefield or a playground.

The numerous symbolic forms operative in human understanding constitute one of the three factors that contribute to psychological relativism. But these forms and images are themselves subject to limitation. Were the same set of symbolic forms universally present to and employed by reason, the limits of sensitivity, perspective, and reason would be the sole basis of relativism. But, as Niebuhr puts the matter, "we are required in our time to recognize the further fact that the reason which operates in this restricted field is itself limited by its

historical and social character."[26] Historical relativism refers to
the fact that the images and patterns that condition human knowledge
are themselves conditioned. They are finite particulars as temporal
as the data they organize. To abstract them from the social-cultural
milieu in which they originate does not automatically give them universal status.

Historical relativism is a logical consequence of relational
selfhood in a network of interaction and change. "There seems to be
no perception of anything which does not contain an interpretation;
and there is no interpretation which is not a function of our social
communication as well as of our interaction with the objects. Communication is a three way process in which an active questioning and answering, interpreting and correcting goes on not simply between speaker
and hearer but between both of these and their common objects. Yet,
further, there are no common objects except in a society in which the
symbolic process goes on."[27] The social-temporal self is never in
precisely the same situation twice, and thus the dialogue between the
symbolic forms of reason and the relationships they serve to interpret
is continual. Furthermore, the emergence and development of symbolic
forms is subject to the joint authorship of the self and its social
companions in numerous triadic relationships. Historical relativism,
as Niebuhr uses the phrase, involves relations in being as well as in
time. It points to the fluidity of images and patterns employed by the
self standing in a particular relation to all others in the temporal
series of events, to all others in a present social-cultural environment, and to a company of social companions that varies from one situation to the next.

In Niebuhr's view, historical relativism does not deny the
reality of that which is known. Rather it takes seriously the significance of the relational standpoint of the knower. Niebuhr, looking
back on his own use of "historical relativism," suggests that "historical relationism" might be more adequate. The former term implies a
subjectivism Niebuhr does not intend.[28] Relativism points to the partiality of knowledge, not the incompleteness or absence of the known.
The relational self can step outside neither the conditions of all human experience nor the particular social-temporal context in which that
experience takes place for it. In acknowledging these consequences of
relational selfhood, relativism does not excuse ignorance and error.
It does deny the possibility of human omniscience.

Another factor in Niebuhr's denial that agnostic consequences
follow relativism is animal faith. "The acceptance of the reality of
what we see in psychological and historically conditioned experience is
always something of an act of faith; but such faith is inevitable and
justifies itself or is justified by its fruits."[29] Without this animal
faith in the reality of the partially known, the self would be para-
lyzed. No new item of knowledge could be trusted and acted upon. This
primitive faith does not justify trust in any and all knowledge. It
must be coupled with criticism. The natural scientist's confidence that
there is some correspondence between human knowledge and the real state
of affairs is not confidence in a particular scientific theory. If that
were the case, the falsification of the theory would end the enterprise.
In fact, scientists normally follow up falsification with renewed efforts
to understand the phenomenon in question. Animal faith and its fruits
are most evident in just such a situation, that is when experience contradicts our previous understanding without shaking our use of reason.

Niebuhr refers to animal faith in several realms of human endeavor, each with its own manner of proceeding critically as well as faithfully. The rational, scientific study of natural phenomena has its own system of checks and balances functioning through particular triadic relationships that manifest a deeper trust. The independent reality of that which is partially known is continually affirmed, challenged, and reaffirmed in the construction and criticism of numerous explanatory theories.

If we turn to the moral realm, we see that Niebuhr's responsibility theory operates on the animal faith that human decision and action are meaningful. It does not question the responsiveness and accountability of selfhood. Rather it asks to whom or to what a particular self is responding and in what community it is accountable. As an instrument of analysis, responsibility theory serves a critical function within the ethical realm. Moral philosophers themselves illustrate this combination of animal faith and critical method. By publishing his analyses and theories Niebuhr invites the criticism of his social companions, other participants in the moral life. Regardless of the forms these criticisms take, they will manifest a basic confidence in the meaningfulness of human agency.

Another instance of animal faith is the primitive confidence that life is worth living. It is Niebuhr's contention that persons do not live without such faith. That this basic confidence in the meaningfulness of life is expressed in a wide variety of attachments is apparent in the plurality of the gods. Niebuhr's analysis of henotheism, polytheism, and radical monotheism reveals the continual process whereby particular objects of trust and communities of loyalty stand the test of adequacy in the face of everyday human experience. Niebuhr argues that divisiveness and frustration undercut the objects of faith but not the faith itself. Thus the rejection of one god is accompanied by the acceptance of another.

Animal faith sustains what Niebuhr calls <u>objective relativism</u>. The self is objectively relativistic when it proceeds with "confidence in the independent reality of what is seen, though recognizing that its assertions about that reality are meaningful only to those who look upon it from the same standpoint."[30] One who proceeds in such a fashion must subject his or her assertions to the criticism of others who have a different perspective as well as those who share the same standpoint. But one need not deny the existence of absolutes nor give up the search for universal truths. Objective relativism does not lead to despair. It recognizes the partiality of human knowledge per se and the particular partiality of individual knowers. It invokes the critical method in order that exclusive perspectives and finite formulations not be mistaken for inclusive wisdom timelessly expounded. The fact that the self always stands in triadic relationships that involve other knowers operates as a natural though not always sufficient check on subjectivism.

<u>Religious relativism</u>. Whereas the first two limitations apply to all human knowledge, the third applies only to our knowledge of the gods. Niebuhr's strongest statement of religious relativism is that "one can speak and think significantly about God only from the point of view of faith in him."[31] Religious relativism has its basis in Niebuhr's definition of God or the gods as objects of faith, objects of trust and loyalty, thirds in the most important instance of the cause triad. Given such a definition, this form of relativism seems to follow

necessarily. If God is the object of faith, how could we know him apart from that faith? God, the objective reality, cannot be separated from faith, the subjective activity. Faith is to God as sense experience is to natural entities.[32]

Relativism in this religious sense seems to have taken on a different meaning or at least more complexity than its psychological and historical counterparts. It is not simply pointing to a limited perspective; it is pointing to the only perspective. Psychological and historical relativism do not deny movement from one perspective to another, communication between standpoints. On the basis of a verbal description I can "see" the Golden Gate Bridge even if I have never viewed a picture of it or visited San Francisco. A skillful historian can enable me to "watch" the Battle of Gettysburg and perhaps even "feel" the emotions of the participants in that event over one hundred years past. But apparently I can only know God from the perspective of faith, my faith here and now. Relativism in this sense asserts that a particular mode of relatedness provides the only access to God. Religious relativism asserts that "knowledge of God is available only in religious relation to him."[33]

Niebuhr argues that there is no such thing as faith neutrality with respect to one's final cause, the center of value in relation to which life is worth living. Faith in life's meaning is always attached to an object. Each god, as a value-center and a cause, determines the context and criteria of meaning for its adherents. Faith in one god prejudices the self's understanding of another god and the community it represents. Faith in the gods of vocation or success distorts one's perspective on the family. If the movement through causes that point beyond themselves stops with nationalism, then the patriot has a warped picture of world community and the requirements for its attainment. So it is that a self trusting in one god among many has, at best, a skewed knowledge of the last reality beyond the many.

Given the lack of faith neutrality and the distorted and conflicting evaluations made with respect to differing value-centers, Niebuhr calls for theological disinterestedness. "Religion demands that God be loved for his own sake rather than for the sake of any value, high or low, material or spiritual, which he is conceived to conserve, promote or increase."[34] This theological disinterestedness, or God-interestedness, is the positive side of religious relativism. Once again relativism is not intended to deny either the reality of universal truth or human access to it. Rather it refers to limitations on that access, and this is precisely the point at which there is a difference between religious relativism and its psychological and historical partners. The self can have knowledge of God only from the perspective of a faith relationship to God.

A further clarification of Niebuhr's position is in order. As a Protestant theologian, "a man who seeks to understand what he believes with the aid of Protestant theology," Niebuhr has a religious interest in God.[35] That is to say, he is concerned with the deity value of God, the value a reality has as the satisfaction of the religious need for that which makes life worth living. The religious question is not "Does God exist?" but rather "What being fulfills the need for God?" Theology and the problem of deity value cannot be separated, and thus the theological enterprise must be carried out in the context of faith. But this does not deny other disciplines the possibility of pursuing a nonreligious interest in the reality that the religious person calls God. "For as an action or a character may be known by the psychologist or historian without recognition of its goodness, or as a picture may be known by a chemist or a physicist without knowledge of its beauty, so the being which religion knows to be God may be known by philosophy, history or natural science without knowledge of its deity."[36] The self can have <u>religious</u> knowledge of God only from the perspective of a faith relationship to God.

To speak of an object in terms of its deity value may suggest a psychologism or religionism Niebuhr does not intend. A being has deity value by virtue of its own characteristics. It is not the human desire for a god nor the self's awareness of its religious need that sustains deity value. This value, like all others, is the consequence of an objective relationship between valued and valuing beings. Values are relative to structure and organic need.[37] They are objectively relativistic, though now that phrase refers to the object rather than the mode of inquiry whereby it is accessible. Niebuhr argues that subjective confidence in the reality of what is seen despite the awareness of a partial view has its basis in the way things actually are. The stubborn independence of reality is exemplified in the conflict and frustration that is engendered by polytheistic and henotheistic forms of faith. The embodiments of these forms go against the grain of the universe.

So it is that Niebuhr can speak of psychological, historical, and religious relativism and at the same time call for <u>religious realism</u>.[38] Religious realism has an objective interest and a critical method. While confident in the independent reality of the religious object, it is aware of the ease with which the relative can be mistaken for the absolute. While related to God in faith and with social companions similarly trusting and loyal, the religious realist is aware of the temptation to make that faith or that community its god. The basis of religious realism and objective relativism in Niebuhr's theology is twofold. The self lives and moves and has its being in the One beyond the many, and the self is social and time-full, even in its relation to the One.

III. Revelation as Organizing Principle and Transforming Power

How does the social, temporal, absolutely dependent self come to grips with its identity and organize its relations so as to act with integrity? The relational self in its psychological, historical, religious relativism raises questions of self-understadning and guidance.

An initial response to these questions is Niebuhr's theory of responsibility. Based on the image of <u>man-the-answerer,</u> it emerges from the particular experience of persons responding to one another in dialogue. Its four elements give expression to the ways in which social selfhood is manifest in moral conduct. <u>Response</u> characterizes all our acts as relational selves. Our <u>interpretation</u> is based on patterns of constancy that exist among I,Thou, and You. <u>Accountability</u> grows out of our capacity to take the position of the other. Interpretation and accountability are dependent upon <u>social solidarity</u> as I-Thou reflexiveness is dependent upon social companions. Responsive action becomes "responsible" when it takes account of the continuation of response-reaction dialogue in time and the continuity of human agency in being, when it traces the intricate webs of natural and personal relation into the future, assuming solidarity in time and being.

Yet responsibility theory is finally an empty framework. It points out but does not erase the discrepancy between one's social companions and the full extent of social solidarity. It suggests that self-integrity might be found in relation to a cause that holds the self accountable in all its other relations, but it does not identify that cause. If it is to do more than reveal the intricacies of human agency, responsibility theory with its symbolism of man-the-answerer must be coupled with an <u>organizing principle</u>, a substantive figure that can give content to the responsible life.

Niebuhr's understanding of faith as trust in and loyalty to a center of value and a cause is another way of approaching the problem of self-identity and integrity of action. The mutual trust and loyalty characteristic of a community of faithful selves manifests the self - social companion - cause configuration of relational selfhood. The object of faith held in common is personal in the reflective sense, a source of self-knowledge and judgment mediated through representative Thou's in a community of social companions. In the object of faith the self finds a landmark by which to orient its interpretations. In representative Thou's and faithful social companions the self finds the judge and jury before whom it stands accountable. In this triad of faith the self has its strongest sense of social solidarity.

We have seen that there is movement and conflict among the numerous cause triads in which the self participates. Niebuhr contends, however, that the self always stands in one preeminent cause triad, a triad of faith whereby one seeks to order all one's other relations of trust and loyalty, even if only momentarily. Herein lies the significance of the theistic forms of faith. Henotheism, polytheism, and radical monotheism are special instances of the cause triad because they refer to the self in its most fundamental confidence and loyalty. The objects of theistic faith are the final centers of value and the ultimate causes. They are the gods. For their devotees they mark the end of the movement through thirds that point beyond themselves. These objects of faith must bestow meaning when all else fails.

Many of the gods to which we attach our faith cannot support meaningful existence in the face of crisis or even through the round of common daily affairs. Such gods cannot satisfy our relgious need for that which makes life worth living. The question of religious need is not whether a god exists, but rather what being or beings have the value of deity.[39] What object or objects of faith sustain a meaningful context for any set of circumstances? Expressed in terms of responsibility theory, the question is what center of value and cause provides a sufficient focus for all our interpretations and an adequate judgment in all our accountability. The religious question can also be understood in light of the forms of faith. "The question about faith is not whether one has it or not but in what form one has it, whether for instance in pluralistic, or closed-society henotheistic, or universal form and what the implications and consequences of each form are.[40]

One's religious need for that which makes life worth living and the struggle among various forms of faith to meet that need relate to the problems of self-identity and integrity of action. Polytheism and henotheistic faiths are frustrating and divisive. Their answer to the question of life's meaning always leaves out some elements of experience, and their exclusive causes fail to integrate all the self's responses. The movement and conflict characteristic of cause triads

is seen here in a tension that seeks resolution in the direction of
the universal. The drive to radical monotheism is the last phase,
or better, the pervasive force in the movement through thirds that
point beyond themselves. The ultimate cause short of which all causes
are limited is the object of radical monotheism. It is the One beyond
the many, the source, sustenance, and end of all being, the inscrutable
power upon which the self is absolutely dependent.

If the object of faith were only a cause in the strictest
sense, that is only an object of loyalty, then perhaps the self could
pledge its allegiance to the One beyond the many simply by taking courage. But the object of faith is also a center of value, a cause that
is trusted. Faith is confidence as well as loyalty, and neither element
can exist by itself. Radical monotheism is radical faith not only because it cause is the principle of being but because that cause is also
its center of value. Radical monotheism rests its confidence in that
last reality before which all things must pass.

How can the principle of being, the mysterious action by which
I am I, be the one in which I place my confidence? How can a self trust
the void at the limits of its existence? How can it say "God" to the
slayer of all its gods? How can that which raises the question of meaning most starkly be the answer? The religious question, and with it the
problem of self-identity, is how faith in the One beyond the many is
possible. The movement of ultimate trust and loyalty from the gods to
the God of radical monotheism requires a transforming power.

IV. Jesus Christ as Symbolic Form

Jesus Christ is, for Niebuhr, the normative instance of revelation. In this historical figure, pictured in the New Testament and
operative as a symbolic form, responsibility is given content and faith
is radicalized. As organizing principle and transforming power, Jesus
Christ manifests universal responsibility and reconciles God and persons.

Jesus' practice of faith, hope, and love as pictured in the
New Testament has its source and integrity in his relation to God.
Each virtue abstracted from the others manifests a personal identity
before God that accounts for the excellence of that virtue and the
others as well. Thus, whether Jesus' virtues are taken separately or
together, "the strangeness, the heroic stature, the extremism and sub-
limity of this person, considered morally, is due to that unique devotion to God and to that single-hearted trust in Him which can be symbolized by no other figure of speech so well as by the one which calls
him Son of God."[41]

But, according to Niebuhr's analysis, this is only half the
moral picture of Jesus Christ in the New Testament. A moral relation
to the Creator is necessarily a moral relation to the creation; the Son
cannot love his Father without loving his Father's children. Jesus'
love of God, his perfect human eros, is also love of neighbor, perfect
divine agape. This double movement from man to God and God to man is
the basic rhythm Niebuhr finds in the New Testament portraits of Jesus
Christ. It is the rhythm of Jesus' moral integrity as he stands at
once in relation to God and persons. Just as the commandments to love
God and neighbor must be held together, so too must Jesus' human eros
and divine agape be understood together. Jesus' love for his neighbor,

his selfless teaching and healing, mediates God's love for His creation. Jesus exists as "the focusing point in the continuous alternation of movements from God to man and man to God."[42]

Niebuhr's preference for the Son of God figure of speech derives from his own attempts to describe Jesus Christ in the New Testament. This relational image emerges from and makes sense out of the conduct and teaching of Jesus. It gives Niebuhr a way of speaking at once about Jesus' incredible devotion to God and his utterly uninhibited service of humanity. It symbolizes the substantial relation from which terms such as double movement and mediation are abstracted. The Son of God is a figure that suggests the compelling authority of the New Testament portraits themselves. The presence of Jesus Christ in the Christian's history is not simply the memory of a great man. It is the contemporary challenge of a living God. "The power and attraction Jesus Christ exercises over men never comes from him alone, but from him as Son of the Father. It comes from him in his Sonship in a double way, as man living to God and God living with men. Belief in him and loyalty to his cause involves men in the double movement from world to God and from God to the world."[43]

The Son of God imagery manifests the same relational form as Niebuhr's triad of faith in which self and social companions are related in terms of a third, an object of trust and loyalty. This third is the reference point in a dynamic set of mutual relations among I's and Thou's. The third is personified in a representative Thou, a figure that stands for the community of trust and loyalty while at the same time pointing beyond it. As mediator in the double movement from selves to God and God to selves Jesus Christ is representative Thou in the preeminent triad of faith. "You and I and our Neighbor, Jesus Christ, and God, the Father . . . Here the structure of faith which appears in all our relationships, it seems to me, appears, in a kind of cosmic form."[44]

The vitality of the New Testament does not rest in its exhibition of a triadic faith structure or a double movement mediated by a third that points beyond itself. Its vitality is in the figure of Jesus Christ as Son of God, as one who draws persons into present relations with God and other persons. As this special occasion that illumines and directs the Christian's life, Jesus Christ functions as a **symbolic form**. " . . . in Christian life Jesus Christ is a symbolic form with the aid of which men tell each other what life and death, God and man, are **like**; but even more he is a form which they employ as an a priori, an **image**, a scheme or pattern in the mind which gives form and meaning to their experience."[45] Jesus Christ exhibits the same duality we have noted in other interpretive images. He is a symbol of the way things are, a mirror of one's actual experience, and he is a guide in one's own activity. He is a factor in the understanding and the shaping of the self's relations.

The figure of Jesus Christ, his teachings, and the events associated with his life, death, and resurrection serve as provocative parables in the dialogical relation of knower and known. The birth narratives with their mixture of shepherds and kings, stars and stables, beckon men to seek God's presence in the midst of life's variety and uncertainty. The one for whom Jesus Christ is a symbolic form cannot neglect the manifold signs in all that is alien. The Gospel accounts deal with prostitutes, tax collectors, soldiers, poor and diseased men and women. The magnetism of this symbolic form is not a little due to its ambiguity, its unwillingness to yield to our preconceptions. It is a personal figure continually urging us beyond our present definitions, pointing out new life where we have failed to look. The personal mystery of Jesus Christ as interpretive image keeps us continually off balance.

Jesus Christ as symbolic form evokes identification. A memory of two thousand years becomes a reality now when a stranger moves into our neighborhood, when the hungry ask us to share our bread, when the political prisoner seeks our support. Understood through Jesus Christ as symbolic form, the needy companion is a "Christo-morphic being, apprehended as in the form of Christ, something like Christ, though another."[46]

Jesus Christ as symbolic form evokes imitation. Some of us have worked very hard at being Christ-like. Sometimes the effort is to adopt Jesus' style. We try to follow his teachings, or copy his conduct, or love as he loved. Sometimes the imitation becomes an attempt to have Jesus take over our lives in a controlling way, making our decisions for us. But whether we want to follow in Christ's footsteps or have him actually take those footsteps for us, we discover again the mystery of this man. He is at once attractive and disconcerting, because in getting to know him we come to know much more than him. We are drawn to this figure like the disciples and like the disciples we discover more than we bargained for.

Jesus Christ points beyond himself. As symbolic form he draws us into encounter with the One before whom we are unique selves. The same Jesus who refuses the title Good Teacher lays bare the particular disobedience of one who has observed all the laws from his youth.[47] A surprising feature of this symbolic form is that in the effort to appropriate it as a model we discover ourselves in a new context. The one whom we had hoped might relieve us of responsibility brings us face to face with the God of universal responsibility.

In the figure of Jesus Christ, responsibility is given specific content. The elements of response, interpretation, accountability, and social solidarity take on concrete meaning. Seen as man-the-answerer, Jesus is in continual dialogue with the last reality before which all persons stand. Instead of trying to escape it or pretend that the encounter comes only in the future, Jesus responds to that final reality in every present. He responds to it as trustworthy. He calls this One in which the many have their being Father. "If then we try to summarize the ethos of Jesus in a formula we may do so by saying that he interprets all actions upon him as signs of the divine action of creation, government, and salvation and so responds to them as to respond to divine action."[48]

In the conjunction of the symbolic forms of Jesus Christ and man-the-answerer the Christian is given an organizing principle for self-understanding and guidance. In Jesus Christ the Christian has a demonstration of universal responsibility. But this demonstration is also the reconciliation of selves to God. As the incarnation of radically monotheistic faith, Jesus Christ is the disclosure of God's faithfulness. As the representative Thou in the faith triad that includes God and persons, Jesus Christ mediates God's concern for humanity. In his own trust and loyalty he reflects the One who is worthy of such complete commitment. What was for Jesus a response to God becomes for his successors a revelation of God. The event that elicits faith as confidence and loyalty is a demonstration of loyalty and the disclosure of a cause. The Jesus in whom faith was elicited himself becomes the elicitor, the Christ, the **transforming power**.

In revelation as transforming power the self is reconciled to the One beyond the many, the One on whom the many and the self are absolutely dependent. The last reality becomes the object of trust and loyalty, the center of value and the cause. The faith that was misdirected to the gods of henotheism and polytheism is attached to being itself. "How Jesus Christ in history, and the symbolic Christ within, reconciles men to God, or God to men, or accomplishes the double reconciliation of each to each, Christians cannot easily say."[49] It is strange that the earthly fate of the one who Niebuhr calls the incarnation of radical faith does not confirm the self's suspicion of the last reality. Everywhere Jesus turns during the final days of his life he is cruelly betrayed. All his followers, only a short while ago loudly proclaiming their commitment, are now rapidly retreating. First they are unable to watch with Jesus at Gethsemane. Then they panic and flee, the strongest of them positively denying any association with the man from Galilee.

The New Testament narratives of the trial before the Sanhedrin and the Procurator are among the most powerful literary depictions of human aloneness. Apparently there was not even that dedicated handful we have seen standing trial so often in our own time. The Passion story is not about the Jerusalem Thirteen, it is about the Jerusalem One. A single word could have reunited Jesus with his friends. Apparently the word that Pilate wanted would not have been a fitting response to God. And so he went on to be hung on a cross, this radically faithful, responsible self. How can this possibly be the event that elicits our trust in the last reality? Jesus echoes our own cry of despair before the One who destroys all our dreams. "My God, my God, why hast thou forsaken me?" Certainly at Golgotha we meet God the enemy.[50]

The miracle with which Niebuhr struggles is a present one. "How is faith in God possible?"[51] How does Jesus Christ as symbolic form work the contemporary transformation from God the enemy to God the companion? Niebuhr's assertion is not that there was a single miraculous intervention of God two thousand years ago. Niebuhr's assertion is that the spirit of the slain Jesus in unconquerable. This is the resurrection, that the one who was faithful even unto death is a present transforming power. The transition from God the enemy to God the friend is inseparably connected with the man whose response of trust and loyalty was answered in resurrection from the dead. "Of that resurrection we may know no more than that he lives and is powerful over us and among us."[52]

For Niebuhr the resurrection, whatever else it may be, is the victory of universal trust over suspicion, of universal loyalty over disloyalty. This victory is won whenever and wherever selves are reconciled to God. The establishment of friendship between God and persons is, for Niebuhr, the key problem in human existence.[53] It is in terms of this problem that Niebuhr understands Jesus Christ as revelation, as that transforming power working in our midst to the end that we may respond to the One beyond the many as friend.

When the relational self finds its identity and its integrity of action in response to the last reality, when it attaches its faith to that One beyond the many, it discovers a community of reconciliation, a body of social companions faithful to a common cause. When Jesus Christ is the transforming power and organizing principle in such a community, he is the self-transcending third in a cause triad that is the church. To follow him is to join a larger community and become a participant in a universal triad of faith that includes God and the world. In this context Jesus Christ is a representative Thou and the church is a revolutionary body seeking to extend the reconciliation of God and persons throughout the universal community of being.

## Notes

1. The Responsible Self (New York: Harper, 1963), p.71. Hereafter RS.

2. "The Ego-Alter Dialectic and the Conscience," Journal of Philosophy, 42 (1945), p.352.

3. RS, p.75.    4. Ibid., pp.72-73.    5. Ibid., p.77.

6. Ibid., p.78.    7. Ibid., p.79.    8. Ibid.

9. Journal of Philosophy, p.356.

10. "Moral Relativism and the Christian Ethic," unpublished preliminary paper for the Conference on Theological Education, Drew Theological Seminary, 1929, p.10.

11. RS, p.83. See also Radical Monotheism and Western Culture (New York: Harper, 1960), pp.21-22. Hereafter RMWC.

12. RS, p.85.

13. The Meaning of Revelation (New York: Macmillan, 1941), p.63. Hereafter MR.

14. RS, p.112.

15. "Life Is Worth Living," Intercollegian and Far Horizons, 57 (1939), p. 22.

16. RS, p.116.    17. MR, p.7.

18. In Niebuhr's discussion of relativism in MR, psychological and historical relativism both appear under the heading "Historical Relativism and Revelation," pp.7-22. See also "Moral Relativism and the Christian Ethic."

19. MR, p.18.    20. Ibid., p.10.

21. "Martin Luther and the Renewal of Human Confidence," unpublished address delivered at the centennial of Valparaiso University, 1959, pp.8-9. See also RS, pp.151-52.

22. Niebuhr acknowledges Cassirer's work, but he does not adopt Cassirer's technical meaning of symbolic form. See RS, pp.151-59.

23. RS, p.152.    24. Ibid., p.67.

25. John Updike, Rabbit Run (New York: Knopf, 1960), pp.7-9.

26. MR, p.9.

27. "Towards New Symbols," unpublished Cole Lecture delivered at Vanderbilt University, 1961, p.4.

28. "Reformation: Continuing Imperative," Christian Century, 77 (1960), p.249.

29. MR, pp.19-20. For an explicit discussion of "animal faith" as Niebuhr uses the term  see Intercollegian and Far Horizons.

30. MR, p.22.    31. Ibid., p.23.    32. RMWC, p.12.

33. The Nature of Religious Experience (New York: Harper, 1937; ed. with J.S.Bixler, R.L.Calhoun), p.112. Hereafter NRE.

34. Ibid. p.102.    35. RMWC, p.115.    36. NRE, p.112.

37. Ibid., p.113.  See also RMWC, pp.100-13.

38. See "Religious Realism in the Twentieth Century," Religious Realism, ed. D.C.Macintosh (New York:Macmillan, 1931), pp.413-28, for a discussion of religious realism in Germany and the United States.

39. NRE, p.114.

40. "On the Nature of Faith," Religious Experience and Truth: A Symposium, ed. Sidney Hook (New York:N.Y.U.Press, 1961), pp.100-01.

41. Christ and Culture (New York:Harper, 1951), p.27.

42. Ibid., p.29.    43. Ibid.

44. "The Triad of Faith," Andover Newton Bulletin, 47 (1954), pp.9-10.

45. RS, p.154.    46. Ibid., p.155.    47. Lk.18:18-24.

48. RS, p.167.    49. Ibid., p.176.    50. Mk.15:34.

51. RMWC, p.116.    52. RS, p.143.    53. Ibid., p.44.

JESUS AND POWER

Frederick Herzog


Duke University


To address Christology today is somewhat of a venture. We
know most of the historical conditions that produced the creeds of the
church. We are also aware of numerous historical circumstances that
account for the shaping of the New Testament literature. It is
obvious that there was a long and complex development from Peter's
confession of Jesus' Messiahship (Mt. 16:16) to Chalcedon's formulas
of the God-man.

For many Christians it is impossible today to repeat the
creeds of the church without inquiring about the base these creeds can
rely on in Christian origins. There is of course the pathetic move of
playing off the simple Gospel against the hellenistic creeds when there
is nothing simple about the Gospel. We shall not fall into that trap.
The real question is: What actually happened which made for that big a
difference in Judaism to trigger a new faith movement called Christianity? The question has been asked many times before. But it has not as
yet been pondered under the shadow of the decline of Western theology.

"Whatever Happened To Theology?"[1] was the question put by
Christianity and Crisis to a number of theologians a few months ago.
The answers vary widely. But the question could not have been raised
had there not been a feeling of a decisive change in Western theology.
That we all experience an incision in theological sensibility cannot be
gainsaid. Business as usual is passé. The hypothesis needs to be ventured that Western Christianity may have spent itself. It would be
surprising if the decline of the West would not involve a decline of
Western Christianity with its theology.

Christianity in the West for centuries has been asking mainly
two questions: (1) In what sense is Jesus the Christ? (2) In what sense
is Jesus also God's Son? Perhaps, in the end, these are questions
theology in the West will still be asking for centuries to come. But
in this moment of change a long-neglected question challenges us with
irresistible force: In what sense did Jesus remain a Jew?

Obviously Jesus was not a Christian. But this factor is seldom given much attention. What happened in Judaism itself providing
the basis for Hellenistic and Roman Christianity and later for Western
Christianity as a whole is, however, of great consequence. We also
need to know the immediate pre-history of church history. What kind of
socio-cultural milieu did Jesus function in? What mainsprings of action
were provided him by his society?

These questions are of course being asked in biblical studies all along. But it is surprising how little they get asked in systematic theology as to their doctrinal implications.

## Grafted Into Israel

Systematic theology easily brushes over the biblical context where these questions manifest their doctrinal import. About the relationship of Gentiles to Jews St. Paul, for example, tells the Romans: "But if some of the branches were broken off, and you, a wild olive shoot, were grafted in their place to share the richness of the olive tree, do not boast over the branches." (R. 11:17) The point is: the Gentile becomes part of Israel. Through faith in Jesus the Gentile becomes a Jew. I should not overstate the point. But according to the usual way of formulating the issue the Gentile needs to become a Christian. One consequence thereof is the frequent expectation that also the Jew must become a Christian.

The expectation of the Jew having to become a Christian is tied to Christianity as a cult religion where Jesus as the Christ has largely turned into a cult figure. Here Christian cult language explains itself through Christian cult language ad infinitum. That is what Christian theology tends to be all about in many quarters. But the systematic theologian needs first of all to understand the immediate prehistory of the Christian movement. The Old Testament is studied carefully by Christian scholars. What we need to consider in systematic theology is what it means that Jesus was still a Jew.

Some things in the public ministry of Jesus we tend to overlook. The strangest systematic theology blindspot is the reason for his end on the cross. Much historical material needs to be sifted before one grasps the reasons for the trial resulting in a death sentence. Scholars are not in agreement as to what really happened. One thing we can all be certain of is that there was a power conflict between Jesus of Nazareth and those in authority. We often tend to overlook this because the cross has been integrated in Christianity as a cult religion. One focuses on its religious significance rather than on its historical causes.

Religion is a many-splendoured tricky thing. One of its tricky aspects is mystification. It often is in the hands of wily professionals who exact tribute from a credulous following. But in Jesus' day there were those in the lower class who were countering the professionals with their official myth and taking things into their own hands. The general mood is reflected in objections to the scribes and the Pharisees: "Woe to you, scribes and Pharisees, hypocrites! because you shut the kingdom of heaven against men; for you neither enter yourselves, nor allow those who would enter to go in....Woe to you, scribes

and Pharisees, hypocrites! for you tithe mint and dill and cummin, and
have neglected the weightier matters of the law, justice and mercy and
faith." (Mt. 23:13.23)

One cannot understand the pre-history of Christianity except
as an internal struggle in Israel between those who had been disadvan-
taged by the religious professionals and these very professionals.
This does not say anything against Judaism as a whole. It's rather
that also in Judaism there were those in power and those who were powerless.

The struggle with the official myth of Israel created all
kinds of intellectual and psychological tensions difficult to disentangle today. But it is altogether clear that the basic struggle was a
power conflict over the visio dei and the imago dei. It was a question
of what all this history of Israel was finally coming to as regards the
character of God and human selfhood.

In general terms, the new vision of God as the waiting God[2]
or as costly love[3] is widely acknowledged. But it is much less understood that the new view of God was interdependent with a new view of
human selfhood. The full implications of both new visions were not
immediately clear. Perhaps it took nearly two thousand years of Christian history in countless interpretation experiments to come to a small
measure of understanding. Especially unclear remained the human selfhood dimension. One only has to take a careful look at the creeds to
get the point. Chalcedon, for example, worries about the God-man relationship and has little to say about who this man is who joins divinity
and humanity in perfect union.

The blindspot pertains to the crucial factor in the power
conflict in Jesus' public ministry. What upset the authorities was
that here unschooled persons took it upon themselves to work out the
meaning of the official myth: "'How is it', they said, 'that this un-
trained man has such learning?'" (Jn. 7:15) A little later we read:
"The Pharisees retorted, 'Have you too been misled? Is there a single
one of our rulers who has believed in him, or of the Pharisees? As
for this rabble, which cares nothing for the Law, a curse is on them."
(Jn. 7:47-49)[4] The blindspot theme is here clearly articulated: the
powerful and the rabble. For the Pharisees, according to this report,
there were persons and non-persons. Some belonged to a worthy in-
group, others were sheer rabble - white trash.

The challenge is to get deep into Judaism in this regard -
and not just into "Christian Christology". The God encounter is here
first of all tied to a particular Covenant context. Within this context something happened among non-persons that might be as paradigmatic
for human history in the West as Chalcedon.

## A Western Paradigm

Among the many interpretations of Jesus of Nazareth in the West, much of the major concern has centered in cross and resurrection. This is especially true of the Protestant tradition, also of the more recent giants of Protestant theology of whom Bultmann and Barth are perhaps the most representative. In Bultmann's famous demythologizing essay it soon becomes clear that the Jesus he is mainly focusing on is the crucified Jesus who "bears vicariously the sin of the world, and by enduring the punishment for sin on our behalf...delivers us from death."[5] This mythological view, according to Bultmann, needs interpretation as judgment of the world, and as judgment and deliverance of man as well. The cross involves a redemptive word. All who hear it need to appropriate it by being crucified with Christ. Concentration on the cross, however, is not enough. Cross and resurrection form a whole. Faith in the resurrection is not belief in a miracle disrupting the course of nature, but appreciation of the saving efficacy of the cross. In the kerygma, cross and resurrection go together. In the preaching of the Word of God both are means of salvation.

Julius Schniewind already observed that in Bultmann's essay "the synoptic gospels are never so much as mentioned as evidence for the kergyma, and John figures only as the satellite of Paul."[6] Bultmann, in turn, complained about Schniewind's metaphorical view that Jesus Christ "incorporates his own in himself as a king includes his people."[7] The debate on demythologizing might have taken on a different character had these reflections been pressed further. Even Bultmann saw Jesus' destiny bound up with that of the whole human race.[8] But the issue of the corporateness of selfhood was not seen as central at that time. Bultmann was still caught up in the centrality of the Enlightenment struggle of "God the Problem".[9] In this orientation his primary concern was whether or not God could act in the "modern world" of cause and effect. He wanted to stress our being addressed by God here and now - being questioned and judged by him.[10] And yet he never took the person of Jesus into account in this regard. The struggle of Jesus in Israel made little difference.

It is almost painful at times to listen to the individualized emphasis of Bultmann's thought. "My existential self-understanding... my concrete encounter, my past and future"[11] are at stake in the preaching of the Word. The presupposition seems to be all along that the self involved in the self-understanding presents no real problem. God somehow has to prove to the self that he can act in the world. But the possibility that the self might be asking the wrong questions on this score hardly enters the picture.

In Bultmann's interpretation we are struggling with the Christian view of the cross as a saving event. We are very much on the "Christian" side of the Jesus story. If one also takes into account

the existentialist mold into which Bultmann was wont to press this
event one becomes sensitive to the possibility of an ideology operative here that might conceal the more radical dimensions of the Jesus
story.

I can no longer simply begin with the assumption that God always
acts in Christian origins about the same way with cross and resurrection
as   hermeneutical norm.  Perhaps the cards are being stacked too
neatly by the Western interpretations of God's action we have become
accustomed to.  Before I answer the question whether God is acting in
history I first need to ask: which action are we talking about?  The
notion that God is acting in history dare not become a matter of
course.  With Bultmann in any case it is tied too quickly into the
cross and the resurrection theme alone.

With Barth it is in principle very much the same, his differences with Bultmann in detail notwithstanding.  In fact, here we have
a much more confident affirmation of God acting in history.  Revelation
is assumed to be taking place all along in the Covenant story.  In the
cross, the Judge finally takes the place of the judged and lets them go
free.  In the resurrection this becomes manifest as truth.  "If it is
the case that Jesus Christ has made our sin His own, then He stands in
our place as the Representative of our evil case and it is He who
answers for it (as ours).  It is then (as ours) the sin which is forgiven us in Him....Made sin for us, He stands in our place."[12]  As the
story of Barth's dogmatics unfolds it becomes clear that Barth accepts
the picture language of the New Testament as a whole.  The Church
Dogmatics is one vast effort of faithfulness to the Scriptural witness.
On its own grounds, this move makes sense.  That is, if one agrees to
the principle one can also agree to most of what is being proposed in
detail.

Somehow in Barth the premise is also the result.  Jesus
Christ becomes the true history not only of humankind, but also of God.
And it needs especially to be underlined that Jesus' history is for
Barth our history: "We have been speaking of Him and therefore of
justified man, of His history and therefore our own."[13]  For Barth,
this is not a merely symbolical or metaphorical way of speaking: "It
is not a mere figure of speech to say that in faith man finds that
the history of Jesus Christ is his history."[14]  It is the direct
ontological truth of history.  This involves in more ways than one a
great difference from Bultmann.  Barth acknowledges a real role of the
person of Jesus.  And yet Jesus as person, in the end, is subject to
the cross-resurrection theme, so that the primary focus of Barth's
doctrines of incarnation and atonement is the transaction between God
and man: God's righteousness is restored, God's justice prevails,
God's grace triumphs, and man is again acceptable in God's sight.

The genuine strength of the paradigm Barth works with cannot
be denied. And in contradistinction from Bultmann Barth lets cross
and resurrection interact significantly with the person of Jesus. What
is more, Barth carefully emphasizes "the one covenant"[15] that binds Jew
and Gentile together. It is only that Barth does not raise the issue
of Jesus' personhood within Israel on its own merit. So here too the
power conflict between the rabble and the powerful is overlooked as
significant factor of theological construction. The point we need to
keep in mind is that the Western paradigm of Christology largely sees
the Christ story as a transaction between God and man: God is satisfied,
and all is well with my soul. The implications of the new man-to-man
relationships in the person of Jesus do not become a decisive factor
for theological reflection.[16] This may seem for many an irrelevant
point. But it may well be that the tradition has so "brainwashed" us
that we tune out significant data from the beginning of theological
research.

### Jesus as Jew

The impression dare not arise that there have been new data
"unearthed" in the Jesus story which now need to be evaluated. It is
rather a question of what to do with data already available. Geza
Vermes, in Jesus the Jew, offers some simple points that delimit the
blindspot of systematic theology fairly well. There is first of all
the contrast between Galilee, the countryside Jesus came from, and
Judea. In one way it is the contrast between rural life and the metropolis: "At home among the simple people of rural Galilee, he must have
felt quite alien in Jerusalem."[17] Jesus came from among those not belonging to the Jerusalem power structure. He was not a member of an
in-group: "It appears that in the eyes of the authorities, whether
Herodian or Roman, any person with a popular following in the Galilean
tetrarchy was at least a potential rebel." Some Jewish leaders apparently felt on edge: "It would seem in effect that during a period
of riots in Jerusalem the unspecified charge levelled against Jesus by
the civic leaders was that as a teacher he had won over many Jews."
So it is understandable "that the first Jewish Galilean version of
Jesus' life and teaching was conceived in a politico-religious spirit."
The Galileans on the whole were considered peasants who carried the
stigma "of a religiously uneducated person." The long and short of
it is that Jesus usurped the prerogative of power. Did a Galilean have
the right to teach the people? "Jesus became a political suspect in
the eyes of the rulers of Jerusalem because he was a Galilean."

Obviously Jesus and his disciples while breaking new faith
ground in Galilee were not working on a textbook of systematic theology.
What we first find in Jesus' words and acts are new shades of meaning,
slight shifts of emphasis, and new relationships between human beings.

And yet in a placid countryside and in the midst of a quiet community a powerful nuclear fission of the spirit takes place. A new dynamics enters the historical process. The rabble claimed its rightful place of sonship and daughterhood before God against the tutelage of the religious professionals. Power was redistributed. It reached even the most wretched and debased. What was happening was not necessarily something absolutely unique to Jesus: "Jesus and the Essenes thought that the social outcasts and oppressed would become the first in the very near divine future."[18] Yet in the person of Jesus what was common to him and other Jews became effectively embodied in lasting relationships in public space. In Jesus the new power distribution found the momentum to persevere in history.

We are not adducing much material, but lifting out what is often overlooked. The God of Abraham, Isaac, and Jacob was struggled with in Galilee in a new politico-religious constellation. He was no longer cooped up in the Jerusalem temple under the sovereign control of the priest and the rulers. He proved sovereign again in the freedom of the people who followed their destiny in the person of Jesus.

What we have here is also a struggle between new and old categories of understanding (cf. Mt. 9:17). Nothing is put neatly in small pieces on a platter of insight. The crucial factor remains the conflict, the striving, the new dynamics. Later on St. Paul will talk about "God in Christ". But this is not a neat formula either. One always has to see its interdependence with a complex context. "God in Christ" first of all is a missionary formula that makes the God of Abraham, Isaac, and Jacob for me as a Gentile my very own, always within the context of the basic power conflict. Here in the person of Jesus a power shift begins. While the immediate consequences were not "world-wide", the process of history was infused with a new change agent effecting a new direction and a new quality of life. The result was a new power balance.

Eugene B. Borowitz, in a paper on "Contemporary Christologies: A Jewish Response",[19] offers us an excellent point of entry for new reflection. He believes that with an approach as that of Barth there is no dialogue possible between Jews and Christians. There is no common ground in a mutually accepted interpretation of Scripture. A dialogue might seem possible, however, at the point where the power shift in Israel is seen by Jew and Christian alike and where both can ponder the effect of the outcast's central place in God's work. The battle between traditionalists and liberals Borowitz sees as central might be transcended at this point.

Borowitz argues the christological issues with a great number of contemporary theologians. Our brief summary of his critique merely seeks to show the lacuna in Christian theology which in part may ac-

count for the lack of encounter between Jewish thought and systematic
theology. The critique points to a reconsideration of material in the
Gospel story neglected too long by the systematic theologian.

A core objection by Borowitz pertains to overemphasis on
individualism. Jesus seems to function only in terms of a personal
paradigm. He is the center of the Christian life. Jewish life is
centered in the people's history and offers a more social context for
individual existence. The question is how Christians can move from an
individual as central cult figure to a sense of social responsibility.
Other issues arise in regard to the irreplaceability of the individual,
the reconciliation of humanity with God, and the capacity to love an
unseeable God. Time and again the Christian emphasis on the uniqueness
of Jesus seems to obscure God's transcendence through its identification with contingency. Even the Christ on the cross theme obscures
this transcendence: Powerlessness as such does not clarify the reality
of God, whereas holiness does.

I am much indebted to the Borowitz analysis. But I am not
going to suggest that Christian theologians now dissociate themselves
from the superstructure of Christian belief that has accumulated over
nearly two thousand years of church history. It is my heritage and I,
for one, intend to stand by it.[20] But it cannot be denied that in many
ways the superstructure has also obfuscated the pristine power of the
originative Christian event. Would it be possible for Jews and Christians to dialogue at least on Jesus as a Jew not as yet caught up in
Christian individualism? Would it perhaps be possible for Christians
to see how he embodied the corporateness of Jewish selfhood in a new
way in that also the outcast and oppressed were acknowledged as part
of the self? And might it not be already at this point that a new
act of God changed the human condition so radically that the memory
of this act never got lost? If there is any point for the Christian
to talk about God's incarnation, it has something to do with Jesus'
Jewishness. To stay with the Christian formula, God did not become
just man, he became a Jew.

The question of course is what this could possibly mean. It
amounts to much more than a merely academic argument. The search for
global human community is taxing us all. Books are written, groups
gather for study, and foundations publish reports. Time and again
these various efforts come down to the question of the character of
human selfhood. A recent Hazen Foundation study puts it in concise
terms: "This concern for the other, this transcendence of self,
whether that 'self' be an individual, nation, class, race or creed, is,
we venture to affirm, the essence of morality. Without such morality,
not only will the human condition remain highly precarious, but the
needed universalism, even if achieved, will prove to be impotent and
without content and the desired humanism will bring more evil than

good."[21]  Both the Jewish and the Christian community need to ask: is transcendence of self indeed the essence of morality?  Is "morality" all we have to be concerned about?  What does our common tradition have to contribute?  Could not the feeling of the need to transcend the self be exactly the problem?  Was Jesus as a Jew perhaps saying that the self is dual or corporate in the first place and need not be transcended, but merely calls for acknowledgment in its true structure?

Might it not be that only in a false arrangement of power we feel the need to "transcend" the self?  It may well be that the self offers the appearance of separateness where human beings begin to lord it over one another, that is, where power is abused to divide humankind into persons and non-persons.  In order to make a clear point here the Christian needs the Jewish understanding of Jesus' selfhood.  This does not mean that we will then immediately solve all problems.  But there might just be a fighting chance that we finally will find a common ground of Scripture interpretation helping "the needed universalism"[22] emerge creatively.  Christianity alone seems incapable of making the contribution mankind so sorely needs today.  Within our Western tradition it will take a concerted effort of seeking to recover our common roots.

The interdependence of the notion of selfhood with the issue of power is the crucial point.  The Hazen report immediately speaks of "the differential in power that exists between nations and cultures." In regard to reconstituting the human community "one of the questions to bear in mind is how to overcome, limit or compensate for the distortions and limitations imposed by the power configurations among nations."[23] To some it might seem that this still leaves us entirely in the realm of _Realpolitik_ (not pertinent to theology).  But this would simply be a misunderstanding of the interlocking of theology and culture: "The flow of culture is often a function of the differentials in power, of political and economic strength, but it can only be maintained if the stronger power is culturally productive as well."[24]  Theology needs to understand that the exercise of power is a function of one's view of selfhood.  As long as the self is able to bracket out segments of humanity as not belonging to the self the power differential will wreak havoc on some members of the human family.  In the prevailing notion of selfhood in Western culture, we usually have value as human beings when in some form we acquire power over others.  We think of making it on the ladder of success which is one way of acquiring power over others. One glorious little self here is still pitted against another not so glorious self.  The resources of the Judeo-Christian tradition are there to be marshalled against this outlook at the point where Jesus as member of Israel created the power balance between human beings by acknowledging the marginals as part of the self.  Power corrupts at the point where the weak, the poor, and the maimed are viewed as non-persons.  And absolute power corrupts absolutely where everyone beside

oneself is viewed as non-existent except as prop for one's self-aggrandi-
zement.

## Theology In Red, White, and Black - and Israel

It is on this background that we need to look once more at the
ethnic struggles Protestant theology went through this past decade.
To some it seemed an exercise in futility.  And yet, in the end, this
was the only we were able to recover the corporate truth of the Christian faith which had escaped us for so long.  It was an overpowering
acknowledgment of corporate selfhood that in New Testament times finally brought Jew and Gentile together in one humanity.  Here the enmity
had been overcome.

Benjamin Reist recently has offered us an excellent overview
of what the ethnic struggles of the past years theologically were all
about.[25]  In the exceptionally creative development of a position of
his own, Reist puts once more before us the fundamental issues.  In a
few bold strokes from the outset he makes it clear why theology can no
longer disregard the color-line.

Initially I will try to draw out Reist's basic point and then
I will seek to extend his argument along the line indicated in my
present essay.  It should be clear throughout, however, that for Christianity the need of overcoming our separations does not lie in the realization of our pluralism as such.  It lies in the originative event,
not because of its primitiveness, but because of its ontological truth.
In Jesus as a Jew the true structure of human selfhood was acknowledged.

How can we best get at the root hermeneutical issue?  Reist
very much begins with an analysis of the historical experience of
American theology: "We hear much talk these days of an American theology.
None worthy of the name will ever emerge unless it has its beginnings as
a theology in red, white, and black."[26]  It is a matter of course to
Reist that there is more to humanity than these three colors: "These
are not all the hues that make up the full mosaic that is humanity.
The attempt is beginning only, envisioning the unfolding one day of
theology in red, white, black, brown, and yellow, against the background
of the blue earth, our mother.  But the process must begin with the attempt at a theology in red, white, and black.  For these are the historic
American components of that full mosaic that is humanity, all of which
is now present in this land.  These are the three components that
initially became indigenous by way of a tragically brutal but nevertheless irreversible process."[27]  It cannot be denied that it was within
this context that the ethnic challenge impacted theology.  But we dare
not overlook how much the Cartesian starting point of theology may still
remain with us unless with forethought we exclude it from our premises.
Are we going to define American theology as theology in red, white, and
black right away at its beginnings or are we going to ground its

beginnings in the originative event?  Theology in red, white, and black
can still appear as basing true selfhood on human experience.  And so
again, in the end, God-certainty might come as an afterthought based on
our experience.  In Christian origins it is first of all the sovereign
God who empowers human beings to acknowledge the structure of selfhood.

Express acknowledgment of "the gospel of Jesus the Christ
that is at the heart of the being of all the churches"[28] comes only
after Reist's significant reflections on red, white, and black have already placed us into our American context.  A little while later Reist
quotes Vincent Harding: "There will be no new beginnings for a nation
that refuses to acknowledge its real past."[29]  By the same token, one
could say, there will be no new beginnings for a church that refuses
to acknowledge its real past.  Reist certainly does not wish to get
caught in not acknowledging the past.  In the end of the book he relates to the originative events of the church as forcefully as one
might ever hope.    But can we afford not to do this relating right
at the beginning?  Does not God's liberation hinge on what he has done
once and for all in the person of Jesus, so that we need to be incorporated into his selfhood before we try to weld together red, white,
and black?

There still is a very fundamental issue at stake in our struggle with the ethnic dimensions of our American existence.  The point of
our identification with black or red today (becoming black or becoming
red) is not general overcoming of the color-line, but specific overcoming of the oppression-line.  The color-line as such is not the problem,but its affording opportunity for one person to lord it over another,
debasing the other person.  Speaking of becoming black or becoming
red[30] is a new attempt to find a contemporary mode for grasping Jesus'
radical identification with oppression.

This is the factor that our focus on Jesus as Jew keeps in-
escapably before us.  The small beginnings of Christianity in Judaism
contain the reconstitution of human selfhood exactly at the point
where the individual self is usurping the power of the corporate self.
It is not built into the created structure of human selfhood that one
individual should lord it over another.  No human being has a right to
prey on the other: "Even the possums and the skunks know better!  Even
the weasels and the meadow mice have a natural regard for their own
blood and kin.  Only the insects are low enough to do the low things
people do - like those ants that swarm on poplars in the summertime,
greedily husbanding little green aphids for the honeydew they se-
crete."[31]  It is their corruption of power that enables human beings to
do the low thing of preying on each other.  Underlying the power corruption is the exclusion of the other from one's selfhood.  The Jesus
event acknowledges the other as part of the self, especially the mar-
ginal other.  The commandment to love the other as oneself is not an
invitation to love an alien other, but finally to discover the other
as co-constitutive of one's self.  This awareness of one's identity in

corporate selfhood emerges in the Judeo-Christian tradition in the
wrestle with the Jesus event at the very base level of Christian origins in Judaism.

Unless we see that our struggle with theology in red, white,
and black has this ethnic bottom-line in Judaism we bypass the basic
ethnic dilemma of Christianity. It is Christian identity in Jesus
that we are time and again unclear about. And this means that we are[32]
unclear about Christian identity in the corporate selfhood of Israel.
In Jesus' corporate selfhood we become incorporated in a power balance
that makes us different human beings. It was in the struggle for this
power balance that in Judea the powers that be decided against the
Galilean liberator. But the power issue was not peculiar to Israel:
"You know that the rulers of the Gentiles lord it over them, and their
great men exercise authority over them. It shall not be so among you;
but whosoever be great among you must be your servant." (Mt. 20:25f.)
This does not mean that Jesus was trying to turn people into lackeys
of the powerful. His concern pertained to mutuality in the corporate
self where there is equality because of mutual acknowledgment of freedom. This reconstitution of power is seldom considered very important,
although the cross finally followed from it.

## Becoming Vulnerable

It is impossible from the Christian perspective to speak of
Jesus as though his cause were a matter of sheer humanism. In his
power struggle God's power is at stake. The fulfillment of the great
and first commandment is interdependent with the second in that God's
presence is involved in the human being. Jesus sought to free human
beings for an adequate imaging of God in balancing power. In the process, God himself proved to be deeply immersed in this effort. He
appeared as the power that undoes the human corruption of power. The
only way human corruption knew to assert itself was the attempt to
destroy the new balance of power. Thus the cross. And then the resurrection. Obviously here new problems emerge. But everything goes
wrong if we pontificate about the presence of God in Jesus without
taking the Jewish context into account.[33] All along the first Jews
who witnessed to the cross did not mean to suggest that now the power
balance had disappeared in sheer powerlessness. Tremendous strength
had been sustained even in the cross. The cross had occurred basically in terms of: "My power is made perfect in weakness." (II Cor.
12:8) It says that power is perfected, not that it turns into sheer
powerlessness.

We cannot go on here without recalling Auschwitz. Any
Christian theology that does not know solidarity at this point has
hardly understood the character of corporate selfhood. Emil L.
Fackenheim has brought this out with great clarity: "A good Christian
suggests that perhaps Auschwitz was a divine reminder of the sufferings of Christ. Should we not ask instead whether his Master himself,

had He been present at Auschwitz, could have resisted degradation and
dehumanization? What are the sufferings of the Cross compared to
those of a mother whose child is slaughtered to the sound of laughter
or the strains of a Viennese waltz? This question may sound sacrile-
gious to Christian ears. Yet we dare not shirk it, for we - Christian as well as Jew - must ask: at Auschwitz, did the grave win the
victory after all, or, worse than the grave, did the devil himself
win?"[34] Fackenheim's point about the difference between Jesus' sufferings and Auschwitz needs to be accepted as premise of any solidarity. The tendency among Christians to make the cross the acme of
human suffering Fackenheim punctures effectively.

Jesus' cross became the occasion for a number of Jews, the
early apostles and their followers, to understand their existence in
a life-affirming way. The cross, in the light of the resurrection,
was viewed as sustaining corporate selfhood through and beyond death.
Here some of the promises to Israel seem fulfilled: Gentiles were
drawn into the covenant.

All my theological tasks as a Gentile hinge on the fact that
my notion of God is rooted in Israel's God. Whatever I do to clarify
my notion of God is an attempt to clarify Israel's notion of God as
communicated to me through the first Jews who were Jesus' followers.
I do not wish to distort the Jewish notion of God. But at the root
of my Gentile faith in God lies a reconstituted Jewish notion of God.
I do not have to decide to become vulnerable at this point.[35] I am
vulnerable. The problem is that I cannot "prove" the involvement of
this God as countervailing force in the power struggle of history.
Christianity itself has certainly not lived up to God's involvement
in history in a convincing way.

Auschwitz seems utterly to contradict God's presence in
history. Emphasis on the powerlessness of God is certainly not the
answer. Instead, there is the immensity of evil to be considered.
The human potential for conspiracy in evil seems limitless. Men do
rise up and play God. Power can be usurped. Arrogation of absolute
power corrupts absolutely. This also became the Christian sin. The
Holocaust is an occurrence for which a Christianized people, the
German nation, became accountable in terms of a demonic usurpation of
power.

Jesus' cross is the exact opposite, a sacrifice of life to
end all human sacrifice, the countering of usurped power by a new
power balance.[36] From Jesus' corporate selfhood, interdependent with
cross and resurrection, power breaks forth that empowers human beings
to create decent power structures. The search for God's presence in
history is thus the quest not for powerlessness, but for countervailing power affirming life and enabling people to exist as persons. Yet
when a Christian theologian suggests that at the cross the mismanage-
ment of power ceases he becomes utterly vulnerable. There is a

credibility gap. Only a Christianity renewed in corporate selfhood might be able to bridge it.[37]

## NOTES

[1]"Whatever Happened To Theology?", Christianity and Crisis, 35:8 (May 12, 1975), 106-120.

[2]As I occasionally have put it, for example, in "Towards the Waiting God," in The Future of Hope: Theology As Eschatology (New York, 1970), 51-71.

[3]Cf. my Liberation Theology (New York, 1972), 179.

[4]NEB

[5]Hans Werner Bartsch (ed.), Kerygma and Myth (New York, 1961), 35.

[6]Ibid., 67.

[7]Ibid., 106.

[8]Ibid., 112.

[9]Title of the book by Gordon D. Kaufman, God the Problem (Cambridge, 1972).

[10]Bartsch, Kerygma and Myth, 196f.

[11]Ibid., 203.

[12]Karl Barth, Church Dogmatics, IV/1 (Edinburgh, 1956), 241.

[13]Ibid., 629.

[14]Ibid., 636.

[15]Ibid., 670.

[16]The only place I know of in Barth where this dimension breaks through adequately is IV/1, 106. But the insight does not begin to function significantly in this volume in Barth's further theological construction.

[17]Geza Vermes, Jesus the Jew (London, 1973), 49. The following quotations are from pp. 49-57.

[18]David Flusser, Jesus (New York, 1969), 77.

[19]Presented at the annual meeting of the American Theological Society, April 4-5, 1975, New York.

[20]Even as Barth is using the Christian dogmatic tradition for the construction of his theological perspective he is aware of its function as "defense mechanism". See IV/1, 127. Cf. Paul Tillich, Systematic Theology, vol. 2 (Chicago, 1957), 141f.

[21]Reconstituting the Human Community, A report sponsored by the Hazen Foundation (New Haven, 1972), 28.

[22]Ibid.

[23]Ibid., 10.

[24]Ibid., 24.

[25]Benjamin A. Reist, Theology In Red, White, and Black (Philadelphia, 1975).

[26] Ibid., 25.

[27] Ibid., 24f.

[28] Ibid., 32.

[29] Ibid., 45.

[30] Ibid., 180.

[31] William Styron, The Confessions of Nat Turner (New York, 1966), 221.

[32] Recently James Wm. McClendon, Jr., Biography As Theology (Nashville and New York, 1974), has offered the significant suggestion of the need to develop an "ethic of character-in-community" (p. 32). Since "Christianity turns upon the character of Christ" (p. 38), it is time and again necessary to recover the dimensions of his self-hood as center of Christian character-in-community. Character is first of all perseverance of commitments in the basic structure of human selfhood. This is what Jesus brings to the fore. The new thinking that is going on right now in recovering the corporate dimensions of theological work finds strong support in the excellent essay by Leland J. White, "Christology and Corporate Ministry," American Benedictine Review, 26:1 (March 1975), 54–74.

[33] It created endless havoc in theology when Schleiermacher declared: "Christianity cannot in any wise be regarded as a remodelling or a renewal and continuation of Judaism." The Christian Faith (Edinburgh, 1928), 61.

[34] Emil L. Fackenheim, God's Presence In History (New York, Evanston, San Francisco, London, 1972), 75.

[35] Carol Christ in "Whatever Happened To Theology?", Christianity and Crisis (May 12, 1975), 114, speaks of being "vulnerable to experience". It may be that the most taxing vulnerability for the Christian theologian comes in the encounter with Judaism.

[36] In order to explain fully what is implied one would need to offer an analysis of the Christian doctrines of the atonement, especially their assessment in the Anglo-Saxon tradition. For a convenient overview see Robert S. Paul, The Atonement and the Sacraments (New York and Nashville, 1960), 135ff. And a dialogue with more recent christological statements would be inevitable. The general tendency still is to orient oneself in the way the issues were raised in the eighteenth and nineteenth century European discussion. Two recent volumes offer helpful foci for orientation: Hans W. Frei, The Identity of Jesus Christ (Philadelphia, 1975); Eugene TeSelle, Christ In Context (Philadelphia, 1975). For the initial impetus of the present essay I am indebted to discussions with Brevard S. Childs and James A. Sanders.

[37] The perspective here proposed has far-reaching consequences. The power balance reality in Jesus pertains beyond the ethnic line also to the male-female relationship. For an overview of the issues see Rosemary Radford Ruether, Religion and Sexism (New York, 1974).

TOWARD A CRITICAL THEOLOGY

Charles Davis

Concordia University

The Meaning of Criticism:

In speaking of a critical theology I have in mind a meaning of "criticism" and "critical" that goes back to Kant, though
with subsequent modification and clarification. Criticism in that
sense may be defined as a process of self-reflection, motivated by
an interest in emancipation. It is a reflection that uncovers and
appropriates the freedom and creative autonomy of the self in its
world.

The self through reflection becomes aware of the formative
processes which create every society and every individual. It
consciously grasps the a priori conditions of every region of
experience, with its objects, actions and interests. The uncovering
of those conditions manifests where and how each type of experience
is grounded and allows an explicit determination of its limits and
validity.

Such reflection is emancipatory, because it dissolves the
apparent necessity of the given world and reveals the creative
potentiality of men for freely constructing their world and themselves,
or, better, their selves in their world.

There is a contrast here between a mythical and a critical
consciousness. A mythical consciousness accepts an order of the
world and society as given prior to man's freedom and imposing
itself upon him as necessary, whereas for a critical consciousness
society and the world are products of human freedom, remaining
subject to the creative power that constructed them. Again, for
a mythical consciousness there is an unquestionable order; for a
critical consciousness everything is under questioning. Criticism
is in principle universal; to limit it is essentially to destroy it.

Kant did not fully recognize the historical dimension of
critical reflection and as a consequence he gave his categories an
uncritical necessity. Nevertheless, his critical philosophy, taken
as a whole, was emancipatory in intent and effect. It should be
interpreted in relation with his writings on history; for example,
the essay, "What is Enlightenment?", where he speaks of the overcoming
of man's self-incurred tutelage.[1]

Besides its dissolution of a mythical consciousness,
critical reflection is emancipatory in two further ways, corresponding
to two tasks explicitly formulated since Kant.

The first is the psychoanalytic task of uncovering the
structures of repression in the individual. These structures block
the freedom of the individual and inhibit his creativity. They put
him in bondage to unconscious drives and systematically distort
his personal actions, their expression and their products. Whatever

213

the hesitations about the particular concepts, hypotheses and theories
of Freud, no critical consciousness can now ignore his contribution
or evade the task his work drew attention to.  That is why the
Germans include Freud among the representative thinkers of the
Aufklärung.  Critical reflection upon any region of human experience
has now to ask how far a genetic explanation shows its form and
contents to be the product of neurotic repression rather than of
uninhibited creativity and freedom.  Not that we can dismiss the
products of neurosis as valueless, but such an origin is relevant
to their critical evaluation.

        Critical reflection is, in a second way, emancipatory in
being a critique of ideologies.  Ideology is a distortion resulting
from social structures of domination and violence, analogous to the
structures of repression in the individual as uncovered by Freudian
psychoanalysis.  The critique of ideologies on the social and
political level carries out the functions performed by psychoanalysis
on the individual level.  In other words, just as on the individual
level a critical consciousness demands that we enquire how far stances,
responses, assertions and decisions are distorted by the blind spots
and inhibitions resulting from repression, so also on the social
level criticism requires us to uncover the hidden, systematic distortions produced by repressive social structures.  A process of
simple interpretation is not enough when dealing with the products
of social consciousness.  Critical reflection must also develop
genetic explanations to account for the ideologies that trammel
social communication.

        Both psychoanalysis and the critique of ideologies can be
seen as parts of a total process directed towards the achievement
of unimpeded communication.[2]  Psychoanalysis is concerned with
internal communication within the subject, communication between the
organic and psychic, namely the unconscious, and consciousness, so
that the two levels work in harmony with a free flow between them.
The critique of ideologies in its turn aims at a liberation that
would establish a communication free from domination, unconstrained
and non-manipulative within society among its various groups.

        In brief, criticism is reflection that brings to conscious-
ness the formative processes behind the individual and society.  It
thus enables men to appropriate their creative freedom and liberate
themselves from the repression and domination that distort their
self-formation.

        A problem thinkers have struggled with since the emergence
of critical reflection is its relationship with tradition.  Historically, it was a question of overcoming the limitations and onesidedness of the Enlightenment of the philosophes.  Here it must
be enough to summarize conclusions.

        Human freedom is not the freedom of atomic individuals
or windowless monads, but the freedom of men in community.  The
individual is not an absolute subject, with other men related to him
only as objects of his thoughts or actions.  The subject of human
thought and action is a social group, a "we".  Not that we should
reify the social group as an entity existing apart from the
individuals composing it, but the individual acts only within and

from out of a network of social relationships. That network, with the interactions it includes and the institutions it creates, is not reducible to any of the individuals it comprises.

Again, human creative autonomy is that proper to an historical subject acting within history. Creation by men is not creation ex nihilo by ahistorical subjects.

Both these considerations converge to show that a primordial relation of participation binds men to traditions that precede them. Since our being is social and historical, we begin within a received culture transmitted as a tradition, and the fundamental way we remain related to the social historical is by belonging. There is no transcendent, neutral point of view, from which we can survey the mess of traditions corrupted by repression and ideology. There is no absolute reason, stripped of all pre-judgements, allowing us to engage in a critical reflection that would dominate the cultural materials through purely objective techniques. Gadamer has argued that at length in Wahrheit und Methode.

However, this should not mean that critical reflection should be exluded and that we should swing back to a pre-critical approach, according to which traditions are appropriated merely hermeneutically by an interpretative understanding from a basis of participation. The traditions we receive as our cultural heritage are not just places of truth and freedom, but places of untruth and unfreedom. Hence there must be a moment of critical distance and an element of discriminating reflection.

Ricoeur in his discussion of Gadamer and Habermas[3] argues that Gadamer's own hermeneutical philosophy implies an element of distance as well as of participation in our relation to tradition; or, in other words, his own position demands a less negative assessment of "alienating distanciation" (Verfremdung) than he gives. Thus, Gadamer's theory of historical consciousness (Wirkungsgeschichtliches Bewusztsein) implies efficacy at a distance, with a tension between the near and distant as essential.[4] His "fusion of horizons" means that "we do not live within closed horizons nor within a unique horizon."[5] Finally, Gadamer's stress upon "linguisticality" (Sprachlichkeit) means that participation in a tradition is through the interpretation of signs, works and texts, and, as Ricoeur argues in detail,[6] the mediation of texts and their equivalents shows that there is an element of distancing in all communication. Human communication is communication within and by means of distance, namely through the mediation of objective texts and works. The objectification constitutive of texts and of meaningful action as socially fixated[7] both allows and demands that we insert explanatory procedures (erklären) into the hermeneutical process and use objective, "scientific" techniques alongside the appropriating procedures of understanding (verstehen). There is, therefore, room for the introduction of critical reflection and the critical distance it implies into our relationship to tradition. Ricoeur, however, insists that critical reflection is not from some non-historical place and, consequently, that, to be fruitful, it must coincide with a creative reinterpretation of our cultural heritage.

The recognition that there is no absolute starting-point distinguishes criticism as dialectical from the abstract critical reason of rationalism and empiricism. Both rationalism and empiricism, though each in its own way, seek to establish some absolutely certain ground on which everything else can be based. Rationalism claims to find it in a set (containing perhaps only one) of necessary, self-evident truths, serving as principles from which all else can be deduced. Empiricism appeals to events observable by the senses and recorded in protocol statements. On the basis of these scientific laws are established and scientific hypotheses verified. Thus, empiricists canonize the "facts" as the only sure and final ground, an absolute, on which all the rest of knowledge must be based. On the first level, scientific laws are based directly on the "facts" or protocol statements; on the second level, theories, which offer unified explanations of many laws, are based on them indirectly.

The rationalist and empiricist viewpoints, though developing methods of real though limited value, are abstract, because they omit consideration of the historical, social, cultural context that conditions all human knowing. Neither reasoning nor observation are ahistorical and unaffected by the social and historical situation of the reasoner or observer.

Freedom can easily become an empty concept, so fluid that it is devoid of consistency or content. To be given a meaning, it must be connected with traditions having an interest in freedom, the traditions from the ideal and concept originally emerged. Again, criticism can become an empty negativity, an exercise in missing the point. To be meaningfully criticized, elements (particular truths or "facts") must be related to the whole of which they are parts and which alone give them meaning. That whole is a tradition as a coherent unity. There are two possibilities. The elements may be criticized from a position of belonging to the tradition of which they are a part. There is then a movement from the tradition to the criticism of its elements and back to the tradition as reinterpreted and reappropriated. Or the elements may be criticized from outside the tradition of which they are parts. In that case they must still be considered in the context of the whole to which they belong, but the critic has the further task of bringing his own tradition or total view into relation with the tradition the elements of which he is criticizing.

Criticism, therefore involves a continuous movement to and fro, from parts to whole and from whole to parts. Critical discourse oscillates between particular truths and facts and over-all syntheses, between the totality of a constructed world and its particular elements.

Because criticism as dialectical refuses the project of finding an absolute starting-point analytically in particular truths or facts and insists upon an unceasing movement from elements of thought and action to their concrete historical context and back, it has the discernment of coherent wholes in the flux of history as a basic task.

What constitutes a coherent whole in the context of which particular elements of thought and action may be understood, criticized and evaluated? A tradition and the social group that carries it; or, in an equivalent formulation, a social group with its tradition.

Tradition here means more than an intellectual scheme. Philosophies and theologies are abstract; they are not concrete wholes, and therefore they are not of themselves fully intelligible. A tradition is a way of responding to reality, including feelings, memories, images, ideas, theories, forms of language, modes of actions, aspirations, ideals, attitudes, interpersonal relationships; in brief, the entire complex that constitutes life within a particular world, a world bounded by an horizon that determines the particular sense of reality that pervades it.

A tradition in that concrete sense is correlative to a social group and cannot be adequately considered apart from the social group which carries it. Tradition and social group determine each other. What unites a social group and distinguishes it from other groups is the tradition it bears. What constitutes a tradition is to be the way of life, the consciousness and praxis, of a social group.

But clearly not all social groupings are coherent wholes, deserving consideration of themselves and not simply as elements of a wider whole, and not all forms of thought and action have sufficient range to be traditions in the sense used. Hence the fundamental critical task of discerning the significant dividing-lines among social groups and their traditions. This discernment is itself subject to modification in the dialectical process.

On the basis of a discernment of coherent wholes, criticism proceeds by uncovering the formative processes that created them, together with the inhibitions and oppressions that in their regard obstructed the working of human creativity and freedom. Then in the light of that critique, it discusses the validity of those totalities and their limits.

A Critical Theology:

By a critical theology I mean a critique of that area of experience commonly called religious. I am therefore using "theology" without putting its theistic implications in the forefront. I use it because I am writing within the context of the Christian religion, though with the aim of achieving a critical distance from it and with an awareness of other religious traditions.

I am using "religious experience" in the comprehensive sense I think it should be used, namely as including all the activities and passivities we call religious. The term, therefore, embraces the creation and use of myth, symbol and ritual, the following of mystical techniques, the holding of doctrinal beliefs, the carrying out of norms of practical, social and institutional activity. It should not be limited to inner events. These, while at the core of religion, always occur in and through bodily and symbolic forms.

The project of critical theology demands that we make a distinction between two meanings of theology, two kinds of activity we call theological.

Theology is first the elaboration and transmission of a religious tradition as an expression of participation in that tradition. It is a directly religious activity as defined by that tradition. Theology in that sense is the meditative assimilation of a particular tradition and the preaching or proclamation of that tradition. The tradition itself is not under question, but is for this kind of theological activity the final point of reference.

Theology in the second sense moves to a critical distance from the particular tradition and endeavours to uncover its foundations and evaluate them. To move to a critical distance is necessarily to adopt a standpoint from which the claims of other traditions come into view and refuse to be dismissed simply by reference to the authority of the particular tradition. Moreover, not every religious tradition, not all forms of the Christian tradition, accepts as legitimate, let alone as a religious activity, the critical questioning of its presuppositions or principles. My conviction, which I have defended elsewhere,[8] is that fundamental theology as critical coincides with the philosophy of religion. Philosophy of religion emerged in the West as the insertion of the critical moment into the theological enterprise. Its distinction from theology was for purely historical and institutional reasons, chiefly the resistance of theology to a critical questioning that did not accept the appeal to authority as final.

The critical enterprise in theology creates difficult questions concerning methods, criteria or warrants, the standpoint of the critic and his own relation to tradition. But before tackling these questions, it is necessary to counter the one-sidedness that restricts critical theology or the critique of religion to the critique of religious assertions.

Critical theology has to identify and discuss religious experience as this is embodied and expressed. The approach, therefore, must be through religious language, if language is taken in the widest sense as the articulation of experience in expressive forms. Whatever may be the essence of religious experience, whatever the element constituting experiences as intrinsically religious, it is mediated and articulated in language, in meaningful actions and in meaningful institutions.

But the language of religion does not primarily consist of doctrinal statements, even less of the assertions of speculative theology. The primary language of religion is found "embedded in such modes of discourse as narratives, prophecies, legislative texts, proverbs and wisdom sayings, hymns, prayers, and liturgical formulas."[9] To these strictly linguistic forms should be added the forms of action, aesthetic and practical, which also enter into first-order religious expression.

Critical reflection upon religion, therefore, presupposes
a poetics of religious expression. The task of such a poetics is to
identify and classify the various literary and artistic forms used
to articulate religious experience. The meaning of religious
expression is determined by the various modes of articulation proper
to each literary or artistic form. To discuss the meaning of
religious language in general is too vague and crude to be fruitful,
and, to avoid this, religious language should not be restricted, as
by some analysts, to doctrinal and religio-metaphysical statements.
In short, critical reflection upon the meaning and truth of religion
simply cannot bypass the preliminary work of a poetics of religion.

The use of the word "poetics" already reflects a critical
choice. It corresponds to the conviction that religious forms,
linguistic and other, are the product of the creative imagination.
By the creative imagination I refer not simply to the picturing
faculty, but, more importantly, to the constructive, poetic
intelligence. "Poetic", because religious images, concepts and
words are not the direct formulation of observational or introspective data. They do not express directly known objects. They
are the indirect and metaphorical evocation and articulation of a
transcendent intentionality or dynamic in human experience. God
is not a known object, but a poetic idea. To suppose otherwise is
idolatry. This is not to dismiss religious language as emotive
and not cognitive, but it is to place its mode of cognition nearer
poetry than empirical science.

However, to establish a dichotomy between cognition and
emotion would be false. Values are apprehended by feelings, and
feelings are not mere emotions or bodily movements; they are
responses that are total in so far as they come from the unity of
the self as an embodied person or personal body. Feelings are
bodily responses that are animated by intelligence and spiritual
affectivity or, conversely, embodied intelligent and affective
responses. Religious feelings are the spontaneous, connatural
responses to religious reality. They are the arousal of our personal
being - our intelligent and bodily, spiritual and material selves - by
religious reality as variously mediated and articulated in the forms
of religious expression. Consequently, a critical approach to
religious forms that simply interprets or comments intellectually
upon its cognitive meaning is inadequate. We have to show how
those forms relate to our sensibility. The critic must not
dissolve them through commentary, supposing that only their meaning,
as reformulated in his interpretation, is relevant, and not their
impact. The critic must, instead, let them be, showing what they
are and facilitating their action upon our feelings. To borrow
Susan Sontag's term, we need an erotics of religion. We can apply
here what she says of literary and art criticism: "The function
of criticism should be to show how it is what it is, even that it
is what it is, rather than to show what it means. In place of
hermeneutics we need an erotics of art."[10]

A poetics of religion and an erotics of religion come
together as a critical aesthetics of religion. Such a critical
aesthetics should be the first stage in any criticism of religious
experience and the presupposition for subsequent critical reflection
upon religion.

In passing it may be noted that the demand for a critical aesthetics of religion is not in any conflict with insistence upon the social and political character of religion, such as is found in the political theology of Metz. One may simply point to the discussion of aesthetics among Marxists and, in particular, to the great importance given to aesthetic theory and criticism in writers of the Frankfurt School of critical sociology, notably Adorno, Horkheimer, Benjamin and Lowenthal.[11] Worth mentioning is also the thesis of Herbert Marcuse concerning the "new sensi-bility" as a political factor.[12] Metz himself has noted the task of developing a new critical aesthetics,[13] and the point has been taken up by one of the critics of his political theology.[14]

The work of critical aesthetics in making clear the nature and functioning of the forms of religious expression in all their variety leads to and overlaps with a critical reflection upon the creative process through which they emerge and articulate religious experience. Further, the attempt to lay bare the formation of religion and its a priori conditions confronts critical reflection with the question of structures of repression that may have inhibited human creative freedom in that area of experience and distorted the process and its products.

Indeed, as is well known, Freud maintained that religion as a whole was a general neurosis, in the sense that the mental processes and kinds of behaviour involved in religion were the same as those associated with neuroses. Freud's contentions are not so easily dismissed as is sometimes thought.[15] But even were we to leave them aside, we should still have to face the more moderate but widespread conviction of a conflict between traditional religion and the creative autonomy of modern men in relation to the world and society. There is, for example, the deeply disturbing thesis formulated admirably by William Lynch in Christ and Prometheus.[16] He argues that the religious imagination in its older form has in fact hindered the emergence of the secular in its autonomy. Traditional religious images stress the conditionality of the world, that is they relate everything to a centre, a principle or condition outside itself, which alone gives it meaning. Such images have blocked the secular project, which he describes as "the march of mankind, in the autonomous light of its own resources, toward the mastery and humanization of the world."[17] The older religious image of the world "could not tolerate the basic secular notion of constitutive autonomy and unconditional, self-contained novelty."[18] It has imposed "its own forms upon the world as final meaning"[19] and in some instances devalued the secular with negative images. Consequently, in the present crisis of religion there has to be a vast desymbolizing process, which will be a "descent into hell" of the religious imagination, as it strips itself of its older images.[20] Then one must struggle for a new image of man and of his secular project.

The question, therefore, arises for critical reflection whether there is not an incompatibility between all traditional forms of the Christian tradition, together with most Christian theologies and the modern process of emancipation with its stress upon human creative freedom. Does not the modern history of freedom, in which critical consciousness emerged and to which it belongs,

mark a shift in human society and culture that has rendered
traditional forms of religion obsolete?

John Wren-Lewis makes a distinction between two cultures
or ways of responding to life: the traditional and the humanist-
experimental. The traditional, represented by most religion but
also by dogmatic materialism, is governed by the supreme need
to reach some truly authoritative understanding of the realities
behind common experience. The assumption is that there is an
order, a grand design, beyond the realities of everyday experience.
The concern is to discern and contemplate it; and then one's duty
and purpose in life is to conform to it. For the modern, humanist
and experimental outlook "the world is simply what we know it to be
in the practical business of meeting, it, handling it, and doing
things in it - not so much a thing, a system, a reality, an order,
as an opportunity, a potentiality for creative action."[21]

One is reminded here of Marx's view of the relation
between theory and praxis.[22] Marx rejected the notion of theory
independent of praxis, theory as a presuppositionless, contemplative
recognition of a stable object. Praxis, ranging from bodily labour
and production to political revolution, was the only source of
meaning. Theory was the consciousness of praxis; and so theoretical
activity like the practical activity with which it is one, is a
product of the changing reality of society and of the relationship
with nature mediated by society. That was the context for Marx's
rejection of religion. What characterized thought as religious for
Marx was its being mere theory divorced from social practice. By
claiming permanent and universal truth in theory as if it were
independent of social conditions, religion uncritically reflected
patterns of social dominance and concealed social reality in
mystifying abstractions. Religion and theology claimed a purely
theoretical centre of reference for their truth and its continuing
identity.

For John Wren-Lewis, traditional religion is a way of
avoiding the challenges and responsibilities of human creativity
and freedom, and, following Freud, he sees the steady decline
of the traditional outlook as "a gradual escape from the bondage
of an age-long state of neurotic inhibition."[23] For Marx religion
was ideology through and through, a denial of concrete history,
an escape into abstraction and a mystification of social dominance.

I refer once more to what will be regarded by some as
all too familiar negative critiques of religion, not to parade
them for acceptance, but to make it obvious that a critical
theology focussed upon the verifiability or falsifiability of
doctrinal statements or concerned with the validity of proofs
for the existence of God and with similar matters is largely
missing the point. Criticism, understood as reflection motivated
by an interest in emancipation, is concerned with religious
traditions as concrete, coherent wholes. It is an attempt to
uncover and bring to awareness the formative processes, both
individual and social, which have created and articulated a
particular tradition. Its interest in human creative freedom
and in unconstrained social communication without domination will
make it sensitive to the distortions due to neurotic inhibition

and social oppression. It cannot be content with intellectual
discussions in vacuo.

Doctrinal or theological statements cannot be interpreted
outside a context. Just as words need the context of the sentence
to give them a determinate meaning and sentences the context of
a particular work, composed according to a literary genre and in
an individual style, to give them their meaning, so also particular
works have to be interpreted in the context of a total coherent
whole, namely a tradition and the social group that carries it.
To attempt to analyse and evaluate religious statements outside
of their total context is to fall into the abstract thinking of
empiricism or rationalism and the myth of some absolute starting-
point. Critical theology as dialectical will pass from an examination of individual statements to the investigation of the whole
of which they are elements and then back from a grasp of the whole
to a further interpretation and assessment of the individual
statements.

The concrete coherent whole to be discerned by critical
theology in its dialectical method will be a distinct religious
tradition as correlative to a social group.

"Religious tradition" has taken on a narrowly intellectual
meaning as an inherited set of beliefs. That is not the meaning
intended here. I am using it to include praxis as well as theory.
In short, as previously stated, a tradition embraces the entire
complex that constitutes life within a particular world; it is
a way, comprehensively considered, of responding to reality.
For the present methodological discussion, it would not seem
necessary to reach a conclusion concerning what makes a tradition
religious.

The term "religious tradition" may mislead by creating
the supposition that the discrimination of religious traditions
is already an accomplished fact in the rough-and-ready division
of the world religions or, in the Christian context, in the
association of each tradition with a particular Church. That
supposition is far from being the case in fact. The discrimination
of different traditions is a delicate task, requiring much detailed
work. An illustration of this is Lucien Goldmann's careful
reconstruction of the tragic vision as a total world-view or
vision of reality, found as such in Pascal and Racine. His book,
I may remark, is methodologically most stimulating and I have
been much helped by it.[23] What it also makes clear is that a
religious tradition as distinctive cannot be identified with
adherence to a particular Church. Descartes and Malebranche on
the one hand and Pascal and Racine on the other were Catholics,
but they represented two very different religious traditions as
ways of responding to reality. In any major Christian Church,
especially over a period of time, there are several substantially
different religions, even if those belonging to them all recite
the same creeds.

A key task of critical theology is therefore to develop
a typology of religious traditions.

We have histories of theology, but these set forth a
eries of similar intellectual schemata, inserted for the most
art simply into the biographical context of their originators.
uch accounts remain abstract and are of defective intelligibility.
o put it bluntly, they do not make complete sense.  Can there
e a "history" of theology, other than a correlation of
ostractions?

There are also some accounts of different ways of doing
heology - typologies of theology.[24]  But are not these again
xercises in abstraction?  Theologies are not pure, uncontaminated
ntellectual enterprises; they are influenced by a variety of
nterests.  They are not self-contained entities, but parts of a
ider whole.  They cannot be intelligently studied apart from
ther writings coming out of the same tradition taken as a whole.
o make complete sense, they have to be replaced in the economic,
ocial, political, literary and artistic life of the social groups
rom which they sprang.  No doubt, formal and logical studies of
heological statements and systems are needed for conceptual
larification, but we should not suppose that such studies enable
s to know what is going on when theologies are produced and
lash.  It is now well recognized that the Trinitarian and
hristological controversies in the early Church do not make
ense apart from the economic, social and political struggles of
hich they were one form of expression.  The difference between
liberal and neo-orthodox theologies or between neo-Thomism and
ranscendental Thomism is not confined to some realm of pure
heological ideas.  The difference in the concrete was one of
ocial, political and religious praxis.  Feminist theology in its
urn has drawn attention to the economic, social and political
nfra-structure of theological images, concepts, statements and
heories.

Therefore, what is needed for critical reflection is
discrimination of traditions as distinctive wholes, not the
sting seriatim or classification of theological schemata or
ocedures.

A tradition is correlative with the social group that
rries it.  What are the social groups to which the different
ligious traditions belong?  To determine these is also the task
critical theology.

We can take different theologies as clues to different
ligious traditions, in so far as a theology is either a direct
, if neurotically or ideologically distorted, an indirect
stract expression of a concrete form of life.  We can then ask
ich social groups produced which theologies.  For example, the
eology of Thomas Aquinas, together with Aristotelian Scholastic
eology in general has been connected with the growth of the
ties and the emergence of the medieval bourgeoisie.[25]  To turn
the contemporary situation, the theology of secularization
s been seen as the ideology of those Christians who socially
d politically intend to conform to the values and praxis of
vanced industrial society.[26]  Clearly, such general statements
st be made more precise and also supported by detailed
vestigations.  When that is done, the particular theology

itself must be merged into a greater whole with other theoretical elements and with social and religious praxis.

A complication of modern times is that theology has increasingly become a form of expression reserved to ecclesiastics. The clergy usually draws its members from different social classes, but these members become to a great extent déclassés and form a distinct social group. Consequently, the discernment of the social basis and functioning of an ecclesiastically produced theology is a question of determining the role and function of the Church at a particular time and place. Clerical theology is carried by the social group that serves the Church as a particular institution with a particular though varying function within society. Hence its lack of appeal to laity and their hostility to some manifestations of it.

Something similar must be said of academic theology, produced in the universities and more or less free from ecclesiastical control. The academic context has been particularly important in the development of German theology. Its social basis has to be determined by examining the role and functioning of the universities. In passing, the recent change being brought about in Catholic theology by its move from the environment of the seminary to that of the university might be noted. A different social group is beginning to develop its theology. Earlier there was the great influence of Blondel, whose religious thinking was done outside the strictly ecclesiastical orbit.

At the same time, if one considers, not the social groups serving the institutions of Church and university, but other social groups within modern society, it is apparent that theology for them has ceased to be the dominant expression of religious thought. Any critique of religious experience today that confines itself to theological writing is playing on the periphery. Even apart from its expression in action, religion today is articulated in other than theological writing, namely philosophical, literary, political and indeed scientific in the social sciences. For example, no adequate account of religion in the nineteenth and twentieth centuries is possible without a study of the novel.

To repeat then: critical theology is concerned with religious traditions and the social groups which carry them; that does not mean with systems of theology and the theologians who produce them. Criticism as dialectical endeavours to discern and evaluate totalities, namely the forms of life and consciousness of social groups.

But what are the criteria of evaluation, once different religious traditions have been discerned?

If one is convinced that theory and knowledge are subordinate to the wider and deeper movement of human existence as an integrated whole, then inevitably one will ask what are the interests in terms of which a particular form of human knowing is justified. Jürgen Habermas distinguished three kinds of interest as fundamental to three kinds of knowledge. First, the strict sciences yield information that presupposes the interest of certainty and technical control. Second, the hermeneutic sciences give an understanding of the social and cultural life-world that presupposes the interest of extending intersubjective communication. Third, there is a critical science, which is an inquiry capable of dissolving the apparent necessity of historical modes of authority and of creating an awareness of the self-formative processes of society and the self and which has an interest in emancipation as its presupposition.[27] For me, critical theology, like criticism in general, is motivated by an interest in emancipation. It will therefore evaluate religious traditions by the criterion of their relation to human emancipation.

However, I should want to interpret emancipation in a fashion similar to Metz's development of the concept of freedom.[28] Human freedom is never simply the self-possession of man, but always at the same time the opening of man to the transcendence of God. To achieve a religious understanding of freedom without losing touch with social and political realities is not easy. All the same, I should maintain that, given a sufficiently profound grasp of freedom, freedom can become the most important interest for men, the key value or criterion in assessing the truth and value of those concrete modes of life I have called religious traditions. It should be added that neither the understanding of freedom nor its use as a criterion can be achieved in theory alone, but only in and through praxis.

Any evaluation of religious traditions will also be partly comparative. In other words, a tradition has the greater claim to truth and value when it can integrate the positive elements of other traditions into itself as into a higher synthesis, while overcoming their insufficiencies and defects. The dialectical method in insisting upon the consideration not just of isolated elements but of totalities always seeks the greater totality as surpassing partial syntheses. Implicit in this comparative criterion is the criterion of adequacy to human experience. The claim to truth of any concrete form of life must be judged by the extent to which it does justice to all the data and exigencies of human experience.

That leaves us with the question of the standpoint of the critic or, to put it in another way, the tradition to which he belongs and from which he engages in critical reflection.

Historically speaking, there is no doubt that the concept of critical reflection I have been expounding and applying comes out of that movement for emancipation and enlightenment which has been a feature of the modern epoch in the West. It belongs to what Metz calls the modern history of freedom (die neuzeitliche Freiheitsgeschichte)[29] or, alternatively the Aufklärungsprozesz or Aufklärungstradition, understood as the attempt of a line of thinkers from Kant onwards to overcome the onesidedness of the abstract reason of the Enlightenment in its first phase, with its rationalism and empiricism, without returning to an uncritical acceptance of tradition or of authoritarian Christianity.[30]

When, however, Christians like myself take our stand within that tradition and engage in a critical reflection that rejects rationalism and empiricism on the one hand and any final appeal to external authority on the other, are we still within the Christian tradition? Is there a Christian form of the critical tradition? Or, is it not more honest to say that insights from the Christian tradition have been integrated with other insights into a higher synthesis, no longer in any authentic sense Christian?

Historically and sociologically, it is difficult to place the modern thrust towards freedom and creative autonomy through emancipatory praxis and critical consciousness within the Christian tradition. Almost every step in the emergence of modern freedom and criticism has been opposed by most representatives of the Christian tradition. Further, traditional Christian imagery is in conflict with modern autonomy, as we have seen in Lynch's call for a vast desymbolization. Moreover, the idea of a once-for-all revelation and final truth, which would seem to be at the heart of the Christian vision of the world and the Christian mode of life, essentially contradicts the changing, experiemental, constructive character of human truth for a free and critical consciousness. Truth for critical reflection, unlike in the Christian conception, cannot be handed to us ready-made for our acceptance; it arises out of the struggle for liberation and is always proportionate to the actualization of our creative freedom.

On the other hand, the tradition of emancipation and criticism is itself in jeopardy today. The difficulty of identifying which social groups now carry it points up the problem of its survival in modern technocratic society. Perhaps the scattered bands of those who still give it their allegiance may in their creative reinterpretation and reappropriation of it in the difficult contemporary situation find themselves drawing upon further resources of the Christian tradition. In which case a deeper affinity than previously suspected between the critical and the Christian tradition may be uncovered.

Nevertheless, critical reflection as its starting-point has the concrete reality of an existing tradition, not the programmatic ideal of some writer. To suppose otherwise is to turn criticism into ideology. Consequently, it has to be said that critical theology comes out of a tradition which is in conflict with existing forms of the Christian tradition, and it is as yet unclear that any of these in reality have the potentiality of developing in such a way as to integrate its values into itself.

# Notes

[1] For an interpretation of Kant that considers the full scope of his critical philosophy against the restrictive interpretations of the neo-Kantians, see Lucien Goldmann, Introduction à la philosophie de Kant, Collection Idées (Editions Gallimard, 1967). For the Kantian revolution as the liberation of reflection against pre-given reality, together with the lack of recognition by Kant himself that critical thought is about history, see Jeremy J. Shapiro, "From Marcuse to Habermas," Continuum 9 (1971), 65-6. An English translation of Kant's writings on history, including "What is Enlightenment?" is given in Immanuel Kant, On History, edited with an introduction by Lewis White Beck, The Library of Liberal Arts (Indianapolis/New York: Bobbs-Merrill, 1963).

[2] I am making free use of ideas from Jürgen Habermas.

[3] Paul Ricoeur, "The Task of Hermeneutics," Philosophy Today, XVII (1973), 112-128; and "Ethics and Culture: Habermas and Gadamer in Dialogue," Philosophy Today, XVII (1973), 153-165.

[4] Ricoeur, "The Task of Hermeneutics," 127.

[5] Ibid., 128.

[6] Paul Ricoeur, "The Hermeneutical Function of Distanciation," Philosophy Today, XVII (1973), 129-141; and "What is a Text? Explanation and Interpretation" in David M. Rasmussen, Mythic-Symbolic Language and Philosophical Anthropology (The Hague: Martinus Nijhoff, 1971), pp. 135-150.

[7] Paul Ricoeur, "The Model of the Text: Meaningful Action Considered as a Text," Social Research, 38 (1971), 529-562.

[8] Charles Davis, "The Reconvergence of Theology and Religious Studies," SR: Studies in Religion/Sciences Religieuses, 4 (1974/5), 205-221.

[9] Paul Ricoeur, "Philosophy and Religious Language," The Journal of Religion, 54 (1974), 73.

[10] Susan Sontag, Against Interpretation and Other Essays, Second Laurel Edition (New York: Dell, 1969), p. 23. Her italics.

[11] For an account of their work, see Martin Jay, The Dialectical Imagination: A History of the Frankfurt School and the Institute of Social Research 1923-1950 (Boston: Little, Brown, 1973), especially Chapter 6: "Aesthetic Theory and the Critique of Mass Culture," pp. 173-218.

[12] Cf. An Essay on Liberation (Boston: Beacon, 1969).

[13] J. B. Metz, "Grond en functie van de politieke theologie," Tijdschrift voor Theologie, 12 (1972), 239-240.

[14] H. Schaeffer, "'Politieke theologie' in een tijd van 'religieuze renaissance'", Tijdschrift voor Theologie, 12 (1972), 239-240.

[15] For a good discussion of the issues, see chapter 6: "Religion and materialism on the psychoanalyst's couch" in John Wren-Lewis, What Shall We Tell the Children? (London: Constable, 1971), pp. 55-73.

[16] Notre Dame, Indiana: University of Notre Dame Press, 1970.

[17] Christ and Prometheus, p. 7.

[18] Ibid., p. 27. Lynch's italics.

[19] Ibid., p. 31.

[20] Ibid., p. 26.

[21] What Shall We Tell the Children? (London: Constable, 1971), p. 21. Wren-Lewis's italics.

[22] For an account of this, together with a discussion of its relevance to theology, see Charles Davis, "Theology and Praxis," Cross Currents, XXIII (1973), 154-168.

[23] Lucien Goldmann, Le Dieu caché: Etude sur la vision tragique dans les Pensées de Pascal et dans le théâtre de Racine (Editions Gallimard, 1959).

[24] A recent example is David B. Burrell, Exercises in Religious Understanding (Notre Dame: University of Notre Dame Press, 1974). At the time of writing I have not yet seen David Tracy, A Blessed Rage for Order: The New Pluralism in Theology (New York: Seabury, 1974), but in David Tracy, "Theology as Public Discourse," The Christian Century, 19 March, 1975, it is said to be a presentation of five major models for fundamental theology: the orthodox, the liberal, the neo-orthodox, the radical and the revisionist.

[25] Cf. M. D. Chenu, Introduction à l'étude de Saint Thomas d'Aquin (Paris: Gabalda, 1950).

[26] Cf. M. Xhaufflaire & K. Derksen, eds., Les Deux visages de la théologie de la sécularisation, L'actualite religieuse, 29 (Tournai: Casterman, 1970).

[27] Jurgen Habermas, "Zur Logik der Sozialwissenschaften," Philosophische Rundschau, Beiheft 5, Febr. 1967; and Erkenntnis und Interesse (Frankfurt-am-Main: Suhrkamp, 1968). For a brief account in English, see Trent Schroyer, "Marx and Habermas," Continuum 9 (1971), 52-64.

[28] J. B. Metz, "Freiheit als philosophisch-theologisches Grenzproblem" in Gott in Welt: Festgabe für Karl Rahner I (Freiburg: Herder, 1964), pp. 287-314. A translation of this essay is given in Philosophy Today X, 4 (Winter 1966), 264-279.

[29] Cf. his essay, "Kirchliche Autorität im Anspruch der Freiheitsgeschichte" in Johann Baptist Metz, Jürgen Moltmann, Willi Oelmüller, Kirche im Prozess der Aufklärung: Aspekte einer neuen "politischen Theologie." Gesellschaft und Theologie, Systematische Beiträge, Nr I (München: Kaiser/Mainz: Grünewald, 1970).

[30] Cf. Willi Oelmuller, Die unbefriedigte Aufklärung: Beiträge zu einer Theorie der Moderne von Lessing, Kant und Hegel (Frankfurt-am-Main: Suhrkamp, 1969); id., Was ist heute Aufklärung? (Düsseldorf: Patmos, 1972).

325